Race C

ALSO BY TODD M. MEALY

Glenn Killinger, All-American: Penn State's
World War I Era Sports Hero (McFarland, 2018)

Race Conscious Pedagogy

Disrupting Racism at Majority White Schools

Todd M. Mealy

Foreword by Terrence J. Roberts
Afterword by George Yancy

McFarland & Company, Inc., Publishers
Jefferson, North Carolina

This book has undergone peer review.

Library of Congress Cataloguing-in-Publication Data

Names: Mealy, Todd, 1979– author. | Roberts, Terrence J,
    writer of foreword. | Yancy, George, writer of afterword.
Title: Race conscious pedagogy : disrupting racism at majority
    white schools / Todd M. Mealy ; foreword by Terrence J. Roberts ;
    afterword by George Yancy.
Description: Jefferson, North Carolina : McFarland & Company, Inc.,
    Publishers, 2020 | Includes bibliographical references and index.
Identifiers: LCCN 2020042084 | ISBN 9781476680330
    (paperback : acid free paper) ∞
    ISBN 9781476641508 (ebook)
Subjects: LCSH: Racism in education—United States. |
    Culturally relevant pedagogy—United States.
Classification: LCC LC212.2 .M43 2020 | DDC 371.829/96073—dc23
LC record available at https://lccn.loc.gov/2020042084

British Library cataloguing data are available

ISBN (print) 978-1-4766-8033-0
ISBN (ebook) 978-1-4766-4150-8

Front cover image by Syda Productions/Shutterstock © 2020

Printed in the United States of America

McFarland & Company, Inc., Publishers
    Box 611, Jefferson, North Carolina 28640
    www.mcfarlandpub.com

For my precious daughter, Adeline

"Actually, we who engage in nonviolent direct action are not the creators of tension. We merely bring to the surface the hidden tension that is already alive. We bring it out in the open, where it can be seen and dealt with. Like a boil that can never be cured so long as it is covered up but must be opened with all its ugliness to the natural medicines of air and light, injustice must be exposed, with all the tension its exposure creates, to the light of human conscience and the air of national opinion before it can be cured."

—"Letter from Birmingham Jail"
Martin Luther King, Jr.,
writing from Birmingham City Jail,
April 16, 1963, Birmingham, Alabama

Table of Contents

Acknowledgments

No one writes a book alone. I accordingly leaned heavily on several people since commencing this project in 2017. The most important was my mom, Maurene Mealy. Grateful is but a word to describe my appreciation for her patience and time spent looking over these pages. My father, Thomas Mealy, also kept his phone line open to hear about the book's progress and to interject a thought when asked. My siblings Tommy and Crissy shared in many of my life experiences that guided me to this book project. Former president of the Pennsylvania State School Board Association Richard Frerichs—full disclosure, he is my father-in-law—offered guidance at the inception of my critical race studies course, which is at the center of this book. My students also deserve much of the credit for the completion of this book. I have benefited from the discussions with each and every pupil that has taken my race, ethnicity, and gender studies seminar. I am grateful to them for encouraging me to write a book about the relevance of Race Conscious Pedagogy by reassuring me how important race-based conversations are for the cause of educational equity.

My boss, Michael Leichliter, believed in this project from the very start. While most people in his position may vacillate about how such a book could run the risk of casting a negative spotlight on the school district, Leichliter saw the value in educating teachers about how to engage White students in text-based race talk. He decisively greenlighted the project while the two of us were out for lunch in July 2018. Sherry Deckman of Lehman College, CUNY, was also at that lunch meeting. She provided sage advice in the earliest stages of this project. Several colleagues have been helpful in either teaching the critical race studies course, collecting data about the school district, or in drafting this book. They are Maria Vita, Jeffrey Taylor, Beth Shenenberger, Jerry Egan, and Streeter Stuart. Gratitude is also owed to Heather Bennett, Director of School Equity Services for the Pennsylvania School Board Association, who accepted me as a member of her Equity Task Force at PSBA. I met Jason Ottley, founder of the Bond Educational Group, near the end of this project. Our conversations and subsequent collaboration on similar projects carried this book across the finish line.

None of this would have been possible without the support and sacrifices of my best friend and spouse, Melissa. She was patient during those times I pulled her away from her own work to listen to me read over a passage I had just written. She offered insight as an administrator in a school district that is predominantly White, but yet as one of two principals at the only building in her district where Students of Color make up the majority. Of course, she also offered a perspective as a White parent of two White children. It has been those two children that have been there to motivate me every step of the way. Carter and Adeline help me each day to see how important it is to give young children the skills to use a critical lens to improve the world.

Foreword
by Terrence J. Roberts

In Bernard Malamud's 1968 novel *The Fixer*, we see the results of imperial domination that have characterized human existence for as long as our memories have recorded the stories. It is in this particular iteration of that narrative that we find a sentence that sums up the predicament of oppressed people in all ages. Malamud writes: "In a sick country, any step to health is an insult to those who live off its sickness." Malamud's protagonist, Yakov Bok, is forced to contend with the sickness of early 20th-century imperialist Russia; Todd Mealy has opted to confront a more salient virus in his home territory of the United States of America in this second decade of the 21st century. In essence, Mealy challenges his readers to imagine a new reality, one without the miasmic, mind numbing, memory destroying approved national narrative that basically tells us, "everything is okay, we just have to follow the script." The unfortunate truth is that only a selected few have meaningful roles in this drama. Mealy uses the classroom at his high school as a crucible in which students can learn to diagnose the race-based maladies and "othering" tendencies confronting us and to join you, the readers, in imagining a reality where all have the opportunity to realize the inherent potential embedded in the DNA of each one of us.

Todd Mealy is not ignorant of the fact that such an attempt will, and has, engendered fiery opposition. He anticipated the backlash even as he created the curriculum for his students. Malamud's prescient statement was, and is, a clarion call to those who guard the edges of the imperial kingdom. No, those guardians of the status quo will not sit idly by while cherished tropes are skewered in the name of healthy progress. Mealy is teaching his students to live with the inevitable tension that arises when competing narratives are suggested. He helps them develop skills of inquiry that lead, eventually, to new ways of thinking about old practices, philosophies, and systems. As they imagine new realities, as they master the skill of critical analysis, the students become keenly aware of their own need to grow and develop beyond the confines of their necessarily limited horizons. Limited because they have all been baptized in the waters of the dominant perspective that tends to inoculate against the acquisition of knowledge that would free them from these pernicious perspectives.

As you read this work, you will be privileged to learn how the historical record is vital to our understanding of lived reality today, why increasing your own awareness about the ways in which people who are deemed "different" continue to be ostracized by law and custom is essential to your optimal functioning as a responsible citizen, and why it is imperative that educators must become more keenly aware of the problems associated with ignorance about issues of multiculturalism. Todd Mealy is not shy about discussing his own pathway out of the fog of half-truths and mythological beliefs that tend to keep all of us locked in mental prisons which function mainly to shield us from the light of objective reality. You will see, in part, how he was motivated to tear down the walls surrounding him and dedicate his life to helping others find ways to escape.

As you share, vicariously, the joy of student-learning, as you note the fear and anger driving those who oppose this process, as you consider your own position vis-à-vis the questions raised, it is anticipated that you will begin to see with clarity why this book is an important addition to the canon. Among other things, Mealy intends to nudge you toward a more objective understanding of the issues associated with facing truths about ourselves and each other. Further, it is his intent to provide guidelines about how to respond to those who choose to remain willfully ignorant, one of which is simply to arm yourselves with fact-based information. It is imperative to note that the acquisition of this information alone will not result in change of ideas or choice of action. Unless there is motivation and willingness to change, things remain static. One of our oldest mythological constructs is that education alone will solve all of our problems. In truth, education is but one of several building blocks needed to construct the new you. Yes, the new you, who by dint of your desire to live the best life possible and to do what you can to ensure that others have the same opportunity, puts you in a class with but few other enrollees. Not that you should despair; a lone candle can dispel the gloom of the darkest cave.

Todd Mealy shows by what he has presented here that he is one of those glowing candles. He opts to shed light on some of the issues too many of us wish to leave hidden away from view. As you peruse his words and imagine a world operating with a different mindset about difference, think about what you are willing to contribute to make it so. And know this, as you make this important commitment, others who witness your dedication may be motivated to emulate your behavior. And just as a building is erected brick by brick, so a new, more accepting and loving community can be built one citizen at a time if we are all willing to take the first step toward this newly imagined reality.

Terrence J. Roberts was one of nine African American students who, in September 1957, enrolled at Little Rock Central High School in Little Rock, Arkansas. First turned away by the Arkansas National Guard and later by an angry mob numbering in the hundreds, Roberts, then a 15-year-old sophomore, and his peers were finally able to attend class three weeks into the school year. Action undertaken by President Dwight D. Eisenhower dispatched soldiers from the U.S. Army to Little Rock with orders to protect Roberts and his eight peers. In 1999, Roberts received the Congressional Gold Medal from President William Jefferson Clinton.

Preface

"Can I take your order?" the waitress asked my four-year-old son, Carter, and me.

Carter turned to me and said, "Daddy, she sounds funny!"

"That's a beautiful accent, isn't it?" I asked. "It's a Chinese accent."

"Yes, I like it," Carter responded.

We asked for the ginmiya duo and egg drop soup. The waitress, politely smiling, wrote the order down and walked away.

Dating back to Carter's second birthday, the two of us have spent most weekends at the local Regal Cinema. On this particular Saturday, we made plans to see the newest *Hotel Transylvania* movie. My son, however, had never been to a Chinese restaurant. There is one establishment within walking distance from the theater. So I made a plan for Carter to have his first Chinese meal before the movie, as we typically time our entrance into the theater with the end of the 20 minutes' worth of movie trailers that precede the feature film. I had a hunch my son might comment on the accent of our waitress. Carter and his younger sister, Adeline, attend a daycare that is 100 percent White. His preschool is overwhelmingly White. Most of the children in our neighborhood are White. While my sister is Korean, she doesn't speak with a foreign accent. Carter has heard Spanish spoken before. So he is used to that. But he's never heard anyone speak English with a foreign accent. Then it happened. "Daddy, she sounds funny!"

After turning red and telling their child, "Shh! That isn't polite!" I think most White parents would shrivel in their seat at that moment. I, however, was proactively prepared to react. After I spoke to my son about why people have different accents, we pulled up videos about China on my cell phone. For 20 minutes we shared our meal of rice, broccoli, scallops and shrimp while Carter learned about China's historic landmarks as well as the country's food culture.

This incident happened at about the time I started brainstorming an outline for this book. So *Race Conscious Pedagogy* is not written because

I am concerned over how my children would grow up seeing the world for its diversity; rather, my motivations for writing this book are largely due to my own experiences teaching a critical race studies class at a predominantly White high school in a predominantly White rural locale of Lancaster County, Pennsylvania. Over the course of these pages, I discuss the importance of creating a class based on Critical Race Theory to teach students how to become informed citizens on matters concerning race. Discussions in such classrooms focus on current events, media literacy, and governance while placing race at the center of history, legislation, education, economics, geography, military, film, fashion, and sports. Teachers who read this will encounter vignettes—both historical and personal—that offer plausible solutions for implementing a race studies course or program into the curriculum at White dominated schools and why such courses should be necessary for secondary level students in the 21st century. A picture will also emerge of how to engage students in solution-oriented conversations around race and racism in American society. Although not a comprehensive diatribe about equity policy for the public school system, it should give a rich picture how to implement Race Conscious Pedagogy and curricula to benefit every child in the classroom.

Scholarship on the intersection of race and education has increased in recent years largely as a result of reports indicating that Students of Color now outnumber White students in K-12 public schools across the United States (Chen, 2018; Krogstad and Fry, 2014). Most books, however, like Howard C. Stevenson's *Promoting Racial Literacy in Schools: Differences That Make a Difference* and Helen Fox's *"When Race Breaks Out": Conversations About Race and Racism in College Classrooms* focus on how professors tackle race and ethnicity with their college students. There are a few publications that concentrate on culturally responsive pedagogy at the primary, intermediate, and secondary levels; these books, however, rarely touch upon the importance of teaching White students about America's racist history. Margaret Hagerman's *White Kids: Growing Up with Privilege in a Racially Divided America* scrutinizes how White students adapt to various cultures while attending schools in diverse settings. *White Kids'* shortcomings, however, lie in how little space is allocated to examine curricular and pedagogical methods of race and ethnic studies programs at America's more diverse schools. Christopher Emdin's popular book, *For White Folks Who Teach in the Hood ... and the Rest of Y'all Too: Reality Pedagogy and Urban Education*, and Zaretta L. Hammond's *Culturally Responsive Teaching and the Brain: Promoting Authentic Engagement and Rigor Among Culturally and Linguistically Diverse Students* both speak to the need for culturally responsiveness as a means to improve standardized test scores, classroom production, and reducing disciplinary and absentee rates among Students of Color. While both books are valuable for providing solutions for dealing with problems in low income, urban schools that have a majority of students with a darker hue, neither Emdin nor Hammond reflect upon how cultural relevant classrooms might benefit students at predominantly White schools, and would thus enrich society at large.

Perhaps the books most resembling *Race Conscious Pedagogy* are Bettina L. Love's *We Want to Do More Than Survive*, Shelly Tochluk's *Witnessing Whiteness*, Robin DiAngelo's *White Fragility*, and Jennifer Harvey's *Raising White Kids*. Each book—one published in 2019, two in 2018, while the fourth received a second printing in 2018—offers solutions for how to create transformational change where antiracism and diversity are valued parts of education. Love (2019) offers White educators tips on how to become "coconspirators" in the fight for educational equity. To illustrate how White instructors can become race conscious pedagogues working alongside Colleagues of Color, she cites the teamwork between Bree Newsome and James Tyson in removing the Confederate battle flag from the South Carolina State House on June 27, 2015.

> As Newsome scaled the flagpole, authorities waited below to arrest her. However, they also had another plan to get her down: to tase the pole with their taser gun, which could have killed Newsome. Her coconspirator, James Tyson, a White man, also waited at the bottom, tightly hugging the pole so that if they tased the pole, they would tase him too. The two had met just days before.... These two strangers put their lives on the line for each other; they were willing to risk it all to symbolically remove racism [Love, 2019].

This story demonstrates how Whiteness works in American society. Tyson's gender, skin color, and privilege, which intersected in the midst of an explosive confrontation driven by racial division, existed as Newson's protection. If likeminded White teachers can cross over similar ridges that cause racial discomfort, coconspirators will reach their White students in a way that will lead to sustainable change in the community. Like Love, Tochluk argues that White teachers are too comfortable avoiding uncomfortable conversations on race because of how they can avoid discomfort through a lifetime spent in White spaces. Tochluk refers to White racial avoidance as a "dis-ease." DiAngelo's *White Fragility* is similar to Tochluk's *Witnessing Whiteness*. In her popular 2018 book, DiAngelo addresses the common reaction from her White peers who feel threatened, angry, even irritated every time the race question arises. She refers to White discomfort as "fragility." Finally, Harvey's book *Raising White Kids* aims to inform White parents about the need to make their children aware that America is full of racial tension; that that tension can be mitigated if White children are raised in households that inform them that race matters. Harvey's book, like those written by Love, DiAngelo, and Tochluk, debunks the post-racial myth that suggests it is best to go through life colorevasive, as if race does not matter.

Together, these academics conjure an analogous message about who shoulders the responsibility for changing much of White America's colorevasive outlook. The message is also one that racial justice educator Debby Irving has upheld since the publication of *Waking Up White: And Finding Myself in the Story of Race* (2014). Irving maintains that White Americans, not Black Americans, "bear the burden" to educate other White Americans about the legacy of racism. Therefore, White educators should carry the weight of dismantling oppressive structures caused by America's original sin. Taking the theories proffered by Love, DiAngelo, Tochluk, Harvey, and Irving into consideration, *Race Conscious Pedagogy* aims to answer four questions: (1) Why should public schools make Race Conscious Pedagogy an integral part of the curriculum? (2) How are our children paying a detrimental price because public schools refuse to implement critical race studies into the curriculum? (3) What assistance should be given to Students of Color to ensure academic success in schools with predominantly White teaching staffs? (4) How can White people that make up America's school districts (parents, students, teachers, and administrators) relinquish power and comfort to create equitable schools? Through both an examination of empirical evidence along with an ethnographic examination of my experiences teaching a critical race studies course at a predominantly White high school, the pages that follow will offer educators advice for handling difficult community members, parents, students and faculty that might resist pedagogical and district-wide changes toward equity. I do so by providing readers a close look at the structure, curriculum, and pedagogy of my Seminar in Critical Race Studies course at a school I will call "Gap High School" for the sake of anonymity.

Introduction

The summer evening of June 20, 1888, a relatively large crowd, virtually all White, gathered at the Chestnut Street Auditorium in Harrisburg, Pennsylvania, to celebrate the commencement of the new male and female graduates of the city's high schools. The keynote speaker that evening was William Howard Day, a new member of the Harrisburg City School Board of Directors. Day was asked to speak that evening in part because he was the first and only African American member on the board. In two years' time, he would become the first African American elected president of the Harrisburg school board, making him the first person of African descent to hold that position anywhere in the United States. It had been 23 years since the end of the Civil War, which meant it had been nearly a quarter-century since Day worked as a recruiter for the United States Colored Troops and just as long since he directed "the military operation of the Underground Railroad," as Martin Delany once described him, during the latter half of the conflict (Rollin, 1883). Although the boys' and girls' high schools operated separately in 1888, this was the thirteenth joint commencement ceremony in the Harrisburg School District's history. The Metronome Orchestra played "a flood of melody," the *Harrisburg Patriot-News* reported, as the relatives of almost three dozen graduates celebrated the milestone accomplishment. It was not often that school board members were asked to give commencement speeches, so Day's 15-minute presentation was significant for multiple reasons.

As Day, known in civil rights circles as the intellectual rival to Frederick Douglass, rose to speak that evening, he had planned to deliver from the rostrum a poignant and contemporaneous elucidation on the state of public education a decade after home rule was restored in the South and after the promise of a second founding for the country following the ratification of the 14th Amendment withered like a flower. "Knowledge of the work in this high school," he declared, "learned by seven years official association with the mode of teaching under your present distinguished principal, Professor [J. Howard] Wert, and his able associates, and the exercises of this afternoon impress upon me with renewed force the idea which is growing in the community, and which has been recently voiced more than formerly, that this is *the people's college*" (Mealy, 2010). Day made it clear as he spoke to an overwhelmingly White audience that the purpose of public education was to serve all people despite socioeconomic circumstance or racial difference. In a charged atmosphere of strained race relations after the failure of Reconstruction and as national political leadership seemed to be leading the country into racial regression, Day made points both sensible and incendiary. His keynote, known generations later as "The People's College" speech, assumed the tone of a firebrand, restrained by the evening's festivity, while driven by emancipating hope.

Day, the former publisher and editor of the revolutionary yet short-lived Antebellum-era abolitionist newspaper *The Aliened American*—a title suggesting both enslaved and free African Americans had been robbed of their very being and citizenship by way of forced servitude and institutional segregation—pushed upon his listeners hard truths: public education, he said, "belongs to the people, and is for the benefit of the people." His audience sat captivated, with nerves tested; but it was a man who had worked 50 years in public education, first as a tutor of the children of fugitive slaves in Ohio and Canada, then as a Freedmen's Bureau superintendent responsible for building schools for freed persons in the South. "Indeed," he said, "no man is born into knowledge and training for duty." At birth, Day implied, White children and Black children possess the same capacity to learn. But social culture, he would interject, disadvantaged poor and Black children; for this is why he declared the public school system to be "the crowning point, the apex" of race and class equity. "It [public schools] borrows its eminence not simply from its curriculum, but from the usefulness with which it is intended to serve the whole people, high or low, rich or poor, in the graded and necessary preparations for American duties." Then Day turned to his memory of teaching children of enslaved persons as the speech drew to its highpoint. "The accidents of birth or circumstances, or matters over which a man can have no control, amount to nothing in considering the interests of the thousands of children committed to your care for tuition and training in the public school—the People's College" (Mealy, 2010). Day caused some discomfort among listeners as he injected racial discrimination so forthrightly into his oratorical reminder about America's democratic promise: "If we acted upon any other idea—if we presumed that some are divinely born aristocrats—that others were divinely booted and spurred to ride upon the necks of others—that others are divinely born to crawl under the feet of those rulers, and that 'divinity hedges a king'—we could have no public schools. Then certain privileged by birth, as we call it, would administer our public trusts; and the man outside of the charmed, kid-gloved, aristocratic circle would be the mudsill of society."

In many ways, Day's 1888 address on the "People's College" exposes many holes that exist in the public school system today as it pertains both to how Students of Color endure a sense of racial isolation and stress along with the price White and Black students pay for the continuance of traditionalist pedagogues in the classroom and monocultural curricula that implies one dominant culture is valued over others. He recognized quite clearly that the default of the education system was set on assuming that the best path forward for every student is to design a teaching and learning model to mimic the values of White, middle-class, cisgender, and able-bodied males. He challenged the employees and taxpayers of the Harrisburg School District to expose White students to race conscious thinking, to help the few Students of Color in the district flourish in the classroom, to ensure just and fair distribution of resources based upon each student's individual needs, and to give teachers strategies for creating culturally responsive lessons. He warned, "Crush a man by the enactments of the conventionalities of society, and in nearly every case you weaken his mental forces; you crush out his manhood. The public school system opens its doors to all the children of the State and the Nation. It says to each and to all—from the age of six to twenty-one, come to the training place for future American citizenship. Come! Enter these portals in the name of God and country and justice and liberty and equality!"

In the rhetorical roller coaster of this provocative speech, Day had three targets in mind: (1) to explain to White parents that their children will acquire a higher level of critical thinking skills when given the opportunity to learn with children of other racial and economic backgrounds; (2) to make a call for action to help African American students excel in a school system that traditionally has been created for White children by White educators; and (3) to refocus curriculum and pedagogy on race consciousness (my term, not his) that would combat generations of miseducation or misrepresentation in the learning experiences of every student. Day's call for equity marked the moment that transformed the Harrisburg School District into a place where African American students could find leaders willing to make educational freedom and social justice part of the curriculum in the last decade of the 19th century. His oration would lead to the hiring of several African American teachers in Harrisburg's schools before the turn of the century. Day would eventually pass away on December 3, 1900; but between his "People's College" speech and death, the teachers in Harrisburg were trained to attack race-based discrimination. His forthright insistence for a brand of pedagogy concentrating on critical race studies propelled others to call for the same in the 20th century, namely W.E.B. Du Bois (1950), who would later warn educators to not forget Day's contribution to the fight for educational equity: Day fought "for the integration into the democracy of America [and] we cannot forget the full life and real service of this intelligent, busy and unselfish servant of man."

It has been over 130 years since William Howard Day addressed the three defects in education policy: racial isolation, monocultural curricula that privileges White students, and colorevasive school policy. What does it say that more than a century has gone by and the school system still defaults to colorblindness? What does this mean for the American educational system in the 21st century that is now challenged to meet the needs of intersectional identity categories, such as race, gender, language, class, ethnicity, religion, ability and queerness?

It would be one thing if the 2020s were the first decade in which educators engaged in a discussion over whether the education system propagates hegemonic colonial systems of society at large. As seen in Day's "People's College" speech, for much of American history intellectuals have argued that the public school system has long existed as the incubator of White supremacy. This was a concept social reformers and critical pedagogues like Frederick Douglass and Henry Highland Garnet to Du Bois and Marcus Garvey to Malcolm X and Ella Baker to Paulo Freire and bell hooks to Gloria Ladson-Billings and Henry A. Giroux have advanced for generations. By the 21st century, education reformers, working in the shadow of those aforementioned, with decades of evidence and education theory about inequity issues at their disposal, still find themselves grappling with educational justice. These social and pedagogical reformers have demanded public education become diverse, equitable and inclusive; that educators teach in a way that deconstructs America's historical and contemporary racist history. Educators who are White (including me) have an obligation to learn about educational justice along with the intellectual theories that address race and racism to understand better the degree of trauma faced by students from marginalized communities that sit in our classrooms.

Rightfully so then and now, Communities of Color are skeptical about how the public school system treats its children. In 1935, just as the National Association for the Advancement of Colored People (NAACP) hired Charles Hamilton Houston to head its new legal strategy to desegregate K-12 schools along with colleges and law schools, the organization's cofounder W.E.B. Du Bois, who had recently resigned from its executive board over his evolving position on Black intra-racial solidarity, expressed concern over the lower levels of support White teachers would provide Black children if all of America's schools were to desegregate. In a controversial article titled "Does the Negro Need Separate Schools?" Du Bois (1935) wrote, "[the] proper education of any people includes [a] sympathetic touch between teacher and pupil." He suggested the teacher must understand students' "surroundings and background" as well as "the history of his class and group." White teachers in the 1930s, he argued, missed the socio-emotional side of African American students and were thus incapable of providing such empathy to Students of Color. "There are many public school systems in the North where Negroes are admitted and tolerated, but they are not educated; they are crucified ... in [the] classroom or on the campus, in [the] dining halls and student activities, or in common human courtesy." These words might sound uncharacteristic for Du Bois, especially considering that he was an ardent champion for racial integration. His concern over equity in education (achievement, fairness, funding, opportunity, curriculum, a sense of belonging), nevertheless, should sound familiar. He addressed this point: "that a separate Negro school, where children are treated like human beings, trained by teachers of their own race, who know what it means to be black ... is infinitely better than making our boys and girls doormats to be spit and trampled upon and lied to by ignorant social climbers, whose sole claim to superiority is ability to kick 'n-----' when they are down." While Du Bois made it clear that he preferred to send Students of Color to racially mixed schools, his priority at that moment was to ensure Black students a proper race conscious education. He said, "the Negro needs neither segregated schools nor mixed schools. What he needs is Education." Du Bois's 1935 question about whether White teachers and majority White schools can effectively educate Students of Color is again at the center of the debate over equity in public education.

Race Conscious Pedagogy is about this Du Boisian element of equitable and inclusive K-12 schools. Similar to William Howard Day's threefold "People's College" thesis, this book aspires to offer all educators—but mostly White pedagogues in predominantly White high schools—ideas to create a classroom that demonstrates solidarity with students of non-dominant cultures while awakening White students to existing systemic barriers that have made the experiences of Students of Color—along with those who are disabled, religious minorities, and LGBTQ+ students—a frustrating reality inside and outside of school. Moreover, a race conscious pedagogic praxis (see figure 4.1 in Chapter 4) calls for more than a commitment by educators to help students find their way in a racist society; it is about the commitment to changing the mindfulness of administrators, taxpayers, and parents about the meaning of educational equity. The mission is to make the fight for justice a community wide effort. This involves partnerships with community foundations and collaboration between school districts and surrounding communities, including nonprofits, businesses, heritage centers, youth centers, and public libraries.

To be a race conscious educator, one must allow for a new style of critical pedagogy that democratizes the classroom by moving away from regulating and managing voices but instead allows students to share what they have learned about the world from their unique experiences combined with assigned texts. This style of teaching that I call Race Conscious Pedagogy (RCP) utilizes the foundations and central tenets of Critical Race Theory, with particular attention given to the intersections of race and policy, race and education, race and sports, race and democracy, race and the military, race and the economy, race and housing, race and popular culture, race and policy, and race and the media. Contrary to traditional banking methods of instruction that often results in conformity, Race Conscious Pedagogy employs a teaching method that both pushes back against cultural normativity while removing authority from the instructor so students can engage in democratized dialogues centered on meaningful reflections about a group of texts related to critical analyses of Whiteness studies, African American studies, Asian American studies, Latinx studies, Arab American studies, the study of First Nations, as well as racialized religions such as Jewish American and Muslim American studies. To quote cultural critic and critical pedagogy scholar Henry A. Giroux (2011), a critical approach enables students to read texts as "objects of interrogation." In the same vein, a critical race studies course postulates that racism is pervasive in American society before interrogating the texts (Lynn, 1999). This point notwithstanding, a course grounded in RCP is committed to finding solutions to America's myriad systemic and dialectic racial problems. A Critical Race Theory lens is utilized to navigate scholarship and prime students as critical agents in work toward social change and policy reform in the realms of race and racism.

This type of restructuring to instruction is important because, for many students representing non-dominant cultures, a safe space for sharing personal experiences tied to an academic reading is more than a mode of expression or a process to solve problems; it is a method of understanding identity. To instruct in a way that enables students to share ideas that might lead them to disrupt dominant majoritarian 19th-, 20th-, and 21st-century thought-styles about the world is, according to Bettina L. Love (2019), Professor of Education Theory and Practice at the University of Georgia and author of *We Want to Do More Than Survive: Abolitionist Teaching and the Pursuit of Educational Freedom*, "how dark students make sense of the unjust world and a way to sustain who they are." The students' various life experiences allow one another to increase racial literacy by seeing the world differently. Herein lies a solution for how predominantly White schools can fully embracing Students of Color while enabling students from homogeneously White, small town environments to develop higher levels of critical analysis about the world because they are provided the opportunity to learn in a setting where they must interact with children from other racial and ethnic backgrounds while also engaging with texts that represent cross cultural experiences.

To be a race conscious educator, one must think deeply about how a racial group that is different than one's own are internalized. As social psychologist Jennifer Eberhardt (2019) says, "Confronting implicit bias requires us to look in the mirror." The most successful educators are those who perform a great deal of self-reflection. Self-awareness will mitigate those moments of acting out biases. Sure, there are certain situations that trigger bigoted presumptions. Educators, however, can confront their own biases by understanding situations that commonly elicit prejudiced emotions. This applies as much to a veteran educator that ponders personal racial presumptions as it does to a new teacher that asks himself or herself why the majority of students failed an exam or why a lesson plan fell flat. Education researcher Yolanda Sealey-Ruiz of the Teacher's College at Columbia University calls this necessary step toward self-awareness the "archaeology of the self." Sealey-Ruiz challenges aspiring educators to examine one's own disposition toward race, ethnicity, sexuality, class, religion, and abilities before interacting with children. "This should be done first," she claims, "before someone examines their pedagogy" (Picower et al., 2017; Future for Learning, 2018). Only after reflecting on one's own biases and what level of empathy they bring to the classroom can a teacher claim to have the students' best interest in mind.

While Sealey-Ruiz understands how the influences of biases in the classroom can result in dysfunctional relationships between teachers and students, Love offers an alternative perspective on how to move teachers closer to becoming race conscious pedagogues. She argues that instructors who avoid deep intrinsic inspection into how they process their racial bias often "spirit murder" students that are African, Latinx, Asian, and Native Americans. In other words, teachers that still believe the education system is just, that racism is not institutionalized, can easily reconcile the fact that they do not care for children the way educators should; this mindset, according to Love, has "their vision ... impaired by hate, racism, and White supremacy" (Love, 2019). This perspective sheds light on a breach in the educational system that must bind the social emotional development of students to learning in schools. She references the Jonathan Edwards cartoon "White Vision Glasses," which offers juxtaposing representations of an African American male. When looking at the figure without the glasses on, the individual is shown holding a cellphone in one hand while enjoying a soda. But racial presumptions prevail when peering through the glasses, as the figure is now carrying a bag of marijuana, wielding a pistol, and drinking a Colt .45. This image augments the points made by Sealey-Ruiz and Love: that if a majorative system of Whiteness (or anti–Blackness) predominates a teacher's subconscious it will often result in the endangerment and devaluation of the lives of Students of Color. Left unchallenged by the school system, these presumptions will infiltrate the minds of each student, resulting in the further degeneration of American race relations, especially as it pertains to systemic problems like the racial wealth gap, academic opportunity gap, curricular success, inequalities in social arrangements like schools and neighborhoods, and the disproportionate crime rate.

While William Howard Day referred to public education as "The People's College," Love (2019) calls schools "the mirrors of our society." This is a beautiful expression linking schools to communities. It means, however, that deeply entrenched racist ideas that produce discriminatory policies in the real world also infiltrate the school system. In the same way the public becomes divided over the fight for social justice as it relates to issues such as voter disenfranchisement, trans soldiers in the military, and the killings of Black Americans by law enforcement, there will undoubtedly be a high degree of resistance to the implementation of an education equity policy and race conscious curricula. Therefore, in addition to seeking out the cultures and experiences of students from marginalized communities, race conscious pedagogues must prepare themselves to withstand attacks from taxpayers, parents, students, and even colleagues while remaining steadfast in the commitment to Race Conscious Pedagogy. Often, the criticisms are of a distressing nature that makes teachers question whether it is all worth it. This book exists as a testimony to say that *it is worth it*. For the few hours or, in some cases, days a teacher will have to cope with a degree of discomfort levied upon him or her by a malevolent community member is nothing in comparison to the unceasing experiences that a child from a marginalized community endures much more often.

This book exists also as a warning to race conscious educators that backlash to any form of equity initiative is inevitable. Since schools have always existed as spaces that abet in institutionalizing White supremacy—even in schools that are populated with a majority of Teachers of Color and Students of Color—there is rifeness in the negative reaction to anything that challenges the existing state of affairs. Personal and vindictive counterattacks are the price that race conscious pedagogues must pay to do the work of challenging a school culture that has for centuries either willingly overlooked or unconsciously ignored racial distortions propagated by curriculum, popular culture, and policy.

In Chapter 1, I introduce readers to Beverly Daniel Tatum's notion of "color silence" to illustrate how silence on racial matters only serves to empower racist ideas and racist structures. This chapter is heavy with data that spotlights the rising rate of hate crimes. I also reference my sister, who is adopted from South Korea, by sharing her experiences growing up in a White household while being racially "Othered" by her peers at school and at work. This chapter ends with the rationality behind the creation of my critical race studies course at a rural high school in Lancaster County, Pennsylvania.

Chapter 2 examines the source of Race Conscious Pedagogy by tracing its history to the ruling of *Brown v. Topeka Board of Education*. In particular, I illustrate how race conscious education was implemented at "freedom schools" built during the 1964 Mississippi Freedom Summer and at intercommunal schools created by the Black Panther Party after 1969. These revolutionary schools left behind a blueprint for cultural responsiveness in the classroom that has been forsaken by educators for generations.

Chapter 3 looks back at the Black student occupation and sit-in movement on college campuses in the late 1960s and an exploration of the prevailing racist culture that has been fostered on college campuses and at secondary schools since the 1970s. I contemplate the many examples in recent years of White students intimidating Students of Color at colleges and high schools across the country. This historical foundation is important for positioning the experiences of students who are African, Latinx, Asian, Native American, Jewish, and Muslim at predominantly White schools in the current era; and it helps lay the foundation for the rationale behind the characteristics, mentality, and instructional approach that comprise Race Conscious Pedagogy.

In Chapter 4, I offer a definition and pedagogical framework for what I mean by Race Conscious Pedagogy. Once RCP has been defined, I discuss at length the three theoretical approaches behind the design of my signature critical race studies class, which I call "Seminar in Critical Race Studies." The framework for my course is based on (1) AP Capstone QUEST curriculum, (2) Critical Race Theory, and (3) Freirean critical problem-posing pedagogy.

In Chapter 5, I offer specifics about the curriculum, classroom policies, the course's thesis, texts, the pedagogical style, grading, and collaborative work norms in my critical race studies course. This chapter is designed to help educators construct classes in a way that is advantageous to Race Conscious Pedagogy while guaranteeing students a quality education that refines skills in critical analysis, research, paper writing, and public speaking. Moreover, I demonstrate how various and often competing constructions of race shape how students engage in the course texts, negotiate the classroom, and eventually refashion their personal conceptions of identity.

Chapter 6 begins with a thorough examination of the ethnic studies debate that took place in the Tucson Unified School District between 2006 and 2017. In 1998, Tucson Unified School District created an expansive Ethnic Studies Program that included departments in African American studies, Asian American studies, Native American studies, and La Raza (Mexican American) studies. In 2006, the Arizona Superintendent of Public Schools, Tom Horne, put the La Raza program in crosshairs. After five years, Horne convinced the state legislature to pass House Bill 2281, which included language banning the La Raza studies program. Parents and teachers immediately sued the state for enacting a law they viewed as "not for a legitimate educational purpose." In the 2017 case, *Gonzalez v. Douglas, Arizona Superintendent of Public Instruction*, the Ninth District Court ruled HB 2281 invalid under the 1st and 14th Amendments to the United States Constitution. While the struggles are not the same, this episode serves as the backdrop for my experiences dealing with problematic parents, colleagues, and students after the launch of my critical race studies class in rural Pennsylvania.

Chapter 7 offers insight into how to deal with the backlash, which is illuminated through my own experiences at Gap High School. I share stories about the moments I have had to deal with public counterattacks to the creation of Seminar in Critical Race Studies. I provide examples of how I have handled difficult members of the community as well as students who protested the existence of my class in various ways.

Chapter 8 details several discussions with my students about controversial topics related critical race studies—which include how students utilize various texts while engaging in conversations about the legal and social construction of race, the myth of racial innocence and Du Boisian double consciousness, and the movement for Black lives. Unfortunately, there is only enough space in this chapter to include three lessons. Among the most noteworthy lessons not included is an examination of the authenticity of White privilege, the politics of race in amateur and professional sports, Colorism, the Myth of the Model Minority, cultural appropriation and the debate over Native American mascots and nicknames, and debates about the Confederate flag and who can say the n-word. The objective of this chapter is to give educators a template for how to navigate uncomfortable discussions with high school students that will prove worthwhile learning experiences across a spectrum of critical race studies topics.

The scope of *Race Conscious Pedagogy* does not allow me to reflect on a broader educational equity program that addresses systemic fixes to funding or strengthens the link between a student's school and home; rather, this book is about transforming pedagogy at majority White high schools by centering courses around Race Conscious Pedagogy and a critical examination of racism in the United States. Conceding that a single race studies seminar will not be the end-all and be-all to dismantling a centuries-old system of miseducation, Chapter 9 moves into the realm of school district-wide cultural competence. This final chapter will offer a series of preemptive methods for administrators and teachers to turn school districts and school buildings into safe and welcoming spaces for Students of Color as well as White students. Readers looking for a sweeping equity plan will find value in this chapter. This solution-oriented chapter is divided into two sections, one for administrators and the other for classroom teachers.

1

To Be Silent on Racism
Is to Empower Racism

Introductory Note: This chapter reflects upon the rise in hate crimes and the increase in racial isolation to explain the rationale behind the creation of my critical race studies course at a rural high school in Lancaster County, Pennsylvania.

A sign that read "No place for hate" was placed on the corner of 4th and East Jefferson streets in Charlottesville, Virginia, where 32-year-old Heather Heyer lost her life in a hate crime. She was killed by a 20-year-old neo–Nazi who drove his car through a crowd of antiracists protesting a gathering of White nationals on August 12, 2017. That part of the street, since renamed "Heather Heyer Way," shares an ominous mystique not dissimilar to the unnerving feeling when seeing the spot on Route 80 where Viola Liuzzo, a White woman, was killed in Alabama by a group of Klansmen for participating in the Selma March. The so-called "Unite the Right" rally was reportedly designed to support a public statue of Confederate general Robert E. Lee, which the city wanted to remove. And yet nothing that transpired during the two-day demonstration had anything to do with the monument to Lee. In truth, even the Sons of Confederate Veterans, a group that mobilizes against Confederate statue removal and upholds the notion of the Lost Cause of the South, was not present at the tiki torch rally on August 11 or the violent fracas of August 12. The group would eventually go as far as issuing a statement condemning the violence instigated by White nationalists on that fatal summer day, claiming the protesters "tarnish[ed] the good and glorious name of the Confederate soldier" (Resnick, 2017). The gathering, then, developed into the largest White supremacist rally seen in the United States in decades. Stanford University professor of psychology and recipient of the MacArthur "genius" grant Jennifer Eberhardt (2019) calls it the "tipping point" during the "summer of hate." An assortment of Confederate flags and swastikas covered the streets of downtown Charlottesville. Those hate symbols were accompanied by racist and homophobic slurs, along with chants of "Jews will not replace us!" The hatred that had besieged the town in and around the University of Virginia peaked with the death of Heyer. The *Washington Post*, which after the fact provided a gallery of photographs of the violence, reported that Heyer's death had "riveted the nation's attention" (Duggan, 2018).

Heyer's death alone was not the reason a national dialogue on the state of race in America took place. After a long two days, it was President Donald Trump who enflamed the racial divide by asserting antiracists deserved as much blame for Heyer's death as the neo–Nazis, going as far as to say there were "very fine people on both sides" and "I think there is blame on both sides."

Some Nazis are good people, the 45th president of the United States fundamentally proclaimed. David Duke, the former Grand Wizard of the Ku Klux Klan, tweeted gratitude for Trump's confirmation: "Thank you President Trump for your honesty & courage to tell the truth about #Charlottesville & condemn the leftist terrorists in BLM/Antifa" (@DrDavidDuke, 2017). And America's foremost White supremacist, Richard Spencer, the Madison Grant of the current era, called Trump's statement "fair and down to earth" (@RichardBSpencer, 2017). The cover of *The Chronicle of Higher Education* called the traumatic episode "A Looming Siege" of White nationalism led by Spencer and Jason Kessler, both alumni of the University of Virginia. White nationalism and far right extremism were now officially in the mainstream. It only took the pretext of a rally in support of a Confederate general to bring that to the surface.

Two days after the Charlottesville violence, Pearce Tefft, the father of one of Charlottesville's White supremacist demonstrators, Pete Tefft, submitted an open letter to the *Fargo-Moorhead Inforum* denouncing his son's decision to march alongside White nationalists. He wrote, "I … wish to loudly repudiate my son's vile, hateful and racist rhetoric and actions [in Charlottesville]." Tefft, of North Dakota, conceded, "We do not know specifically where he learned these beliefs," claiming further, "He did not learn them at home." Tefft also affirmed that he taught "all of my children" that all of God's creations are created equal, adding, "we must love each other all the same." Apparently, he penned, his son "has chosen to unlearn these lessons" (Tefft, 2017; Tatum, 2017).

The letter, as heartbreaking as it might appear to parents who blame themselves for their children's shortcomings, evokes bravery for Mr. Tefft, who repeatedly criticized his son's leanings toward neo-fascism. Tefft declared that his son, Pete, was no longer welcome into his home until the hateful beliefs were renounced. For as commendable as the letter is, one line stands alone: "We have been silent up until now." In other words, Tefft had conceded his failure to raise his children in a race conscious household. He added, "Now we see that this was a mistake."

"We have been silent up until now." This is an admission of a profound recklessness that, I am sure, would indict most White parents in 21st-century America. For example, one survey (Kotler et al., 2019) of more than 1,000 educators and 6,000 parents of children ages three to 12 conducted in 2019 by Sesame Workplace and the Non-Partisan and Objective Research Organization (NORC) at the University of Chicago makes it strikingly clear most White parents avoid talking to their children about racial and ethnic identity. Nearly three-quarters (74 percent) of White parents admit to speaking with their kids about race and ethnicity either "rarely" or "never." The same survey shows just six percent of White parents "often" discuss race and ethnicity with their children, while 21 percent do so "sometimes." Tefft's public repudiation of his son is not the isolated ranting of a lone disconsolate White father, but simply the most recent, and the most visible, shot taken at a racist family member. His sentiments are widely held among a number of White Americans who have family members caught in racist tirades gone viral—it is not unusual to hear some White progressive and working-class members themselves joining Tefft's denunciation of family at the office and fitness centers across the United States. But Tefft's comment about remaining silent when it comes to race until it was too late is most notably expressed in the infinite silence of White America.

To be silent on racism is to empower racism. And there is a mound of evidence indicating that negligence on the part of liberal and well-meaning White Americans has advanced many of the hardships troubling Communities of Color. In recent history, an NBC News poll (Arenge, Perry, and Clark, 2018) released shortly after ABC canceled its *Roseanne* reboot when the lead character, Roseanne Barr, tweeted racist comments about Valerie Jarrett, an African American senior adviser to former president Barack Obama, indicated that 64 percent of Americans think racism in the United States is getting worse. A plurality in the same poll believes "too little attention is paid" to race relations. While profound, that NBC News poll reports 30 percent of Americans "say that racism is not a major problem," although a consensus agree "racism exists." Though this particular survey did not reveal results for how the viewpoint of Black and White respondents varied, a 2019 Pew Research Center study indicates that People of Color are more likely to view racism as a major issue than their White counterparts (Horowitz et al., 2019). Since one's environment shapes views on race, and because the same poll shows that Whites have little social interaction with Persons of Color, it is less likely for Whites to view White supremacy as a problem in America, and consequentially evoke strategies to avoid the topic altogether (Sue, 2015).

White America's cultural incompetence is clearly demonstrated in the results of the *Hate Crime Statistics* report (FBI, 2018) released by the Federal Bureau of Investigation (FBI) in 2017. The report indicates that the number of hate crimes reported to the FBI's Uniform Crime Reporting Program increased 17 percent since the previous year. According to the Bureau, the most common hate crimes in 2017 were directed toward "race/ethnicity/ancestry" (59.6 percent), followed by religion (20.6 percent), and then sexual orientation (15.8 percent).

The Pew Research Center released data in 2017 buttressing the FBI's annual report to show that race relations have progressively worsened each year since Obama's election as president in 2008. In the last year of President Obama's second term, only 19 percent of Americans said "race relations are improving" (Dimock, 2017). On the contrary, 79 percent in 2017 said race in America either worsened or stayed the same during Obama's two terms. When broken down by race, 61 percent of African Americans and 58 percent of Latinxs say race relations grew worse by the time Obama left office.

The most current data about the state of race relations in America provided by the Pew Research Center is a 2019 study that surveyed 6,637 randomly selected adults via a self-administered web survey. The report, published at the beginning of a peak period of nationwide discourse over the increase in White supremacist violence in the spring and summer of 2019, bookended by the White nationalist shootings that left 51 dead at two mosques in Christchurch, New Zealand, in March and the August 3 mass murder of 22 people at a Walmart in El Paso, Texas, that occurred because the shooter aspired to stop "the Hispanic invasion of Texas," showed 71 percent of African Americans and 56 percent of Whites had negative views about racial progress in the country. Almost three-fourths (73 percent) of African Americans suggested the Trump Administration was responsible for the deterioration of race relations, compared to less than half of Whites (49 percent). In a remarkable revelation, the 2019 poll indicated 65 percent of those surveyed believed, "It has become more common for people to express racist or racially insensitive views" (Horowitz et al., 2019). Additionally, almost half (45 percent) of the survey's participants said it has become "more acceptable" to express racist views since Trump's election.

According to the two aforementioned Pew Research Center reports, skepticism overall about the state of race and ethnic relations—and how religion is mediated through that lens—is worse off today than after the Los Angeles riots of 1992 when an ugly wave of violence traversed the country. The FBI's numbers of hate crimes validate those concerns. For example, reported hate crimes against Muslims in the United States have reached unprecedented numbers (FBI, 2018). In 2016, there were 127 reported victims of anti–Muslim hate crimes. This number does not include the 141 acts of intimidation toward Muslims in America during the same year. These numbers indicate a 19 percent increase of Islamophobic hate crimes since the previous year (Kishi, 2017; Beydoun, 2018). Also of note are the 684 anti–Jewish hate crime incidents reported to the FBI in 2016 alone. The number of anti–Jewish hate crimes jumped to 938 in 2017, a 37 percent spike from the previous year (FBI, 2018). Of course, violent acts of anti–Semitism are nothing new in American history. There have been attacks on individual Jews dating back to the 1915 lynching of Leo Frank. The growing presence of European refugees in the United States after World War II put Jews and Gentiles in close proximity to one another, producing a surge of violent hate crimes, which include the bombing of the Hebrew Benevolent Congregation in Atlanta in 1958, and the shootings at Temple Beth-Israel in Gadsden, Alabama, and St. Louis, Missouri's Brith Sholom Kneseth Israel Synagogue in 1960 and 1977, respectively (Fattal, 2018). Then there is the murderous rage of lone wolf White supremacists at Pittsburgh's Tree of Life Synagogue in October 2018, resulting in the deaths of 11 worshipers and six others injured, and at the Chabad in Poway Synagogue north of San Diego in April 2019 that left one person dead and three more with injuries.

Having faith in parents alone to discuss the circumstances surrounding race and cultural literacy with their children is not enough. A point has been reached in the history of the American education system that school districts must offer students—Black and White, but especially White—programs and courses that develop cultural literacy and racial tolerance for fear that the racial divide will expand at an alarming rate and racially incentivized violence becomes more deadly.

White Racial Isolation

Why should educators in America's schools embrace the responsibility to engage students in a race conscious education? It is because America is still a White space where racism has the ability to adapt to its surroundings much like a chameleon. In neighborhoods that are growing in color, studies have shown that the trend is for Whites to avoid moving in. In a sort of 21st-century White avoidance phenomenon, suburban Neighborhoods of Color have actually grown more segregated since the year 2000. While the so-called "White Flight" migration of the early 20th century found White urbanites fleeing to the suburbs once Black Americans moved into their neighborhoods following the Great Migration, then again after World War II when the government subsidized White relocation to the suburbs, White families have now increasingly fled their suburban Neighbors of Color in new ways that sociologist Daniel T. Lichter (2015) created the term "exurbs" to describe this self-segregation. Driven by darkening populations settling in the suburbs, Whites are now either restructuring their suburban neighborhoods in a way that is more and more gated or finding remote locations to move farther away from increasingly Black, Brown, and immigrant suburbanites. In 2015, Lichter used decennial census data on 222 metropolitan areas between 1990 and 2010, each with 1,000 Whites, African Americans, Latinxs, and Asians in locations that included Atlanta, Los Angeles, San Jose, San Antonio, Hartford, Philadelphia, Memphis, Cleveland, New York, Newark, and, among many others, the District of Columbia to study racial segregation within and between metropolitan areas. Lichter's research shows that, although more People of Color have moved to the suburbs, segregation inside suburbia has increased substantially during the first two decades of the millennium. The new color line, Lichter (2015) suggests, is "best expressed in the geographic separation of racial groups" where instead of the more traditional occurrence of White depopulation by means of White flight patterns, neighborhoods are now either establishing unincorporated, or walled-in, housing developments as a method of maintaining racial boundaries or finding places "into the fringe" of the metropolitan countryside.

Two studies issued by demographer William H. Frey and the American Community Survey in 2016 and 2018 confirm Lichter's residential segregation research. The reports published by Frey's team suggest that the suburbs have become the most highly segregated areas of the country, especially in northern metropolitan areas (Lichter, 2015; Frey, 2016; Frey, 2018; Chang, 2018). Over 50 percent of Whites say they will not live in an area that is more than 30 percent Black. The results of an investigation of Chicago, Seattle, and Baltimore by sociologists Lincoln Quillian and Devah Pager (2001) indicate that Whites avoid living in communities with Black neighbors because of the "perception of crime." They conclude that stereotypes associating African Americans, in particular, with crime leads to the false presumption that the greater the dark-skinned population in a community the higher the crime rate. While the study conducted by Quillian and Pager dates back to 2001, Jennifer Eberhardt's (2019) groundbreaking research on racial bias and stereotyping echoes this very point. "The sheer presence ... of blacks," the award-winning professor of psychology observes in *Biased: Uncovering the Hidden Prejudice That Shapes What We See, Think, and Do*, "is taken as a true indicator of danger, distorting safety perceptions and biasing people's sense of risk." The nearly 20 years combined worth of research proffered by Lichter, Frey, Quillian, Pager, and Eberhardt, each underscore the reality that media depictions and historical stereotypes such as African Americans are insatiable sexual deviants that are prone to violence, or that Latinxs are drug dealers, or the belief that Muslim Americans are both unflinchingly anti–American and operatives in a global terrorist network, function as an alternative reality in the absence of empirical data for the White populace.

The principle cause of racist behavior is the threat that Whiteness might be eroded by the presence of Blackness. Exurbs preserve White America's long tradition of evading Communities of Color, especially African Americans. As a result, White people live in a society insulated from racial stress and sequestered from racial trauma. White men and women go through each day free of racial discomfort; therefore, enjoying an existence wherein the feeling of entitlement to social, economic, and political advantages endures generations. The implication has been a new wave of White people calling the police on darker hued individuals for simply *being* in White spaces: a Starbucks, at a grill in a public park, a golf club, a school corridor, or at a public pool. The result is the reaffirmation that schools, coffee shops, college dormitories, and even sidewalks are spaces still controlled along racial lines. Cultural illiteracy is one of the inescapable consequences of residential, occupational, and scholastic segregation. Racial isolation, which fosters mistrust toward People of Color, perpetuates a fishbowl mentality.

If people with dark skin do not exist in a White person's fishbowl, then there is no need to learn about America's various social dynamics that operate around race, such as class, gender, ethnicity, and color. Figurative fishbowls shelter White people from even being aware that diverse cultures exist in other areas of the country Martin Luther King, Jr., once described as "a type of colonial area ... too hot, too crowded, too devoid of creative forms of recreation ... an emotional pressure cooker" (Carson, 1998). Existential problems are just that—external and fundamentally not American. Why then is there the need to talk about race? Why learn about race? Why even think that race matters? Why consider that the life of a Black individual is valued less than the life of a White individual? Why think that a Black community is policed any differently than a White community? Why think that White students are advantaged by the education system and Black students are not? Or why try to understand that a microaggression toward a Person of Color is actually one of countless intentional and unintentional insults that often result in an individual's resentment, distress, anxiety, and despair?

Critical Whiteness scholar Robin DiAngelo (2018) contends that life in a racial fishbowl—she uses the term "isolation"—destructively socializes Whites "into a deeply internalized sense of superiority." She claims that Whites "either are unaware of or can never admit" that their privilege exists. So when confronted with the smallest amount of racial stress, Whites respond defensively with "emotions such as anger, fear, and guilt" and "behaviors such as argumentation, silence, and withdrawal." DiAngelo has a name for this range of defensive responses: *white fragility*. This is a concept, she believes, that is "born of superiority and entitlement" (DiAngelo, 2018).

White critical theorists like DiAngelo have spoken about race for decades. Sadly, the White public has remained notoriously defensive and willfully ignorant when confronted with conversations about implicit bias, White privilege, meritocracy, and White supremacy. One of the most common responses I receive when raising the topic with my White peers is a nasty scowl and unapologetic proclamations indicating that they are most certainly not a racist. Shelly Tochluk (2010), author of *Witnessing Whiteness: The Need to Talk About Race and How to Do It,* calls the discomfort displayed by Whites a "dis-ease." While Tochluk's theory is a close association to DiAngelo's concept of white fragility, dis-ease addresses the inability of Whites to be "good witnesses of our own whiteness." She writes:

> White people in general are ill-at-ease over issues of race…. Unfortunately, many of us choose a colorblind, transcendence-seeking optimism that ends up stifling the honestly difficult dialogue we need to have in order to deal with the very real racial dynamics that continue to play out in our interactions. The strategies we use to avoid dealing with race, sadly, then allow us to behave offensively without awareness.

The "colorblind, transcendence-seeking optimism" that Tochluk speaks of is in fact *silence.* This explicit and implicit decision to remain silent actually says more to our children about where one stands on racial hierarchies. If we choose not to talk about America's racist history—and how that history applies to contemporary racial dynamics—then our children will fail to see racism as a problem that needs fixing. Moreover, our children will grow up assuming that all kids regardless of race, ethnicity, or gender will share the same experiences. Accordingly then, when race is brought up in a conversation, the kneejerk reaction by a White individual is one of denial or contempt.

What is the best way to characterize white fragility and dis-ease? According to Beverly Daniel Tatum (2017), it would be to call White Americans "color-silent." Tatum's characterization of White America's certainty in the myth of racial innocence is a damning indictment of the current status of the American democratic project. To uphold oneself as colorevasive, which is the meaning of Tatum's allegation, is the implicit choice to avoid engaging in uncomfortable truths about America's racist culture. To paraphrase Ibram X. Kendi (2019), the founder of the Antiracist Research and Policy Center now at Boston University, the ability to recognize race allows individuals to see America as a racist society, as a nation made up of racist policies, as a country inhabited by a majority of people who possess a combination of racial apathy and racial intolerance. But unfortunately for the mental health and physical safety of People of Color, recent social psychology studies on race show a majority of White Americans claim "they don't see race." Psychology of race experts like Phillip Mazzocco (2017) argue that racial color-blindness "is associated with higher levels of prejudice," which often produces physical and emotional harm to individuals of non-dominant cultural groups.

Color silence is born of the dereliction of White parents and White teachers to place racial and cultural literacy at the forefront of a child's development. Color silence is a political and ideological action that perpetuates the post-racial myth, that we live in a society wherein race has no relevance in daily occurrences—and thus White individuals have no responsibility to acknowledge its existence. This is an easy concept to propagate since the United States no longer has a racial order or set of Jim Crow laws that maintain a color line between the races and cultural groups. Yet the decision by White teachers and White students to avoid conversations about uncomfortable race topics actually declare loudly feelings about living contently in the privileges conferred by their Whiteness while People of Color are left alone to deal with structural disadvantages, like economic exploitation, social marginalization, powerlessness, cultural imperialism, and even violence (Young, 2004). The default for White educators is to proclaim to be colorevasive, that race and ethnicity have nothing to do with how they teach or discipline students. Colorevasive teachers believe they treat all students the same. This, of course, is wrong because to be a colorevasive teacher in America means that students of non-dominant cultures are treated as if they should be White, middle class, heterosexual, and able-bodied (Irvine, 2003).

Speaking to a New York City audience about the Vietnam War one-year before his death, Martin Luther King, Jr. (1967), said, "A time comes when silence is betrayal." Though a harsh criticism of the public's inaction over American military actions in Southeast Asia, King's April 4, 1967, speech is one way of seeing how destructive apathy can be at critical intervals of American history. Silence from educators on the topic of White supremacy is deafening and literally endangering to lives ranging from African Americans like Trayvon Martin to white antiracist activists like Heather Heyer.

The Racial Generational Gap

I was born in a small Pennsylvania city named Bradford in 1979. My family moved to Harrisburg, the capital of the Commonwealth, when I was five years old. Near the banks of the Susquehanna River, I was raised in the city's first planned development named Bellevue Park, an economically advantaged and predominantly White neighborhood on the city's eastern edge. Although my neighborhood was an upmarket piece of urban suburbia, my parents gave me the freedom to roam throughout every end of the city, from chic Uptown to eclectic Allison Hill. Always concerned about the increasing amounts of violence in the city, they had one rule: I could go anywhere and hang out with anyone as long as they knew where I was and whom I was with. If they discovered I was somewhere that I did not tell them I was going to be, that trust would have been broken and I would have spent my formative

years staring out of my bedroom window watching my brother play basketball with friends in our driveway or tackle football with our neighbors in our
front yard.

This was the 1990s. It was a time when I had never even heard of White
privilege. Neither had my parents. They maintained a naïve attitude and faith
in the Civil Rights Act and felt that it must be working to outlaw discrimination. They also were caught up in the problems and concerns of issues
that directly affected their work, family, or friends. My mother worked in
healthcare. At that time, breast cancer and HIV/AIDS were the field's main
concerns. Not racial issues. My father worked for the City of Harrisburg and
although he dealt with many labor issues, he never brought work home.

My parents also trusted that if they set a good example their children
would somehow absorb the same multicultural qualities of tolerance and
interest. Knowing that sometimes children have trouble listening to their
parents or hearing the intent of conversations, consistently leading by example would be a worthwhile route. Building on this concept, they used sports
to create opportunities to practice and play with kids of different cultural
backgrounds: to build a sports family so to speak. I had African American,
Asian American, and transgender coaches. Through these sporting activities
of baseball, basketball, soccer, and football, I built meaningful relationships
with friends and adult mentors from other races, many of which I still have
today.

While race was certainly an issue in my hometown, especially after the
violence that followed the acquittal of four police officers caught assaulting
Rodney King on a homemade video recording made its way to my Harrisburg neighborhood—both my brother and I were harassed on separate occasions while walking home from a 7-Eleven and school, respectively—my
parents still avoided discussing America's racial dynamics with me. Another
opportunity was thwarted when the O.J. Simpson verdict profoundly divided
America along lines of Black and White in the mid–90s. I know now that my
parents engaged with their colleagues at work about these topics. Why avoid
the elephant in the room with my siblings and me?

Silence also emanated from my teachers. My teachers, who were always
ever so willing to share their thoughts on dicey issues ranging from Clar-
ence Thomas's Supreme Court nomination to the Clinton-Lewinsky scandal,
never spoke a word about race to my classmates. Of course, all of my teachers were White and overwhelmingly female. None exhibited any desire to
take an active role in offering my peers and me insight on race-relations or
multiculturalism. In one sense, it was okay, even normal, to engage in material and discussions about the contentious issue of abortion. I still possess a
vivid recollection of having to endure a video of a performed abortion in my
eleventh-grade religion class. Even with classrooms full of curious teenagers,

never had any of my teachers broached the topic of race as I moved through my primary, intermediate, and secondary schooling. Not in English Lit. Not by any of my Social Studies teachers. Not in government classes. Perhaps it was because both the primary and high schools that I attended had a good cultural mix that educators did not see the need to tackle the subject. But that idea is naïve. My four years in high school were an era everyone was supposed to be colorblind. My White teachers believed that the country had achieved post-racialism because there were more Students of Color than ever before sitting in their classrooms. The fact of the matter is, they understood little about race and likely believed talking about it was rude.

I would also make my way through four years of preservice training to become a teacher, at a distinguished Pennsylvania teaching institute no less, without a single engagement in race and ethnic studies or discussion about cultural problems that might arise once I formally entered the teaching profession. I started my vocation in secondary education as a high school Social Studies teacher in September 2001. Two weeks into the school year—just days into my teaching career—I had my second period American history class full of sophomores interrupted by a colleague who burst into my classroom urging me to turn on the television. He said two airplanes had flown into the World Trade Center towers in New York City. It was an act of terrorism, he conveyed, but we did not know yet who orchestrated the attack. I stopped teaching, choosing to sit down with my students to watch the news. Soon the towers would collapse. I realized watching CNN coverage of the tragedy that the worldly experiences for my students—not just those with me in that moment, but the students I would teach over the next three decades—would be much different than mine. I admit that I did not know yet just how much life in America was going to change for my current and future students, but I knew I was totally unprepared for the changes that were about to begin in America.

Christine Marie is my younger sister. We call her Crissy. She was a senior in high school when the September 11 terror attacks occurred. Crissy was adopted into my family from South Korea after her first birthday and naturalized as an American citizen after her second birthday. Not once during my adolescence had I ever thought about her being any different than me. This was foolish. Of course she is different. Apart from the obvious gender difference, she is Asian and has all the facial features of a Korean. My sister is beautiful. She has fair skin, a prominent jaw, high cheekbones and slightly slanted almond shaped eyes. She has the darkest hair, long and shiny. And her last name is Mealy (well, was Mealy, she is married and an Eby now), so I assumed she would never face overt insults or veiled racial abuses that would cause her pain and fatigue. How naïvely colorevasive was I?

It mattered not how much she tried to assimilate into the culture of the

Mealy household in terms of her speech, dress, and tastes; anytime she left our home she was instantly "Othered." She had more problems socially than I had because regardless of how hard she tried to remind everyone she was a member of the Mealy family, her White peers always found ways (intentionally and unintentionally) to remind her that they were White and she was not. Crissy was in a unique situation: one that I thought little about. Like many children in her circumstance, she felt like she was too light for her dark peers and too physically different for White people.

Meanwhile, the burden of living up to expectations of the so-called model minority myth placed unnecessary pressures on Crissy to exude principled cultural values and achieve highly in school. The term "model minority" was coined in 1966 by sociologist William Petersen in *The New York Times* to highlight the socioeconomic success of Japanese Americans. Petersen used Japanese Americans to disparage other "problem minorities," namely African Americans who had spent the previous decade agitating White spaces in an effort to achieve equal rights. Petersen characterized every racially minoritized group except Japanese-Americans as having "poor health, poor education, low income, high crime rate, and unstable family pattern[s]." The Japanese American, he measured, just twenty years removed from wartime internment camps, "challenges every such generalization about ethnic minorities" by exuding an exemplar work ethic, stable families, and good hygiene (Petersen, 1966). In other words, Petersen applauded Japanese Americans—and, over time, every other Asian ethnicity by default—for the group's assimilation into White American tradition.

Author and editor Ijeoma Oluo (2018) calls the model minority myth "active racism" that substantially harms Asian Americans and disconcertingly disregards the fact that Korean, Chinese, Japanese, Cambodian, Laotian, Burmese, Bangladeshi, Indian, Pakistani, Hmong, Vietnamese, Samoan, Pacific Islanders, and Native Hawaiians are varying ethnicities within the racial group. In addition to fundamentally dismissing these contrasting Asian cultures in the United States, the author of *So You Want to Talk about Race* charges William Petersen's model minority myth of discounting war refugees, H-1B visas, and Asian Americans with disabilities.

When guests entered our home, Crissy was considered White. Outside of our home, however, she was seen as a foreigner. She bore the burden of not living up to the standards of the model minority stereotype while accepting the idea that any academic and economic shortcoming had nothing to do with structural forms of discrimination in school and at work. Her identity was in a perpetual state of flux. Everyone in our household could have benefited from reading the work of Chicana cultural theorist Gloria Anzaldua. In her groundbreaking book, *Borderlands/La Frontera: The New Mestiza*, Anzaldua (1987) writes about the "borderland" as a physical and spiritual marker of an open wound where historical and cultural oppression impedes the identity development of those representing non-dominant cultures. Anzaldua expresses further that figurative borders prevail in a culture that devalues racial and gender minorities. Experience, identity, and history, Anzaldua believed, amalgamates to give those "living in more than one culture," multiple and "often opposing messages [that] causes *unchoque,* a cultural collision." Though writing about the U.S.-Mexican border, where Mexicans were stripped of their Mexican citizenship with the enactment of the Treaty of Hidalgo, Anzaldua's "borderland theory" should also be taken as an abstract explanation of "two worlds merging to form a third country, a border culture." Anzaldua was a Queer Feminist Chicana living in Texas and along the Mexican border with limited fluency in English. *Borderlands/La Frontera* is about her search to achieve "new higher consciousness" while striving to overcome an internal struggle with identity in the midst of harsh gender expectations and American colonialism. The borderland concept relates to the experiences of my sister, who knew she was an outsider stuck living in a perplexing culture where her constant code switching evolved into a state of depression. At times Crissy was treated as if she was too White, while some peers saw her as not White enough. To explain the state of mind of those like my sister caught between two worlds, Anzaldua suggests, "A border is a dividing line, a narrow strip along a steep edge. A borderland is a vague and undetermined place created by the emotional residue of an unnatural boundary. It is in a constant state of transition." Crissy channeled her depression into solitude. It caused her to separate herself from our family during her years in college.

In this way, Crissy saw herself as an individual born in South Korea, adopted by a White American family and brought to the United States, where she endured life in a cultural borderland. Like Anzaldua's struggle, Crissy figured out that achieving White, Christian, and middle-class authenticity was impossible. But to say Crissy temporarily disowned her parents and siblings is to miss the point of what she set out to do. She needed reprieve from the code switching, from the dueling identities inflicted on her by peer groups. Crissy needed to find a new *Crissy* that was comfortable belonging to an ethnic group about which she knew little. The level of unfathomable pain and confusion caused by her being "Othered" was something that nobody in my family understood. At the time, it had been almost 25 years since the publication of Anzaldua's seminal book. For individuals like my sister, Anzaldua's words could be as lifesaving as ever.

The experiences of my sister's generation and that of Generation Z is defined by racial animus triggered by the September 11, 2001, terrorist attacks. Many of my current students were pre-teens when Barack Obama was elected president of the United States. It was a peculiar moment when both liberal and conservative pundits prematurely agreed that America had finally attained post-racialism with the election of the nation's first African American president. Actions by a small yet active subculture in White America indicated otherwise. Over a thousand (1,018) hate groups operated in the United States four years after Obama's 2008 election (Stuyk, 2017). In 2009, the Tea Party emerged as a right-wing rebuke to "big government folks" like those in the Obama Administration and Democratic lawmakers occupying both houses of Congress during Obama's first two years in office (Skocpol and Williamson, 2016). This new conservative movement proclaiming to be "taking the country back" had success impeding much of Obama's domestic agenda, including attempts at immigration and gun reform after sweeping victories in the 2010 midterm elections. Tea Partiers would later embark on a campaign to disenfranchise those Black and Brown voters that played the most important role in placing Obama in the Oval Office. An Associated Press study of the 2012 election reported that for the first time, "the black voter turnout rate exceeded the white turnout rate." The study revealed that African American voters made up 13 percent of the electorate despite making up just 12 percent of the population (Weiner, 2013). The AP report was noticeably troubling to Republican and Tea Party conservatives that uproars over alleged "voter fraud" transfused the country. Gerrymandering efforts increased. The number of voting precincts dropped. As of 2018, 34 states had laws mandating voters show some form of identification at the polls. The biggest impact in voter ID laws and other suppression efforts is found in traditionally red states like Texas, Georgia and Mississippi where there are large numbers of Voters of Color. In *One Person, No Vote*, public policy expert Carol Anderson (2018) found no evidence that indicated voting irregularities that would warrant laws restricting voters' rights. She calls this a "No Vote" strategy concocted by the Republican Party aimed at suppressing the annual turnout of Democratic voters and Voters of Color that put a Black American man in the White House. Another 6.1 million Americans were kept from voting in 2016 because of state and felony disenfranchisement laws restricting voting rights for those convicted of felony-level crimes (ACLU, 2018).

There are more disturbing events that forced young people to think about their racial identities. In February 2012, 17-year-old Trayvon Martin was fatally shot by neighborhood watch coordinator George Zimmerman. Fifteen months later, Zimmerman was acquitted after an emotionally taxing trial. Shortly after the exoneration of Martin's murderer, social reform activists Alicia Garza, Patrisse Cullors, and Opal Tometi living at different ends of the country used their respective Twitter accounts to launch a social justice movement called #BlackLivesMatter (#BLM). Energized around Martin's case, the women designed #BLM as a movement with decentralized leadership working to raise awareness about anti–Black institutional racism based on the relative circumstances of specific locations in the United States (Khan-Cullors and asha bandele, 2018). The heroines' efforts expanded during the summer of 2014 when Michael Brown in Ferguson, Missouri, and Eric Garner in Staten Island, New York, were killed by police officers (Wallis, 2016). While the protests aimed at gathering support for the prosecution of the two officers responsible for taking the lives of Brown and Garner drew more support for Black lives across the country, neither law enforcer was indicted for the killings after lengthy grand jury investigations.

Over the next two years, several incidents between Males of Color and the police unsettled the country. In Cleveland on November 22, 2014, 12-year-old Tamir Rice was shot by a police officer (Lowery, 2016). Then the death of 25-year-old Baltimore resident Freddie Gray while in police custody in April 2015, followed by the public and eerily ritualistic killings of Alton Sterling and Philando Castille on July 5 and 6, 2016, created a breaking point for Communities of Color as disturbances between protesters and law enforcement covered on national media outlets made it impossible to bury one's head in the sand when it came to the steady fracturing of American race relations. Sadly, data indicates that White children did not discuss prejudice reduction or implicit bias with parents or teachers in controlled environments after these tragic events.

The Pew Research Center suggests it is easier to jump online to engage in race dialogue than to get into an uncomfortable face-to-face conversation with loved ones. One month after the deaths of Sterling and Castille, Twitter served as the key catalyst for conversations about race. There were 995 million tweets—an average of 2.1 million tweets per day—posted about American racial issues between January 1, 2015, and March 31, 2016 (Anderson and Hilton, 2016). Indeed, 60 percent of those tweets discussed #BLM, with issues ranging from the racially motivated mass shooting at Emmanuel AME Church in Charleston, South Carolina, to a Trump supporter punching a Black protester at a campaign rally. After using Crimson Hexagon software to analyze the tweets, it was discovered that the number of posts condemning #BLM dramatically exceeded the number of comments hailing the social justice movement (Anderson and Hilton, 2016).

If Black Lives Matter disruptions failed to make students think about race and positionality in White dominated spaces, the Trump campaign between 2015 and 2016 produced an anxiety complex among America's Students of Color. In April 2016, a Southern Poverty Law Center (SPLC) report found "an alarming level of fear and anxiety" arose among Students of Color. Even though 33 percent of the survey's participants admitted they had observed an increase in anti–Muslim and anti–immigration sentiment in schools, more than 40 percent of teachers refused to teach about the election's impact on race in America (SPLC, 2016). Evidence suggested that Trump's campaign comments about paying the legal bills for anyone who beat up a Black Lives Matter protester, or banning Muslims from entering the United States, or labeling Mexican immigrants as criminals engaging in sexual assault and drug smuggling hastened the degeneration of American race relations.

A second SPLC survey conducted after Trump's Electoral College victory reported an increase in "hate violence and incidents of harassment" around the country. The report stated, "a wave of incidents of bullying and other kinds of harassment washed over the nation's K-12 schools" (Potok, 2017). The SPLC recorded 867 hate crime incidents in the first 10 days after Trump's election; 323 instances occurred on university campuses or in K-12 schools. The instances covered a cross section of Americans. People who were immigrants, Arab Muslims, African Americans, Jews, LGBTQ+, and women were bullied or physically assaulted during that period. Though Fox News network coverage discredited the report, claiming that none of the evidence connected the hate crimes with Trump, the SPLC pointed out that the largest number of incidents occurred on the day after the election. The report adds that 37 percent of offenders of hate crimes referenced Trump, his Access Hollywood sexual assault tape, or his campaign slogan, "Make American Great Again." Ninety percent of respondents told the SPLC that school climates had been "affected negatively by the election" as slurs, derogatory language, and extremist symbols like the swastika pervaded schools. Over 8,000 respondents, or 80 percent, reported that Students of Color were "worried about the impact on them and their families" (Potok, 2017).

Absent of pushback from the Trump Administration, violent White nationals felt emboldened to march en masse with tiki torches—a symbolic homage to the Ku Klux Klan's tradition of burning crosses—through public streets without masking their identities. The defiance in Charlottesville was a tacit warning that right wing extremists were not afraid of legal retribution or social ostracism. Fourteen months after the "Unite the Right" rally, on October 27, 2018, a White nationalist armed with an AR-15 walked into the Tree of Life Synagogue in Pittsburgh and killed 11 people. The shooter said, "I just want to kill Jews." It is the deadliest attack on the Jewish community in American history. Another anti–Semitic shooting at a synagogue, this time near San Diego, occurred six months later.

From these tragic events and the struggles of my sister, I began to reposition myself in my role as teacher. In particular, these events prompted me to question the ways in which White parents and White teachers discuss race with the youth. Moreover, my engagement with critical race theory as an American Studies doctoral student at Penn State University's Harrisburg campus helped me to consider the ways that White adults and White youths avoid uncomfortable conversations about race both in their classes and private lives beyond the walls of Gap High School, where I have taught since 2007. My desire to understand and improve the conditions of White Americans and Americans of Color led me to obtain a Ph.D. in American Studies with a subfield in race and society, and to approach the Gap School District administration to create a race studies course for 10–12 grade high school students.

When the principal at Gap High School came to me during the spring semester of 2017 to ask if I would be interested in teaching the Seminar course for the newly implemented AP Capstone program, I saw an opening. AP Seminar teachers have the flexibility to choose one or more themes for the class as long as students engage in "deep interdisciplinary exploration" that allows them to problematize local or civic issues (College Board, 2016). I chose race, ethnicity, and gender as the theme for my course. For my students, most of whom are White, interdisciplinary studies in race and gender would likely exist as a fresh topic to hold their interest as I taught them AP Capstone mandated curriculum. This was particularly challenging for many reasons. One, the course runs in block schedule for a full year, or two semesters. The Gap School District has a strict 28-credit graduation requirement that limit the number of electives students can take. A full year course is a significant disadvantage as students can rarely afford to have a single class occupy an entire block over the span of two semesters. Second, I am obligated as a teacher of the Commonwealth of Pennsylvania to prepare students for the standardized tests known as the Keystone Exams. Though Social Studies is not a tested subject in Pennsylvania, our district policy has been to have non-tested subject teachers assist our English, Math, and Science colleagues with cultivating our students' formal nonfiction reading skills that they will need to perform proficiently on standardized tests. Lastly, I was about to launch this course at a rural high school with a student population that was 75 percent White (1,218 out of 1,624 students), a teaching staff that was 99 percent White, an administrative team that was 100 percent White, and a school board that was 88 percent White and 100 percent registered Republicans. None of this means, of course, that White teachers and moderate or conservative school board members cannot believe in intersectional inclusivity. It is, however, an indication of the school district's conservative and racially muted reputation. The school is situated in Lancaster County, which is an area the conservative media outlet *The Daily Caller* ranked the 97th Most Conservative Friendly County in the United States (Palko, 2010; Gap School District, 2019). I was sure the existence of this class would lead to a degree of resistance from students, parents, colleagues, and board members for challenging the district's status quo.

While it might on the surface seem more difficult to achieve these goals in traditionally conservative areas, the fact remains that liberal areas are also woefully lacking in implementing race-based studies despite the outward appearance of being far more empathetic to achieving educational justice. Despite the challenges, the critical race studies course I created at Gap turned out to be a pants kicker to school district officials. In fall 2019, the district's administration commenced the process of implementing an equity initiative. For the first time, the decades old phrase "culturally responsive pedagogy" entered the lexicon of many of the district's teachers and administrators. Relying on parents alone will fail to do the job of creating a culturally competent populace. Despite the good intentions to address race at home, the opportunities are limited many times to only building relationships, good or bad—as seemingly was the case for Mr. Tefft and his son. This is why formal education is needed to speak to racial history and culture. It is this tenet that underpins my approach to this book.

First, we must examine the roots of race conscious pedagogy by exploring the work of civil rights activists who spent the summer of 1964 building schools throughout Mississippi. For African Americans, school desegregation following the United States Supreme Court's ruling in *Brown v. Topeka Board of Education* proved to be disappointing. The unanimous opinion was the African American dream of racial barriers being dismantled: if Black and White children could go to school together for eight hours a day without the supervision of their parents, then surely other public facilities could do the same. But after years of most school districts either procrastinating or finding ways to obstruct racial integration altogether, the reality was that the Supreme Court's decision did very little to create a level playing field between White and Black students. Moreover, the few integrated schools had virtually no Teachers of Color. In the classic post-racial ethos of well-meaning White individuals, desegregation meant that White students did not have to change their attitudes about race, though Black students were expected to conform to the norms of the White student body—to kowtow or be bullied out of the school.

Ten years after the landmark ruling, college-age members of the Student Nonviolent Coordinating Committee joined the Mississippi Summer Project to register African American voters and build unaccredited summer schools, officially known as "Freedom Schools" for African American students at every end of the Magnolia State. Many antiracist White college students from Ohio and other parts of the North whose privileged racial and socioeconomic status drew unprecedented media attention to the project traveled south to volunteer. By the end of the summer in 1964, Mississippi Summer Project volunteers developed a curriculum and pedagogical approach designed to teach Black students how to examine race prejudice in various American institutions, such as the economy, the criminal justice system, and, among other things, legislative policy. Their work was a way of deconstructing the majorative system of Whiteness while at a school setting in order to challenge it in their community. Today, I call a curricular program designed as such race conscious pedagogy; in the 1960s, however, it was revolutionary teaching.

2

Revolutionary Teaching and the Origin of Race Conscious Pedagogy

Introductory Note: This chapter examines how critical pedagogy derived from the Freedom School experience during the Mississippi Freedom Project of 1964. For contextual purposes, the chapter begins by reflecting on the reaction to the 1954 Brown v. Topeka Board of Education *decision.*

Thirty years after the landmark 1954 *Brown v. Topeka Board of Education* decision that desegregated America's public schools, Linda Brown Thompson, the woman who was once the schoolgirl at the center of the case, admitted to the *New York Times* reporter, Walter Goodman, the legal victory "was not the quick fix [to segregation] we thought it would be" (Goodman, 1984). Chief Justice Earl Warren's ruling failed to deliver essential details about how desegregation would work. Warren's oversight was weighty considering schools in the South had never been integrated. No easy steps could be taken to convince school boards, administrators, teachers, students, and parents to comply with the culture-altering decision. The Supreme Court now had to decide on rules, a timeline for desegregation, and a punishment to schools that dared to violate the federal decision (*Brown v. Board of Education of Topeka*, 2018).

It would take a second hearing on *Brown* in 1955 to decide how desegregation would work. In *Brown v. Board of Education II*, commonly called *Brown II*, Warren offered a subsequent decision that the NAACP saw as an affront to the opinion given the previous year. In a unanimous decision, Warren wrote that schools should desegregate "with all deliberate speed." The effect of Warren's new ruling created a misleading sensation about the high court's intentions. School districts in places like Orleans Parish in New Orleans, Louisiana, implemented a step-ladder system of integration, requiring districts to complete the desegregation process within 12 years. The idea was that one grade throughout the district would integrate per year. The *Brown II* ruling, nevertheless, was accepted in some locations, yet rejected in most. Most year-at-a-time integration plans failed to integrate southern school districts for generations. Otherwise stated, the court's judicial placation to the South resulted in what Goodman called "all deliberate delay," as local, state and federal lawmakers, as well as private citizens threatened what U.S. senator Harry F. Byrd named "massive resistance" (Goodman, 1984; Shreveport, 1962).

With the high court's failure to impose a deadline for beginning or completing integration, school desegregation was met with vigorous opposition almost immediately. In July 1954, less than two months after the first *Brown* ruling, 35-year-old Robert "Tut" Patterson, a former football player from Mississippi State University and World War II veteran, organized with the help of five other men the country's first White Citizens' Council (WCC) in Indianola, Sunflower County, Mississippi. Patterson and his crusaders in the WCC aimed to preserve "the Southern way" of segregation keeping schoolhouse doors closed to African American students and preserving voting restrictions on Black Mississippians (*Alabama Tribune*, 1956). "Segregation is not immoral, it is not unChristian," Patterson told a crowd of 500 in Lowndes County shortly after he launched the Indianola Citizens' Council, "our forefathers believed in it and what was good enough for them is good enough for us" (*Greenwood Commonwealth*, 1954). Within five months of the first *Brown* ruling, more than 260 WCCs formed in 25 of the state's 82 counties and, in October, members formed the statewide Mississippi Association of Citizens Councils. Patterson was voted to be its first executive secretary. Under the broad-shouldered redheaded war veteran's leadership, the Mississippi Citizens' Council sought to counter every move of the 250,000-member NAACP. In his own words, Patterson proclaimed the mission of the White Citizens' Council "to have some organization to withstand the NAACP" by growing its membership four times the size of the civil rights group, electing Citizens' Council members into local and state offices, publishing an official newspaper titled *The Citizens Council*, and using peaceful means to preserve segregated schools (*Greenwood Commonwealth*, 1955; Hills, 1955).

Patterson defended any criticisms of the WCCs as an act of altruism, an undertaking every bit as important to the welfare of Black Mississippians that most members had "the interest of the Negro at heart." Patterson reasoned that he had 35 African American families living on his plantation. As such, "go out and talk to any one of them, and they'll all tell you I'm the best friend they have," he told a group of journalists in 1955. Patterson explained that six of his sharecroppers departed to the North but returned after a few weeks, claiming, "they'd never leave the South again." He explicated further: "If we integrated schools right here it would mean putting 20 white children into a classroom with 80 Negro children. That will never happen in Mississippi" (Brown, 1954). One month after Patterson became the most influential grassroots segregationist in the state, Benton County Citizens' Council member E.B. Golding, the former superintendent of the Benton County School District, was elected Mississippi's auditor general. The Citizens' Council then unleashed a torrent of counterattacks on school desegregation activists that Patterson had earlier branded "troublemakers" and "communists" (Price, 1954). When members of the NAACP filed petitions to integrate various Mississippi school districts, the Citizens' Council responded by working with county WCCs to place advertisements in local newspapers disclosing the name of every petitioner. Accordingly, Black and White petitioners commonly lost their jobs. Black businessmen were boycotted by White clients, lost distributors, and were denied credit and loan renewals by banks. Moreover, Patterson's Citizens' Council threatened to unseat board members that voted against the interest of the status quo. The Citizens' Council was so effective that similar organizations were launched in most states throughout the South. By December 1954, Alabama had four WCC chapters, including one in Dallas County where spokesperson Graham Kirkpatrick empathically advanced Patterson's anti-integration mission, warning that desegregated schools would lead to the erosion of American society since "the Negro is just two steps ahead of the jungle" (*Montgomery Advertiser*, 1955). If Kirkpatrick's words were any indication, everyone involved in maintaining the color line considered this a work in public safety (Adickes, 2005; Ingram, 1954).

The effort to keep Black students out of White schools was not limited to the actions of private citizens. Late in the winter of 1956, over one hundred United States congressmen representing southern states reaffirmed constituents that they would use the power of high office to resist the decrees of *Brown I* and its corollary, *Brown II*. Impeded by national mourning over the lynching of Emmett Till in Mississippi yet rejuvenated by the anger at the Montgomery Bus Boycott and the reelection of Dwight Eisenhower in 1956, South Carolina's U.S. senator Strom Thurmond and Georgia's state representative Richard Russell authored the Southern Manifesto, as it was informally known, claiming the decision in *Brown* was an "unwarranted exercise of power" and only created "chaos and confusion" throughout the South (Day, 2014).

The manifesto was first published in the *Southern School News* on March 11, 1956. One day later Georgia Senator Walter George read it aloud on the Senate floor. "Without regard to the consent of the governed, outside agitators are threatening immediate and revolutionary changes in our public school system," the Southern Manifesto read (Thurmond and Russell , 1956). "If done, this is certain to destroy the system of public education in some of the states."

The modern civil rights movement defined by tactical nonviolence and participatory democracy as it is now understood had not begun before or immediately after the *Brown* decision. The absence of a grassroots movement in the aftermath of the Supreme Court's "all deliberate speed" policy allowed massive resistance to flourish. Without an organized oppositional force, the Southern Manifesto buoyed the efforts of governors and state level lawmakers to maintain segregated schools regardless of federal support for one-grade-per-year step-ladder integration strategies. Pledging "all lawful means," the manifesto's signees slowed the timetable for the implementation of public school desegregation and slowed down federal civil rights legislation for a decade. Author of *The Southern Manifesto: Massive Resistance and the Fight to Preserve Segregation*, John Kyle Day (2014) explains, "Jim Crow largely came on White southern terms." The public declaration by national lawmakers emboldened voters to unseat lawmakers that refused to divulge positions on the school segregation issue. Political pressure placed on local officials throughout the South led general assemblies to defund public schools that were trying to integrate. After President Eisenhower sent soldiers to Little Rock, Arkansas, in the fall of 1957 to protect nine African American students that had enrolled at Little Rock Central High School, the governors in Virginia, Tennessee, and Arkansas shut down desegregated public schools altogether. If schools were closed in the first place, how could the federal government intervene? The proponents of massive resistance abandoned public education by casting votes for politicians who supported the idea of reallocating public funds to private all-White schools called "Segregated Academies." In the years following the issuing of the Southern Manifesto, education for White students continued in subsidized private segregated academies while African American children either returned to the all-Black school if it was still operational (which was no guarantee), or moved in with relatives in another state to enroll in a school, or received no education at all (Lassiter et al., 1998; Badger, 1999; Douglas, 2012).

There was no state like Mississippi where, under the guidance of the statewide Citizens' Council and four governors, James P. Coleman (1956–1960), Ross Barnett (1960–64), Paul B. Johnson, Jr. (1964–1968), and John Bell Williams (1968–1972) the entire state had maintained segregated colleges until 1962, and quasi-segregated K-12 public schools until 1970. Rather than going with the lower court order of allowing students to attend a school on the basis of residence, the Mississippi Department of Education, and accordingly, the state's 30 school districts, had adopted a "freedom-of-choice" method of giving students the option to attend any school in their school district. Harvard legal scholar Charles Olgetree (2005) claims the method "repeatedly failed to yield any significant desegregation." Mississippi's response to *Brown* with a freedom-of-choice plan was not inimitable. These plans proved nearly bulletproof against judicial reviews throughout the South, as school boards proved in circuit courts that "freedom-of-choice" plans did not perpetuate segregation and thus did not violate the Civil Rights Act of 1964 or the Equal Protection Clause of the 14th Amendment. The state was in the process of "equalizing" education, as was the argument in desegregation cases (Hale, 2016). Olgetree explains that courts typically ruled "[r]acial separation under *free choice* can only result from the individual's school selection." In other words, Mississippi's response to *Brown* was suitable for the courts.

The freedom-of-choice approach placed the burden of integrating schools on Black families that lacked resources to attend any school that was previously predominated by White students, as White parents made no effort to enroll their children into schools populated by Black students. Integration in Mississippi, consequently, transpired into nothing more than a few Black students at White schools. In *The Hardest Deal of All: The Battle Over School Integration in Mississippi, 1870–1980*, historian Charles C. Bolton (2017) explains that Black parents taking steps to enroll their children into White schools were regularly intimidated. The few "token" Black students entering into a White school, writes Bolton, "faced the wrath of generally unsympathetic White teachers and students." Much like an extension of the controlled and alienating experience in society at large, Black students tried to remain inconspicuous in an attempt not to offend a White teacher who possessed the power to humiliate or expel them from class. Bolton also claims freedom-of-choice schools "proved essentially meaningless" to integration in the state.

During the summer of 1962, a local civil rights activist, Jesse Harris, who first participated in the Jackson sit-ins the previous year, told 19-year-old Howard University student Charlie Cobb that Mississippi was civil rights' "war zone" (Hale, 2016). At the time, Cobb, who hailed from Massachusetts, traveled through the Mississippi Delta on his way to a Congress of Racial Equality (CORE) convention in Houston, Texas. The conversation alone convinced Cobb to drop out of Howard and remain in Mississippi until 1967. While in Jackson, Cobb developed an enlightened outlook on Mississippi's racial problems, which, he said, originated in the state's "impoverished educational system." African American made up 57 percent of Mississippi's student body yet, according to historian Jon N. Hale (2016), received 13 percent of state funds. Thought it had been 10 years since the ruling in *Brown I* and *II*, the state was still appropriating almost a hundred dollars more for White students than their Black counterparts. Moreover, Black schools were in session just half the time of White schools. Accordingly, Cobb went on to champion the effort to open up non-traditional schools for Black youths in Mississippi. "What we have discovered [in Mississippi] is that oppression and restriction is not limited to the bullets of local racists shotgun blasts," he wrote to SNCC members in the North, "but it is imbeded [sic] in a complex national structure." As a Bay Stater, Cobb's (1963) indictment of Mississippi spoke directly to the state's "grossly inadequate" commitment to Students of Color, post–*Brown*. He declared, "Negro education in Mississippi is the most inadequate and inferior" compared to any other state. Cobb said schooling in Mississippi produced a "social paralysis," or inferiority complex, in Black pupils while accusing classrooms to subsist as an "intellectual waste land." As for the few Black students in freedom-of-choice schools, Cobb reported, many were kicked out of classes for writing term papers about the freedom rides and for asking teachers to explain how registering to vote works. Black teachers, meanwhile, lost jobs "for saying the wrong thing." Something had to change. Cobb made clear the best foot forward was to amalgamate the civil rights movement's politics of social activism and self-determination with changes to curriculum and pedagogical approaches.

Cobb introduced an alternative to the traditional educational institution in Mississippi. In 1963, he submitted a proposal to SNCC's headquarters in Washington, D.C., that aimed to offer African American children a summer school experience designed to counter the state's traditional "sharecropper education." In "Prospectus for a Freedom School," he called for an army of SNCC and CORE workers to join the voter registration efforts already underway in Mississippi to build progressive "freedom schools" for the state's under-resourced Black students. Utilizing a theoretical approach that would later become "Decolonial Theory," known by contemporary education scholars as an approach to instruction that rejects the public school system's Eurocentric tradition, the mission of the freedom school movement aimed to prepare "student[s] as a force for social change in Mississippi" by deconstructing colonial and racial subjects from around the state and make connections between the experiences of African Americans in the 49 remaining states (Hale, 2014; Cobb, 1963). In a word, Cobb wanted to educate Black students in African American history, the basics in letter writing, public speaking, and techniques for civic crusading. Cobb told volunteer teachers, "the value of the Freedom School will derive from what the teachers are able to elicit from the students in terms of comprehension and expression of their experiences" (Pearlstein, 2001). Teachers were to utilize what Brazilian education philosopher Paulo Freire would later call "pedagogy of freedom." At the center of Cobb's Freedom Summer Project was the conviction that Black Mississippians had "to make decisions about and take charge of things controlling their lives." He, however, did not have a resourceful name for the type of instruction teachers and students would engage in at the freedom schools. He simply considered it self-discovery work.

The aim of the Freedom School curriculum will be to challenge the student's curiosity about the world, introduce him to his particularly "Negro" cultural background,
and teach him basic literacy skills in one integrated program. That is, the students
will study problem areas in their world, such as the administration of justice, or the
relation between state and federal authority.... The whole question of the court systems.... Students will be given practice activities to improve their skills with reading
and writing. Writing press releases, leaflets, etc. for the political campaign is one
example. Writing affidavits and reports of arrest, demonstrations, and trials, etc.
which occur during the summer in their town will be another [Pearlstein, 2001].

Simply put, the design of freedom schools was to train local grassroots
political agitators. Everything the teachers taught and everything discussed
in classes aimed at preparing students to become active participants in the
Mississippi freedom struggle. In other words, students would spend the summer engaging in discussions about their daily experiences with segregated
housing, voter disenfranchisement, inaccessible health care, and seemingly
nonexistent job opportunities. At the end of the summer, they would graduate
into an advanced level of participatory activism with enhanced skills to challenge the status quo. Harry Bowie (1964), SNCC member focusing most of
his time on voter registration drives, praised freedom school problem-posing
pedagogy while criticizing the traditional manner of teaching, a banking
method that involved teachers depositing information into students' minds
in the form of uninterrupted lecture. Bowie said that brand of pedagogics was
"meaningless" for its attempt "to flood the student with information he cannot understand." In true Freirean practice, "questioning" in freedom schools,
Bowie believed, "is the vital tool" for social activism preparation.

Cobb (1963; 1964), Bowie's SNCC associate, candidly said at the opening
of the freedom schools that education without freedom pedagogy was time
spent learning that "silence is safest," and demonstrates that "volunteer[ing
means] nothing." His vision at the very start of Freedom Summer 1964—a
presidential election year—was to provide students with the skills and disposition to agitate for institutional change. His schools existed as "a preparation
for participation in living."

Before summer's end, 41 freedom schools were operational in structures ranging from churches to abandoned buildings, each with an interracial faculty consisting of five to 15 teachers and accommodations for 25
to 50 students, totaling about 2,135 students—twice the number of schools
and students Cobb had anticipated at the start of the summer—ranging in
age from eight to 82 (Shaw, 1964; Hale, 2016). Young children ages eight to
12, learned reading, writing, spelling, African American history, and general mathematics. Students age 13 and older spent five weeks engaging in
a "Citizenship Curriculum" fixated on Decolonial Theory. The curriculum,
which was designed to disrupt Western Europe's influence on conventional
standards of learning, comprised of African American history, sociology,

mathematics, cultural activities, and leadership development (Lehew, 1964). Freedom school students wrote poetry, published a newspaper, and wrote a draft of the Mississippi Freedom Democratic Party's platform for the election cycle. At the end of the course, students were expected to take their newfound knowledge into the Black community to educate Students of Color by tutoring citizens on the literacy test and to register Black voters by offsetting the cost for the poll tax. Classrooms existed as spaces for Black Mississippians to compare their lives to their White counterparts as well as to contrast their living standards with Black Americans in the North.

The Citizenship Curriculum fell into six categories (Fuso, 1964): (1) an examination of race relations in Mississippi, (2) comparative study of living conditions in the North, specifically the Black ghetto and residential segregation, (3) White cultural hegemony, (4) the method at which Southern Democrats, known by then as Dixiecrats, wielded power in Congress, (5) comparison of the plight of Black Mississippians to poor Whites in the state, and (6) a critical inspection of the civil rights movement, namely the freedom rides and sit-ins. At the center of the course were these discussion questions: (1) What does the majority culture have that we want? (2) What does the majority culture have that we don't want? (3) What do we have that we want to keep?

When reading over the Citizenship Curriculum during orientation, volunteer teachers were reminded that they must "design a developmental curriculum that begins on the level of the students' every lives and those things in their environment that they have already experienced…. Our purpose is to encourage the asking of questions, and the hope that society can be improved" (Pearlstein, 2014). Though Cobb, Bowie, and other SNCC leaders offered teachers a how-to guide for structuring classrooms grounded in open-ended dialogue and Decolonial Theory, it was perhaps SNCC member Stokely Carmichael, a recent Howard University graduate who had relocated to Mississippi to work on voting rights projects under Robert Parris Moses and Fannie Lou Hamer, who gave the best rendition of a Citizenship Curriculum lesson that featured students in a discussion about colonial vestiges in the English language. In a teaching performance that is duly covered in the 2007 reprinting of Carmichael's 1971 autobiography *Stokely Speaks: From Black Power to Pan-Africanism*, he started one speech class with eight divergent sentences on the blackboard.

"I digs wine"	"I enjoy drinking cocktails"
"The peoples wants freedom"	"The people want freedom"
"Whereinsoever the policemens goes they cause troubles"	"Anywhere the officers of the law go, they cause trouble."
"I want to reddish to vote"	"I want to register to vote."

Carmichael then asked, "What do you think about these sentences? Such as—'the peoples wants freedom'"?

A student named Zelma replied: "It doesn't sound right. 'Peoples' isn't right."

"People means everybody," said a student named Milton. "Peoples means everybody in the world."

Two students jumped in the conversation. The first was Alma: "Both sentences are right as long as you understand them." Then Henry added, "They're both okay, but in a speech class you have to use correct English."

Carmichael then wrote "correct English" on the blackboard. He asked, "Does anybody you know use the sentences on the left? Are they wrong?"

Zelma replied, "In terms of English, they are wrong."

"Who decides what is correct English and what is incorrect English?" asked Carmichael. After a response from a student pointing out that people in England made the rules, Carmichael (1971, 2007) said, "You all say some people speak like on the left side of the board. Could they go anywhere and speak that way? Could they go to Harvard? Will society reject you if you don't speak like on the right side of the board? If society rejects you because you don't speak good English, should you learn to speak good English?" The conversation continued on with Carmichael following responses with another question as he drew the students closer to the conclusion that "correct English" is a product of the social order. Most people, one student claimed, use some form of "incorrect English." Why then, the class pondered, is it embarrassing to speak in broken English? A student named Alma offered the most profound insight at the end of the conversation: "If the majority speaks on the left (incorrect English), then a minority must rule society. Why do we have to change to be accepted by the minority group?"

Carmichael's "incorrect English" seminar still holds particular resonance with critical race pedagogues. "Enslaved Africans formulated new languages in nearly every European colony in the Americas," Ibram X. Kendi wrote in *How to Be an Antiracist* (2019), his acclaimed treatise on race in America, which has quickly become the manual for how to think and behave as a race conscious individual. Kendi's case is to call a "cultural racist" anyone who deems as inferior the dialect of a racially minoritized group. "Whoever creates the cultural standard usually puts themselves at the top of the hierarchy," writes Kendi. Thus, to render "broken" English "incorrect" is cultural racism. To describe Ebonics, which is a blending of various African languages with English, and other Black languages in countries like Jamaica, Haiti, Brazil and Cuba, as "broken" or "improper" is as "culturally racist as the idea that languages inside Europe are fixed."

The argument in Carmichael's freedom school lesson, and the same idea extended by Kendi in 2019, challenges Americans to remove themselves from the shroud of Whiteness to see that even the English language, which has its origin in other Romantic languages, is similarly an incorrect dialect of Latin, Greek, and Germanic languages. And to impose a single cultural standard on how a racial group must adapt to the language of the dominant cultural group is a pretense of White supremacy (Kendi, 2019).

Of course, Freedom Summer did not go as smoothly as the aforementioned paragraphs make it sound. Heartbreak struck the movement before a single class was taught. On June 20, 1964, arsonists had burned down Mt. Zion Church, one of the Freedom School annexes. After learning of the crime, a team of volunteers, including Andrew Goodman, age 20, Michael Schwerner, age 24, and James Chaney, age 22, went to inspect the crime scene and meet with congregants of Mt. Zion Church. Goodman and Schwerner were White CORE volunteers from Ohio who traveled to Mississippi for the Freedom Summer Project. Chaney was an African American man from Meridian who had become a hardened civil rights activist after having participated in two freedom rides. The three men were arrested and jailed on June 21 for speeding through the county seat of Neshoba County, a city with a little more than 5,000 residents called Philadelphia. At 10 o'clock that evening, the three were reportedly released from the Neshoba County police custody. They were never again seen alive.

The disappearance of the Freedom Summer volunteers did not deter the start of classes that summer. In fact, the entire freedom school experience was bookended by the vanishing and discovery of Schwerner's, Goodman's, and Chaney's bodies, with a series of drive-by shootings, fire bombings, and violent threats in between. And still, teachers and students pressed onward. In Natchez, Freedom Summer organizers stored guns in a shack near the Freedom Summer headquarters after a bomb blast demolished a Black-owned tavern in town. At night, volunteers with shotguns and pistols kept "fire-bomb watch" at freedom school sites. Writing in his memoir, *This Nonviolent Stuff'll Get You Killed*, Charlie Cobb (2016) admitted, after the three civil rights workers went missing, Freedom Summer organizers believed a conspiracy existed between police officers and Klansmen to kill or scare out of Mississippi every CORE and SNCC volunteer. It was only after a storm of protests demanding justice for the three men that over 150 FBI agents and 200 sailors from the Meridian Naval Air Station traveled to Philadelphia to investigate the matter. On July 30—well after the freedom school semester commenced classes—an informant told the FBI that the bodies could be found at a construction site in Neshoba County. Schwerner, Goodman, and Chaney were discovered side by side nearly 15 feet into the earth on August 4, six weeks after they first went missing (Dittmer, 1994; Watson, 2010; Hale, 2016).

The Mississippi Freedom Project coincided with the signing of the Civil Rights Act on July 2, 1964. The Voting Rights Act followed over a year later on August 6, 1965. The two bills eradicated Jim Crow from publicly funded institutions and removed all remaining voting barriers. The freedom schools in Mississippi consequentially never reopened. The conclusion of the freedom schools, however, did not mean the end of freedom pedagogy. It just meant that the curriculum would migrate north and its teachers would become solely Black. In the wake of the civil rights movement's legislative victories was a movement that emphasized racial pride and self-sufficiency called Black Power. Additionally, in 1965, a six-day disturbance known to most as the "Watts riots" but described by those in the freedom struggle as the "Los Angeles Uprising" resulted in the deaths of 34 people and $40 million in property damage, shifted further away from the call for integrated social justice work like what had occurred during the 1964 Mississippi Freedom Summer (Horne, 1995). Reality is that the civil rights movement had neglected economic inequality as well as Northern issues of residential discrimination and unjust policing. Swarthmore College graduate, Judy Richardson, a newly enlisted member of SNCC in 1964, distinguished between the needs of oppressed Northerners and Southerners when she told SNCC's Executive Committee: "[freedom] to the southern kid meant the vote, education, eating where you wanted to, etc. But 'freedom' to the [Northern] kids meant getting out of the ghetto" (Richardson, 1964). Freedom pedagogy consequentially moved north where groups associated with the newly begun Black Power struggle took over the revolutionary schools.

At first, SNCC recruited Black and non–Black Students of Color from colleges and universities to draft up revolutionary schools in places like Los Angeles and Chicago. But in 1966, Jimmy Garrett, a veteran SNCC and CORE activist, freedom rider, and original believer in the open-ended inquiry and fieldwork pedagogical vision of the Mississippi freedom schools, was now convinced that college students needed to get organized on campus before entering cities to mentor young people. Garrett arrived at San Francisco State University in the spring of 1966 to persuade students to create a Black Student Union that eventually amalgamated with the Latin American Students Organization, the Pilipino American Collegiate Endeavor, the Filipino-American Student Organization, the Asian American Political Alliance, and El Renacimiento to create a coalition called the Third World Liberation Front (TWLF) (Watkins, 2005; Perlstein, 2002). The TWLF functioned as a social and political mouthpiece for Students of Color on San Francisco State's campus. Within two years, it existed as a radically transformative medium working to shape the educational experiences of San Francisco State's Students of Color in a way that enabled Educators of Color to influence teaching and learning.

At the forefront of the inter-affinity group's mission was the creation of an interdisciplinary ethnic studies program that offered either major or minor degrees. By 1968, the lobbyist efforts of the TWLF yielded a Black studies program. Clinical psychologist and sociologist Nathan Hare, a 34-year-old boxer turned educator, arrived at San Francisco State to work as the university's first chairman of the Black Studies Department after having a contract terminated at Howard University for on-campus activism (Ross, 2016; Rogers, 2012; Hobbs, 1968; Dum, 1969). When the TWLF and Black Studies Department finally took shape at San Francisco State, Garrett's agenda with Hare's leadership to create a dark utopia on that majority White campus caught fire on other campuses across the country, as similar ethnic studies programs along with Black student unions, Afro-American societies, and Black action societies were formed on predominantly White liberal arts colleges as well as at historically Black colleges and universities stretching from coast to coast.

The frenzy for "a better and Blacker education," as Philadelphia-based Black Panther Mumia Abu-Jamal put it in an interview with Omari L. Dyson (2014), author of *The Black Panther Party and Transformative Pedagogy*, filtered down to the high school level almost immediately. On October 26, 1967, students at Simon Gratz High School and Bok Vocational High School in Philadelphia, Pennsylvania, walked out of school as a sign of solidarity with their collegiate peers. The students demanded Afro-American history courses, the right to wear African garb in school, and freedom to not salute the American flag without having to face reproach from teachers and peers. When the Panthers opened a chapter in the City of Brotherly Love, students were provided with the Peoples' Free Library, in addition to afterschool programs that focused on African cultural celebrations. It was common for town-gown relations between residents of a city's Black neighborhood and Black students from a nearby college. The collegians were simply students that saw an adjacent Black community as a home away from home; a social outlet where friendships could materialize and benevolence could be paid forward. High schoolers in cities throughout the country were beneficiaries of the movement toward non-traditional multicultural education, as opportunities to engage in theater and music that celebrated African traditions were plentiful in many places.

Even Stokely Carmichael shed his allegiance to SNCC's old guard that had once given responsibility to the students to come up with a political understanding of the world by drawing from their experiences. Where Garrett's objective was to organize students into organizational forces to be reckoned with, Carmichael adopted a new mode of academic instruction that encouraged repudiating assimilation in favor of revolutionary behavior. Carmichael's Black Power classes included decolonial curriculum with direct instruction from teachers. Indeed, Carmichael now called for a banking model of teaching and learning that concentrated on Afrocentrism and empowered African Americans with the skills to control Black political, cultural, and economic institutions unbounded by ruling class intrusion. This was an education initiative motivated by the prospect of a social revolution, not social activism. In support of Carmichael's Black Power new school of thought, Eldridge Cleaver (1970) argued that this new mode needed to educate "our children on the nature of the struggle and ... transferring to them the means for waging the struggle." The "struggle" that Carmichael and Cleaver validated found consolation in a new political organization formed not too far from San Francisco State's campus: the Black Panther Party for Self Defense.

On May 15, 1967, Huey P. Newton and Bobby Seale—two companions of Jimmy Garrett—released a set of guidelines to the newly formed Black Panther Party called the "Ten-Point Program." The Black Panthers had been founded by Newton and Seale months earlier, on October 15, 1966, to monitor police officers entering Oakland's Black community and raise funds for community programs ranging from free breakfast for school children to legal defense counsel. Beyond demanding freedom, full employment, and decent housing, the Panthers' Ten-Point Program demanded "education for our people that exposes the true nature of this decadent American society [and] that teaches us our true history and our role in the present-day society." Point No. 5 in the program echoed Garrett's and Carmichael's Black Power approach while adding a taste of distrust toward integrated schools and society. Newton said in the earliest weeks of the Black Panther Party: "We believe in an educational system that will give our people a knowledge of self. If a man does not have knowledge of himself and his position in society and the world, then he has little chance to relate to anything else" (Newton and Seal, 1967).

The Panthers made the vision of Garrett and Carmichael a reality when it launched its two-pronged education program. The first was the construction of unaccredited community-centered liberation schools for the general public that taught Black Power ideology, African heritage, and skills to volunteer on the Panthers' community survival programs. Granted, liberation schools were not as numerous as the Mississippi freedom schools. In fact, liberation schools were typically held at Black Panther Party headquarters, which doubled as a party member's home or at a community center. Nor did liberation schools have the type of academic apparatus that SNCC in the Magnolia State benefited from in 1964. Yet the Panthers were determined to educate adults about Party ideology at evening meeting held at no less than seven locations, which included the Bronx, Philadelphia, Chicago, Seattle, Berkeley, Oakland, and San Francisco (Bloom and Martin, 2016). These locations do not include the unofficial Panther chapters formed at the same time in cities as small as

Lancaster, Pennsylvania, and as large as Cleveland, Ohio. According to party member Regina Jennings, Panther teachers taught that "the needs and interests of African people determined our perception of the world" (Jones, 1993).

The second facet of the Black Panther Party's education initiative was the creation of accredited intercommunal youth institutes that educated primary and secondary aged students in general academic courses along with the skills needed to engage in political activism. In June 1969, the Panthers opened its first accredited school for children in Berkeley, California, called the Intercommunal Youth Institute (IYI) (Pearlstein, 2002). Weeks later, the Panthers' San Francisco chapter established a second IYI. Huey Newton explained that IYI schools avoided lessons "about a jive president that was said to have freed the slaves, when it's as clear as water that we're still not free." Instead, he said, pupils in these intercommunal schools learned about the heavy topics of "racism, capitalism, fascism, cultural nationalism, and socialism." Students also engaged in the culture of Africa: theater, dance, music, and material culture.

In 1971 and 1972, the Panthers in Oakland opened two accredited elementary schools. The first was originally called the Huey P. Newton Intercommunal Youth Institute, later renamed Oakland Community School. The second IYI opened in East Oakland called the Samuel Napier Youth Intercommunal Institute. In their landmark book *Black Against Empire: The History and Politics of the Black Panther Party*, Joshua Bloom and Waldo E. Martin, Jr. (2016) call Oakland's Huey P. Newton IYI the Black Panthers' "flagship" intercommunal school. Its inaugural class had 28 students engaged in direct instruction on Party ideology and conducted fieldwork that involved distributing the *Black Panther* newspaper and attending court hearings for political prisoners. One Huey P. Newton IYI student bragged, "at this school we don't have to salute the flag … they teach us about what the pigs are doing to us."

Such language coming from Panthers, not to mention their teenage pupils, was threatening to the majorative culture. It was especially unnerving to hear students speak in such provocative ways because many elder Panthers in various parts of the country had been arrested or were in deadly shootouts with law enforcement officials. Historian Daniel Perlstein (2002) aptly said, "militant displays of Black manhood degrading into macho thuggery," which forced new leadership in the 1970s to rebrand the Party's education initiative along with many other Panther community programs. The rebranding meant the abandonment of, as historian Tracye Matthews notes, "militaristic style" in the Panthers' schools for more progressive tactics that resembled the type of instruction provided to students in the Mississippi freedom schools (Joseph, 2006). By the early '70s, intercommunal school students learned English by writing to political prisoners. Civics lessons were inspired by the 1964 tradition of open-ended problem-posing pedagogy in addition to fieldwork in Black neighborhoods. Pupils learned mathematics on field trips to stores wherein they received change for a purchase. Vocabulary lessons emanated from "words we used around town [and] at home," one student described. No longer was the Panthers' teaching styles aimed at telling students "*WHAT* to think," said Bobby Seale in 1973. Rather, they created a pedagogical practice "to teach our children *HOW* to think!" (Seale, 1973). Panther liberation and intercommunal schools evolved into a group-think model that entailed engaging with texts written by philosophers and historical figures followed by a seminar style discussion with a certified teacher more involved in steering students in the direction of debating solutions for how to fix a community's problems. In an interview with a writer from the *Los Angeles Times* in 1972, Huey Newton explained, "What's really interesting about our school is that in addition to learning the basic skills from accredited teachers, they learn political awareness. When we send them to other schools after they graduate they do well because we've equipped them; they will be the political organizers of the future" (Diehl, 1972).

Conclusion

What can 21st-century educators working at majority White schools learn from schools of revolutionary teaching? On this question and others the Mississippi Freedom Project's freedom schools and the Black Panther Party's liberation and intercommunal schools demonstrate that there truly exists a different outlook toward course material taught in traditional classrooms. The aims of revolutionary schools were made explicit. They produced a critically engaged citizenry while traditional schools then and now enable racists. Marvin Lynn (1999) is one of a handful of critical education scholars who suggest "liberatory" pedagogues must utilize several classroom approaches: teach students about African history and culture; make critical dialogue an integral part of the classroom; engage in daily self-affirmation with students aimed at countering stereotype threat; and actively challenge texts that "advocate hegemonic and counteremancipatory messages." Educators must also ask themselves, is there such a thing as a politically neutral education? Either all education is subjective, including mainstream curriculum and pedagogy, or either all education is objective. It is just as political to not include a piece of information as it is to include it, or, it is just as political to not talk about race as it is to talk about race. This dynamic is especially illuminated in the configuration of the education system in Mississippi during the sixties as Black "sharecropper" schools were both restrictive in its Eurocentric curricula and in the duration those schools were in session.

The efforts of revolutionary teachers of the 1960s underscore this prevailing question about objectivity in pedagogy as they taught against the standardized curriculum that defaulted to Eurocentric culture that existed as a fundamental devaluation of the lives and experiences of Black Americans. White schools before *Brown* and the few desegregated schools post–*Brown* declared loudly to Black and White students: those ideas we are not teaching (slavery; Reconstruction's failure; the argument for reparations; the historical and political factors that created economic inequality; decolonial literature) are inferior and thus not worthy of curricular attention. By definition, that is a political act (Giroux, 2011; Gottesman, 2016; Kendi, 2019; Ladson-Billings, 1999; Ladson-Billings, 2003). Revolutionary schools taught children it was okay to challenge the 19th- and 20th-century colonial framings of the world; to not accept as normal racist policy as it stood in 1964; that there exist many cultures in the world and that for America to live up to its democratic promise each culture and each lived experience should be taught. The idea of revolutionary learning endures today so that all students can receive the tools—community organizing skills, abilities to disrupt, and the dexterity to critically think—to extract power from the racist practices, racist policies, and racist institutions that influence their lives.

3

The Era of the Takeover
and the Struggle for Diversity,
Equity and Inclusion
in Secondary and
Postsecondary Education

Introductory Note: As more and more Students of Color enrolled at predominantly White institutions in the late 1960s, issues related to diversity, equity, and inclusion were exposed in higher education. This chapter examines the history of the 1960s Black campus movement and the backlash that resulted in the subsequent decades. Near the end of this chapter, attention is given to racial dynamics and diversity, equity, and inclusion issues at the high school level.

In the early morning hours of April 18, 1969, almost a hundred African American students took over Cornell University's Willard Straight Hall and held it for 36 hours. The students protested the racist climate on campus and insisted on creating a Black studies program. About midway into the takeover, after a group of White students snuck through a window in an attempt to wrestle the occupiers out of the building, and because an external threat was developing outside the student union building, two men in a yellow car delivered "two packages of guns," including, according to one report, rifles, shotguns, and bandoliers. Some of the protesters inside the building without guns fashioned pool sticks into spears (United Press International, 1969; Ginzberg and Dawson, 2016). To end the takeover, Cornell's vice president, Steven Muller, agreed to give the students complete amnesty. Following the takeover, university president James Perkins issued a statement that any student in "possession of a weapon would be suspended" and any organization found to have firearms would "lose its university recognition." The takeover was followed by condemnation reaching as high as the United States Congress when West Virginia senator Robert C. Byrd, suggesting the Black college students engaged in "anarchy" while having "interests ... far from academic," introduced a campus disorder bill that threatened to levy imprisonment and fines on students "who interfered with the operations of any school receiving federal funds" (Tiede, 1969; *Charleston Gazette*, 1969).

The Black student takeover at Cornell served as the highpoint in two years' worth of similar disruptions on college campuses. In this post-civil rights era of Black Power, many African American students and some White allies considered this uncompromising tactic a tool in an otherwise righteous new paradigm of social justice work; particularly as it pertains to obtaining Black studies programs and cultural acceptance at colleges and universities throughout the country. These disruptions mostly resulted in administrative bodies yielding to the students' requests. A six-day student strike commenced at Harvard University the weekend before Cornell's incident. Three Northwestern University students collapsed during a hunger strike the same day the Cornell incident had ended. African American students assumed veto power over Black faculty appointments at Lake Forest College in Illinois. One month after the sit-in at Cornell, seven professors were held under duress inside a classroom at Franklin and Marshall College located in Pennsylvania. Other institutions of higher education, large and small, faced their own episodes of building seizures or student strikes in both 1968 and 1969: San Francisco State's student strike and subsequent takeover led by Black Studies coordinator Dr. Nathan Hare and English professor George Murray lasted five months; Brandeis's Ford Hall was occupied for 11 days; students commandeered Swarthmore's admissions office for eight days; and 24-hour takeovers occurred at Duke, Cheyney State, Boston University, Rutgers University-Newark, and North Carolina. Additionally, City College of New York, Pittsburgh, Voorhees College, Wilberforce, and Howard University were among approximately 150 campus takeovers, boycotts, strikes, and uprisings during a 15-month period (Ross, 2016; Mealy, 2017; Rogers, 2012; Joseph, 2006). A few hours into each disruption, students offered a list of demands centered on conceptualizing Black identity on campus. The demands typically included a campus climate that fostered a sense of belonging as well as culturally appropriate academic offerings that would help students challenge problems plaguing their home communities. Among the issues were racial zoning, employment injustice, police brutality, health care, inequitable education, and intergenerational poverty. Additionally, students insisted on the creation of Black studies departments and the hiring of more professors and advisors representing the non-dominant cultures on campus.

Historian and Director of the Center for the Study of Race and Democracy at the University of Texas, Peniel E. Joseph (2013), describes the takeover phenomenon as "the greatest political and pedagogical opportunity" to fundamentally alter power relations in the American education system. Indeed, Joseph, author of four books about 1960s Black Power including *Waiting 'Til the Midnight Hour: A Narrative History of Black Power in America* claims that the tactic launched a cultural rebirth on campuses; a revolution precipitated by Pan-Africanism, Black consciousness in the urban North, and decolonial efforts in several African and Asian nations, plus Cuba, during the 1950s and 1960s. In America, urban rebellions resembling anticolonial uprisings taking place overseas had occurred in Watts, Harlem, and Detroit. It was only a matter of time that tempestuous discourse taking place in urban America figured prominently in the minds of Collegians of Color who considered themselves as colonized and ghettoized on campus as they were in America's cities.

So, why do anything extreme? Why an urban rebellion? Why takeover a building on campus? A few days after visiting Watts in the midst of tumult in August 1965, Martin Luther King, Jr., told CBS's Mike Wallace, "a riot is the language of the unheard." He lamented Black Power radicalism is "a reaction to the reluctance of White power to make the kind of changes necessary to make justice a reality for the Negro" (Rothman, 2015; Carson, 2001). Like an urban rebellion, the action of occupying an administrative office in 1968 and 1969 removed power from the hands of the college faculty who were personally inconvenienced and threatened so issues related to racial division on campus were clearly exposed. Administrators were backed into a corner; consequently compelled to respond to demands that were valid, reasonable, and doable. Historian and antiracist educator Ibram X. Kendi (Rogers, 2012) notes that Black campus activism forced officials in higher education to draft new policies that addressed "a series of historically marginalized academic ideas." This form of activism, he suggests, resulted in "a profusion of racial reforms" on America's campuses. Building appropriations were a new and effective form of dissent conducted during a period of 14 months that yielded results. The act alone was both risky for activists and frightening for everyone else. It understandably garnered greater attention to the cause and forced a tangible response from those in power.

It is important to acknowledge that Cornell and other predominantly White institutions (PWIs) in the 1960s forged new standards in higher education pertaining to recruiting and enrolling Students of Color. And yet for ordinary men and women who arrived at those historically White spaces during this troubled era, they found their experience on campus so suppressive that they could bespeak of themselves as aliened Americans—subjugated in a ghetto amidst an ivory tower that still suggested it was a space restricted along racial lines. Such was the case at Cornell in 1969, where just 250 of the university's 14,000 students, or not quite 2 percent, were African American (Troy, 2009). No matter the college, Collegians of Color faced contested emotions. In the classroom there was faculty contact, pedagogy, and curriculum. All, however, lacked cultural relevance. The other consisted of social experiences, wherein most fraternities and sororities were both racially segregated and sexually coarse. Despite every college's high-minded mission, Students of Color were effectively as alienated on campus as they had been in the communities from which they arrived.

Backlash to Darkening Campuses

Not only did college administrators respond to Black student activism, so did White students in a way that projected anguish over the slight advancement toward racial inclusivity on White campuses in the 1960s, 1970s, and 1980s. In what one can interpret as a racially provoked response to the subtle blackening of liberal arts campuses, White students in colleges North and South mocked their racial counterparts, which remained vastly outnumbered—and still do—by personifying racist stereotypes in acts of amateur blackface minstrelsy. While only coming to the surface during the winter of 2019 with damning evidence of White frat brothers engaging in racist mockery in the form of blackface, set off by the revelation that Virginia Governor Ralph Northam appeared in his 1984 Eastern Virginia Medical School yearbook page in blackface and while another man wore Ku Klux Klan regalia (or vice versa)—Northam would eventually claim he was neither individual in the photo—researchers began rummaging through college yearbooks from the Baby Boom generation. The searches discovered behaviors so vile and disparaging that race relations at present fractured. One University of North Carolina yearbook photo discovered by Colin Campbell, editor of the *North Carolina Insider*, showed two collegians in 1979 from Chapel Hill's Chi Phi fraternity dressed as Ku Klux Klan members lynching another man in blackface (Campbell, 2019; Ross, 2016). If blackface minstrelsy was the wedge still keeping Blacks and Whites separate after the demise of Jim Crow, the mission of liberal arts college, it was assumed by some, was the thing that could awaken the consciousness of White collegians, pulling Blacks and Whites closer together, to function as a people's college where young adults of all races, sexes, and creeds could obtain knowledge to create a better and more just society. And yet institutions of higher education are "some of the most racially hostile spaces in the United States," explains Lawrence Ross (2015) in his seminal study of the Black American experience living and surviving as students at PWIs, "these African American students will learn that their White university, their White fellow students, and their White faculty are not automatic allies in their journey toward educational success."

Ross is one of a few scholars who has investigated the claim that PWIs are diverse spaces of post-racial harmony, proving such assertions to be misleading. In *Blackballed: The Black and White Politics of Race on America's Campuses*, he details racially induced incidents at the University of Pennsylvania in 1980, at the University of Cincinnati in 1981, the University of Oregon in 1982, at the University of Mississippi in 1986, Purdue University and Wesley College in 1987, and Stanford University and Louisiana State University in 1988. These were cases of ghetto-themed and Martin Luther King, Jr.-themed frat parties gone full racist, arson attacks on Black fraternal homes, and Confederate battle flag parades. Though typically dismissed by the administration at each PWI as "a series of disconnected incidents," these racially charged episodes were, and still are, Ross observes, part of a perpetual "racism crisis" on America's campuses. The harsh reality is that racist incidents still occur at colleges and universities across the United States. At the University of Texas in February 2015, Phi Gamma Delta hosted a "border patrol" themed party where guests arrived wearing sombreros and ponchos while some members of the frat house dressed as border patrol agents. That same year, students in the University of Oklahoma's Sigma Alpha Epsilon were videoed singing: "There will never be a nigger at SAE [clap, clap]. You can hang 'em from a tree, but he'll never sign with me. There will never be a nigger at SAE [clap, clap]." Ross's retelling of these shameful incidents is suggestive that "throwing costume parties to mock other cultures" has seemingly been a tacit "rite of passage" for White students while existing as a revolting "reality of black students on campus."

But the mocking does not end with Greek life mischief. In 2016, a group of African American freshmen at the University of Pennsylvania were added to a GroupMe text message account named "Nigger Lynching." According to university officials, the GroupMe account included "violent racist and thoroughly repugnant images and messages." One text message invited the students to "a daily lynching ceremony" (Reilly, 2016). Though later found that three people from Oklahoma, and not Pennsylvania, were responsible for the cyberbullying, the episode left each 18-year-old and 19-year-old African American student at Pennsylvania unnerved (McCrone, Lattanzio, and Chang, 2016). Then there was the hate crime that occurred at American University in May 2017 when at least one White student hung from trees on campus bananas tied to nooses. The incident transpired after the institution swore in its first female African American student government president (McLaughlin and Burnside, 2017). Written onto each banana peel in black marker were either the initials "AKA" for the college's predominantly African American sorority Alpha Kappa Alpha or "Harambe bait," referencing the gorilla that was killed at the Cincinnati Zoo after a three-year-old boy fell into its enclosure and was dragged through water.

On Halloween in 2019, at least five male student-athletes at Franklin and

Marshall College (F&M), a small private liberal arts college about the same size as American, attended a costume party dressed as Asian and Mexican stereotypes. Once the images of the costumes appeared on Instagram, the uproar by the college's Students of Color and White allies grew intense. After a campus-wide forum designed to discuss the matter and for the offenders to issue apologies fell short of reconciliation, the protests peaked on the evening of November 8 when several scores of students occupied the gymnasium floor, ultimately forcing the college's athletic director to postpone the season-opening basketball game between F&M and York College. The following morning, student protesters disrupted an open house visit for high school seniors that were on campus to weigh whether or not F&M would be a good fit to pursue a postsecondary degree. According to the list of grievances and demands filed by a consortium of the college's student groups, White F&M students had worn "racially charged stereotypes" as costumes each of the three years before the 2019 incident; all of which went unpunished (College Reporter, 2019). "We are tired, F&M," the students wrote, of racist actions occurring "without consequences." In the month following the incident at the private liberal arts college in Pennsylvania, a series of anti–Semitic and racist incidents followed by campus-wide protests demanding punitive action were reported in the mainstream media. At the University of Georgia, swastikas and the words "All Heil" were drawn on the doors of multiple residence halls. At Iowa State, a swastika was carved into a door of a dormitory and a picture surfaced of a student government advisor in blackface. More racist slurs against African Americans and Asian American, as well as anti–Semitic graffiti and a white supremacist manifesto was AirDropped to students' cellphones across Syracuse University, leading to several days of sit-ins and the suspension of a fraternity.

The Fusion of Racist Ideas and School Policy

While occurring at varying times and on different campuses, this bigotry-driven behavior is interconnected through an umbilical cord that joins institutionalized racism with the collegiate culture that abets and bolsters racist actions. Perhaps the best way to think about how institutional racism influences the behavior of teenage and young twenty-something coeds is by considering how legal scholar Khaled A. Beydoun (2018) describes "dialectical" Islamophobia to explain how anti–Muslim beliefs are "shaped and reshaped" by anti–Muslim cultures "embedded in government institutions," including rhetoric and policy, which thereafter embolden private citizens to perpetuate and perform anti–Muslim acts. In similar form, a broad system of racism and racial dehumanization on display by the structural body—vis-à-vis school district policy that disenfranchises racially minoritized students will have a resultant effect on racist bullying by White members of the student body or a college administration that only gives a slap on the wrist to White frat brothers caught singing about lynching African American people—will justify the torment and violence against people of non-dominant cultures on college campuses and high schools. A school district or an institution of higher learning that has a problem of hate crimes or smaller episodes of racial and religious intolerance, where students of the non-dominant culture lack opportunity, where there exists through the enforcement of zero tolerance disciplinary policies the expulsion or arrest of greater numbers of African American and Latinx students compared to Whites, where curricular microaggressions or racial abuses are left unchallenged, where racist acts go unpunished, and where Educators of Color cannot be found, suffers the most from a culture of dialectical racism that influences the actions of White students to mock and intimidate Students of Color without thinking twice. So, as Black students historically left their still segregated neighborhoods only to navigate PWIs like Eastern Virginia Medical and North Carolina, where racist culture had been allowed to flourish by administrations that either ignored or simply slapped fraternity and sorority members on the wrist after each racist act, it is apparent that the experience on campus was just as devaluating as the segregated communities from which they arrived.

Of course, those White students knew putting on blackface or Klan hoods was wrong. Then again, the environment on many majority White campuses is one in which White students refuse to challenge one another on this type of behavior; largely because no one—neither parents nor college professors—had ever spoken to them about how blackface minstrelsy has historically articulated grotesque and depraved representations of African Americans. This authoritarian-like comportment exuded by White collegians only further suppresses the Black presence on campus. The fact that pictures of White students in blackface and Klan robes holding nooses made it beyond countless yearbook editors immediately following the civil rights movement—and just years after Martin Luther King's assassination—indicates both the absence of empathy and the subsistence of willful ignorance that could have been subdued through a race conscious education. Blackface mockery by White coeds in history or those in the 21st century who question why it is racist to wear blackface to a Halloween party has shown that the rejection of critical race studies at every level signals what education researcher Christopher Emdin (2017) describes as "a systemic denial within institutions built upon White cultural traditions that oppress and silence" the history of Students of Color.

The feeling of alienation concerning dark-skin students at PWIs is not limited to higher education. Students of Color at K-12 public and private schools across the country have endured the same level of racial trauma, isolation, and stereotyping by White student bodies as well as educators that are either colorevasive or explicitly racist. This is illustrated by alarming news stories of White schoolteachers using the N-word while ranting about Students of Color or by forcing African American students to act as enslaved persons for mock slave auctions wherein White students place bids on their African American peers (Griffith, 2019). One of the most disturbing examples of resistance and contempt against racial inclusivity by a White teacher is the March 2018 case of Citrus County School District middle school teacher, Dayanna Volitich, who admitted to superiors that she hosted a White nationalist podcast called "Unapologetic" and managed an accompanying Twitter account. Working under the pseudonym "Tiana Dalichov," Volitich used the podcast to declare that science has proven the White race is superior to others and to peddle the idea that Muslims should be exterminated from the earth (Love, 2018; Stevens, 2018). She boasted on "Unapologetic" that she taught her students racist tropes at Chrystal River Middle School, where 88 percent of the student body is White, according to the Florida Department of Education. She also appeared as a guest on "27Crows Radio with Bre Faucheux," a popular White nationalist podcast in Alt Right circles, to brag she is "not PC" with her students and to call the culture of public schools "so anti-red pilling," which is an internet term taken from the movie *The Matrix* and commonly used by White supremacists to shame those who advocate for multiculturalism, gender equality, and racially inclusive environments (Stern, 2019; @ HuffPost, 2018; Pearl, 2017).

That same month, the conclusion of a five-year investigation involving theft of school district funds along with a racist text message scandal described as "extensive, repetitive, and extreme" by the grand jury report rocked the Coatesville Area School District in Chester County, Pennsylvania. In the fall of 2013, Coatesville superintendent Richard Como and athletic director Jim Donato were relieved of their jobs when it was discovered they used school district-issued cellphones to send one another racist and sexist text messages calling students the N-word, the high school's Mexican American football coach a "Shoe shining coconut," "Burro," and "Taco," and several female teachers the C-word and "pieces [of a--]" (Grand Jury, 2014). The text messages were discovered when a grand jury launched an investigation into Superintendent Como for theft and other ethics violations, including taking money from the high school's student government, summer school tuition, and a donation to the school district. At the same moment Volitich went under fire for the discovery of her White supremacist podcast in Florida, Como received up to 23 months in Chester County Prison and three years' probation. The sentencing judge also ordered Como to pay

$4000 to the high school's student council and almost $7000 in fines (Bond, 2018).

Attacks on racial inclusivity are not limited to White educators who possess supremacist presumptions. Many videos of White students in White spaces disparaging their Peers of Color went viral in what felt like a record setting pace in 2018 and 2019. Among the most highly publicized videos (there are plenty) is one posted in January 2018, when University of Alabama freshman, Harley Barber, repeated the use of the N-word in a video she shared on Instagram. Her post began, "I don't care if it's Martin Luther King Day," followed by three recitations of the racial slur. Barber, who hails from New Jersey, added, "I'm in the South now bitch, so everyone can fuck off." She closed with another sortie of N-words. Then, in the middle of 2018, an African American graduate student at Yale, Lolade Siyonbola, was reported to the campus police for napping in the Hall of Graduate Studies after a White female student called the authorities. The officers that arrived on the scene ended up admonishing the student who called the police, and Siyonbola was let go.

Two episodes at the end of the year left many disturbed and frankly nauseous. On December 10, 2018, Columbia sophomore Julian von Abele was recorded yelling, "White people are the best thing that happened to the world." Seemingly intoxicated while hassling a group of African American students, von Abele bellowed, "We invented science and industry and you want to tell us to stop because, 'Oh my God, we're so bad! … We built modern civilization! White people are the best thing that ever happened to the world'" (Steinbuch, 2018). Just days before Christmas, there was a more public racist attack on an Afro-Puerto Rican male high school student. Andrew "Drew" Johnson, a 120-pound wrestler from Buena Regional High School in New Jersey, was forced to cut off his dreadlocks by a referee with an apparent history of using the N-word. Johnson had just stepped onto the mat for his match when the official informed him that he would be disqualified unless the hair was cut within 90 seconds. Johnson's coaches appealed to the official to withdraw the directive; it was then that the 16-year-old decided to cut his hair. The fact that he went on to win his match was dwarfed by his body language seen in the video of the incident that went viral showing him shrunken, understandably degraded as his humanity was taken by an unenlightened person with no knowledge of or sympathy for how hair has existed as a tool of oppression. Some took to Twitter to praise Johnson for being a team player. But to Johnson, and virtually all People of Color, dreadlocks are an extension of the Black body that has been controlled and violated by White supremacy for centuries (Oluo, 2018; Washington, 2019). Jamil Smith, senior journalist for *Rolling Stone* whose work has also appeared in *The New York Times*, *Esquire*, and *The Washington Post*, posted on Twitter what many were feeling: "It is clear that @MikeFrankelSNJ (Mike Frankel, sports director for South New Jersey Today—who has since expressed regret for the tweet) saw Andrew Johnson choosing to have his dreadlocks cut off as a selfless, All-American sacrifice. But to ignore how wrong it was for that choice to be forced—upon a child, no less—isn't merely White blindness. It is journalistic malpractice." The riffs and rants engaging on social media following the publication of the story showed one side—overwhelmingly White—insisting racial animus had nothing to do with the referee's decision; one tweet appraised Johnson: "Very humbling this kid took the high road to be a team player!" Others railed that an assault had been inflicted on the teenager; that a real reflection of a team player would have been if every member of the team stepped forward in some manner to defend Johnson. Even Bernice A. King, the daughter of Martin Luther King, Jr., implored the media to "discontinue framing this as a 'good' story." She claimed, "It's actually a reflection of bias and acquiescence to bias" (Smith, 2018; Frankel, 2018; McKinley, 2018; King, 2018).

The history of SNCC's freedom schools, the Black Panther Party's intercommunal and liberation schools, along with sit-ins, occupations, and strikes by Black coeds have created indisputable possibilities for restructuring pedagogy and curriculum in the more than 50 years since Stokely Carmichael's historic open-ended lesson on the English language in 1964. Since the 1960s, however, little attention has been paid to providing White students a formal race conscious education. Although broader changes to teaching and learning have evolved, race-centered education has never been a point of emphasis in the educational system. For instance, in my home state of Pennsylvania, according to the Department of Education's Academic Standards for History (2002), which saw its last revision in 2002, curricula scarcely touches upon the civil rights movement. Race relations are introduced at the elementary level; however, in grades nine through 12, the civil rights movement is only a subtopic in a much broader category labeled "How Continuity and Change Have Influenced History, Social Organization" (Duncan, 2020). Under another standard statement, "Conflict and Cooperation Among Social Groups and Organizations," teachers are expected to cover "Ethnic and Racial Relations." This standard is an apropos to race consciousness; however, ethnic studies classes are mandated by neither the Pennsylvania State Department of Education nor the state legislature. Therefore, the only time words like xenophobia and nativism, or an examination of collective and individual social reform actions appear in a class would be during independent lectures about societal issues of the 1920s, 1950s, and 1960s. The topic appears in passing, with no weight placed on texts, context, or subtext. The terms "social justice," "white privilege," "colorism," "institutional racism," "meritocracy," and "implicit bias" do not appear in the document. Neither do the standards mandate that teachers deal with such important contemporary life subjects such as Islamophobia, anti–Semitism, racial zoning and residential discrimination, or the model minority stereotype. Despite the subtle praise for linking expectations with teaching materials on the state standards, the Pennsylvania Department of Education and the Commonwealth's educators received a D by the Southern Poverty Law Center (SPLC) report "Teaching the Movement 2014: The State of Civil Rights Education in the United States" on state teaching standards. As alarming as the 2014 grade is, the D was an improvement from the F Pennsylvania received from the SPLC's 2011 report card. "Pennsylvania does not require students to learn about the civil rights movement," the SPLC reported. "This represents a missed opportunity to set high expectations" (Costello, Shuster, Jeffries, and Stern, 2014; and Mitchell, 2011).

The problem with civil rights history showing up in state standards is not limited to Pennsylvania. A 2020 CBS News study on social studies standards in all 50 states and the District of Columbia revealed that seven states "do not directly mention slavery" and eight states fail to mention the civil rights movement (Duncan et al., 2020). The report also found that just two states allude to White supremacy, while 16 states list states' rights as a cause of the Civil War. Another problem area exposed by the CBS News investigation is the lack of a national curriculum for United States history. The resultant implication for social studies education is shown by a "politicized" process when states policymakers adopted state standards. This explains why some textbooks still claim enslaved Africans were immigrants to the New World.

For many reasons—and for a long time—authentic racial discourse with children is either nonexistent or narrowly practiced by parents and educators. The rise in hate crimes (discussed in Chapter 1) and the SPLC's report cards were just two of the reasons why I felt the need to create a critical race studies course for students at Gap High School, the place where I have been employed since 2007. Among other reasons, I was disturbed and forthrightly nervous about how a resurgence of student disruptions on college campuses in 2015 and 2016 might filter down to the Gap student body unless teachers and administrators were willing to take initiative to seek out student concerns. In 2015, a student disruption over a series of racially motivated hate crimes at the University of Missouri hurled the media pundits and citizens back into debate over the seriousness of student-led protest at predominantly White institutions. In September, after student body president, Payton Head, was allegedly threatened with violence by White men in a pickup truck, about 50 of Missouri's African American students rallied around Head with a demonstration the protesters named "Racism Lives Here." Weeks later after a vandal smeared feces in the shape of a swastika on a dormitory wall, female organizers of "Concerned Student 1950" student group and Jonathan Butler, a graduate student willing to starve himself and whose resolve was shown in an updated will and a do-not-resuscitate order, called for university president

Tim Wolfe to resign for apparent unwillingness to address the growing racial concerns on campus. The students' efforts were augmented on November 8 when the football team announced it would boycott the remainder of the season unless Wolfe tendered his resignation and the administration made promises to make policy changes to minimize existing macro and micro racial aggressions on campus (Lee, 2016). Missouri's successful student protest inspired students at Brandeis University to conduct a 12-day takeover of the Bernstein-Marcus Administrative Center, which includes the university president's office, before receiving demands that included new Student of Color and Professor of Color outreach as well as an action plan to address discriminatory social patterns in the daily routines on campus.

The struggle of the past has been the focus of this and the previous chapter. This history serves only as context. It is necessary to see this backdrop clearly to understand something very troubling: things have changed slowly in the United States when it comes to attitudes about racial uplift and intersectional social justice. Students representing non-dominant cultural groups have reached an age in high school where they can make sense of how prevailing hardships inflicted upon their racial or ethnic group outside of school are occurring to them inside of school where their trauma is often downplayed or wholly dismissed by their peers and teachers. As a student of history, the episodes at Missouri and Brandeis sounded all too familiar. These events were alarming as I went to work each day in the fall of 2016 and spring of 2017 at a place where Students of Color are vastly outnumbered by White students and where there are no Teachers of Color. I was concerned about disturbing behaviors I observed from time to time at Gap, where many in our community hold narrow notions of racial, ethnic, and sexual identity. More often than not, many in the Gap School District adhere to an aggressive culture that remains, in crucial ways, uncomfortable with the increasing visibility of our People of Color and lesbian, gay, bisexual and transgender peers.

Conclusion

In his award-winning book *The Critical Turn in Education*, Isaac Gottesman (2016) tells us that critical pedagogy has been shaped by "radical ideas" of the 1960s and 1970s along lines of class, race and gender. Indeed, credit goes to those involved in the struggles of that earlier moment for bucking the trend in education, as well as to intellectuals like Henry Giroux, Stuart Hall, and Paulo Freire (a subject in the next chapter) that produced a pedagogical revolution that affixed terms like critical race studies and race conscious pedagogy to education reform. The varying approaches by leaders from the freedom movement ultimately provided educators a blueprint for how to shift pedagogy away from traditional teacher-dominant methods to critical theory instruction wherein students problematize issues afflicting America's marginalized communities. K-12 education still fails when it comes to decolonizing curriculum as well as taking new approaches to empower students with a pedagogical method that steers them toward improving home communities after graduation. While not the only cause, the gap in race-centered instruction is a big reason why racial episodes persist at the collegiate level. At the current juncture in education theory, organizations like the National Association of Multicultural Education (NAME), the Critical Race Studies Education Association (CRSEA), the White Privilege Conference, the Phi Delta Kappa annual conference through its National Institute on Central Office Leadership, and Teaching Tolerance exist to increase educators' consciousness around race, ethnicity, sexuality, gender, and disabilities, as well as awareness of problems related to diversity, equity, and inclusion. It is now a matter of whether contemporary educators are willing to redesign pedagogy that will improve the diagnostic abilities of White, African, Latinx, Asian, and Native American students in a way that will help them deconstruct institutional racism in America.

4

Making a Course

*Theoretical Framework
for a Course Grounded
in Race Conscious Pedagogy*

Introduction

Gap is a 113 square-mile rural school district in Lancaster County, Pennsylvania. Total residential population in the district is estimated at 41,376. It has an average student population of 5,405 that attend seven elementary schools, two middle schools, and one high school. Employed full-time in the district are 381 teachers and 244 support staff, with an additional 250 employees that work seasonally or part-time (Gap School District, 2019). According to numbers provided by the district's central administration, only four faculty members in the entire school district represent racial/ethnic groups other than White as of 2019. In any case, this low number is alarming. But when isolating the focus on the Gap School District, a district with a diminutive yet tangible history of racial alienation, the breakout of a racial confrontation between student-to-student and teacher-to-student is only a hairsbreadth away. The most notorious racially motivated clash at Gap High School occurred in 1997 when the school made headlines after a group of White students wore white t-shirts as a show of racial unity and an effort to intimidate their Peers of Color. At the time, just two percent of Gap students were African, Latinx, Asian and Native American.

While the teaching staff has seen little transformation since 1997, the student demographic composition of the school district has changed rapidly. As of 2020, the student body is 73.7 percent White, 15.2 percent Latinx, 4.9 percent African American, 3.0 percent multi-racial, 2.9 percent Asian American, .17 percent Pacific Islander, and .05 percent Native American. When considering the district's special programs, almost 17 percent of students have disabilities, 2.1 percent of students qualify for services under civil rights law

Section 504, and 2.4 percent have limited English proficiency. Of the district's 5,405 students, 269 are enrolled in gifted and talented programs. When the gifted program is broken down by race and ethnicity, 88.8 percent are White, 5.2 percent are Latinx, 3.0 percent are Asian, 2.2 percent is African American, 0.4 percent is Native American, and 0.4 percent identify as mixed race. Gap School District Superintendent (Gap School District, 2019) has begun implementing an equity standard for the district in addition to designing a Teacher of Color recruitment and retention plan, and admits, "Gap School District's faculty/staff does not reflect its student body." He acknowledges, "while excellent teachers are not defined by their gender, race, or ethnicity, it is important for students to sit in classrooms reflective of the diversity of our commonwealth." Despite its agricultural appeal, the school district sits on the edge of Lancaster City, where the largest ethnic group is Puerto Rican (29.2 percent), followed by German (21.2 percent) and African American (12.8 percent). The high school, in fact, shares property with the city's School District of Lancaster. This unique geographic dynamic has diversified Gap's student body in ways not anticipated 10 to 15 years ago.

In my role as an educator, I wanted to be proactive on the race topic. With a burgeoning non-dominant population deprived of racial, ethnic, and cultural affinity student groups and culturally responsive classes, along with the deteriorating political climate around issues of race since 2016, I anticipated problems that might resemble the student body walkouts or campus sit-ins of the late 1960s. It is against this historically familiar backdrop of social justice activism that I provide a contextual descriptive analysis of my critical race studies course. In particular, this chapter will provide a detailed description of the theoretical framework used to construct the course. Through this description, I aim to highlight my race studies course's distinctive features, as well as the ways that it might be incorporated into any high school's required course load. Such an analysis might draw attention to the relevance Race Conscious Pedagogy has on teenage high schoolers. At least, I hope that it does.

Race Conscious Pedagogy Framework

The need to disrupt racist ideas infused within White student bodies while providing Students of Color culturally relevant learning experiences is at the core of Race Conscious Pedagogy. Neither, of course, can be achieved if educators refuse to believe that a matrix of oppression operates within institutionalized policies and practices of the school system. Because hegemonic systems saturate the learning environment, only proactive challenges to notions of colorblindness and token integration by White pedagogues can awaken White students from their monolithic view of the world. Only those educators that recognize that race matters and can intersect race with gender, class, sexual orientation, national origin, religion, and ability/disability can gain the trust of marginalized students. I call such a capacity a state of *race consciousness*. The practical application of these ideas embedded into a class taught with a critical race lens underpins Race Conscious Pedagogy (RCP). The key assumptions of RCP described herein are also shown in figure 4.1.

At the bottom level of the RCP Pyramid, neither equity nor race consciousness is understood by the educator. Therefore, the concept of Tier 1 is referred to as WAKING UP. In such a category, the educator possesses a fishbowl worldview, and thus assumes that all students share the same lived experiences (see Chapter 1). This initial approach toward race consciousness exists as a level where the educator realizes—primarily because discussions about equity and racial bias are taking place in accordance to school district policy—an exploration into topics about race and equity must begin. Moving left to right on Tier 1 of the RCP Pyramid, the educator upholds racist beliefs based on the post-racial ethos of colorblindness; which, of course, is assumed to be a good thing. Early on, the educator also maintains innocence—both implicitly and explicitly—as it pertains to the ability to see White supremacy as the problem in a racialized country. As the educator reaches the middle trait of this bottom tier, the realization that race, in fact, does matter in American society is ascertained; accordingly, a sense of responsibility for social and legal injustices emerges. The Tier 1 educator commonly perpetuates stereotypes by unknowingly treating all students as if they are White, middle-class heterosexuals. Traits in this category include colorblindness, unchecked implicit bias, racial identification, a race matters mindset, and guilt.

The educator grows into a TRANSACTIONAL pedagogue in the second tier of the RCP Pyramid. In the second level, the educator begins the practice of almost daily self-reflection, which enables the acceptance of owning past racist beliefs. The educator also recognizes the existence of white skin privilege. A level of empathy empowers the educator to be more patient and sympathetic to Students of Color. Despite good intentions, however, the educator in this tier maintains racist emotions and ignorance on issues perceived in Communities of Color to be racist, while allegations of racism are challenged by most Whites; vis-à-vis, wearing blackface at a Halloween party. A "white savior" attitude fundamentally makes the mission of the transactional educator all about himself or herself, and is thus blinded to the actual needs of Black and non–Black Students of Color. Therefore, the belief in educational equity within the school system, like curricula, early school programs, school discipline, culturally proficient training for teachers, technology, transportation, and allocation of funds is not considered by the educator as a foundational aspect of the school culture. The traits of self-reflection, white skin privilege awareness, empathy, and a White liberal mentality make up this level. While these qualities appear to be regressive, this is a vital stage in making progress toward race consciousness.

The Tier 3 educator becomes an INTEGRATIONIST with an attitude that endeavors to integrate a sense of belonging for non-dominant cultural groups. This is a practical movement by the educator who has chosen to be informed on equity principles and has acquired the language to feel relatively comfortable engaging students in race talk. By this point, the classroom has on the surface transformed into a culturally responsive space. The educator's curriculum is reassessed to remove racial abuses, commonly referred to as microaggressions that offend Students of Color. Additionally, because of the changes in the teacher's curricular and pedagogical approach, students of the dominant culture become sympathetic to the lived experiences of their Peers of Color. Tier 3 traits are culturally responsive pedagogy, decolonized curriculum, and a word-to-world teaching-style wherein the educator begins to use race-based narratives and counter-narratives to fuse scholarship with the students' lived experiences.

The pedagogue becomes a TRANSFORMATIVE educator with a revolutionary mentality in the penultimate tier of the RCP Pyramid. In the role of a transformative educator, the instructor now exists as an archetype of cultural equity, setting an example of social justice crusading that inspires the students. The Tier 4 educator realizes there is no middle ground between racist and antiracist, to such an extent that proactive measures are undertaken in using the classroom to contest institutionalized oppression. Upon reaching Tier 4, this revolutionary educator now understands the default of the school system has always been the perpetuation of stereotypes that inflict harm on Students of Color and accordingly champions social justice causes in the school community. The educator is fundamentally willing to take risks that challenge the status quo of the school district and to serve the needs of under-resourced students. The revolutionary educator, irrespective of the discipline, makes critical race theory the framework for the curriculum. By designing a course that enables students to dismantle institutional racism through dialogue and reflection, the educator's classroom becomes a space featuring the use of texts and assignments designed to study the intersection of race with public policy, sports, religion, literature, geography, popular culture, the economy, psychology, music, science, education, and performance arts. Qualities in this level include the commitment to utilizing Critical Race Theory in the curricula while making antiracism a standard of living.

TRANSCENDENCE is achieved when an educator reaches the apex of the RCP Pyramid. This means that the educator has become the best version of himself or herself by realizing that race intersects with other identity categories: gender, class, ability, age, religion, and sexual orientation. Race consciousness, in other words, is the ability to create an inclusive learning environment that generates a sense of belonging for everyone in the classroom. The teacher accomplishes this by acknowledging and valuing the intersectional differences of every student. Because in a lower tier of the RCP Pyramid the educator recognizes there is no middle ground between racist and antiracist, it is now realized there is also no state of neutrality when it comes to classism, sexism, ableism, homophobia, or religious bigotry. The race conscious pedagogue does not grow comfortable with the school system as it stands intolerant of same-sex and same-loving individuals, nor does the educator become totally satisfied with the development of under-resourced low-income White students, being as every aspect of student performance along with school culture can advance closer to perfection. The only trait for this tier is race consciousness, the vital awareness that social categories face very similar systems of oppression because the various non-dominant racial, economic, sexual, and cultural identities overlap; to understand the issue of racism should make the race conscious pedagogue an ally of the LGBTQ+ community, religious minorities, and students of all marginalized groups.

Yet we cannot merely change the mentality of White educators who will then transform the attitude and disposition of White students; we must fundamentally alter how curricula, classroom culture, and teaching styles are designed. We must reimagine how we engage White students in the decolonial resources. We must reconsider how the leadership of a school district— its school board members, superintendents, and principals—is advised that Race Conscious Pedagogy is a good path forward for the school community. According to the Race Conscious Pedagogy Pyramid, the objectives of Race Conscious Pedagogy are (1) to make Students of Color aware that their cultures and their voices are valued features of the classroom; (2) to acculturate White students to diverse world experiences and break through the walls of colorblindness and color silence to establish a healthy and honest classroom dynamic; (3) foster critical thinking skills through narratives and counter-narratives as well as structured class dialogues that result in self-determination and original analytically-based ideas (Moses, 2002); and, most importantly, (4) to foster race conscious pedagogues that can enhance and advance the quality of learning in the classroom by nurturing a sense of belonging for *all* students.

For many reasons, ethnic studies, race studies, and gender studies have existed as lightning rod topics for K-12 teachers and administrators. This is why there are so few race/ethnicity/gender studies courses offered at the primary, intermediate, and secondary levels (this will be discussed in Chapter 6). Knowing that I would face counterattacks from those within and

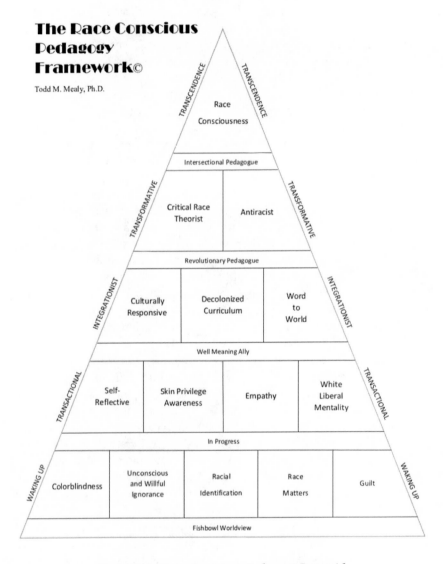

Figure 4.1—Race Conscious Pedagogy Pyramid

outside the district no matter how the course was constructed, I decided to craft a curriculum that avoided singling out any one racial or ethnic group. An African American history course was too narrow to attract enough students to enroll in the class. Latinx studies would likely trigger complaints that the class is designed only for Latinx students and allegations that the course might turn students into angry radicals. The term Whiteness is too inflammatory for many people in the district of European descent to create a critical Whiteness studies course. This brought me to the broad topics of race, ethnicity, and gender. Indeed, I designed a course that offers an interdisciplinary examination of ethnic history and culture in the United States wherein students are expected to analyze scholarly publications, music, film, folktales, books, and other academic and anecdotal resources in an attempt to problematize the post-racial and post-cultural disposition of the United States after the election of Barack Obama.

To make the language in this book easy to follow, I will only concentrate on the race component of the course. The class I created explores the intersections between race and law, race and the media, race and the economy, race and popular culture, race and housing policy, race and religion, race and education, race and the military, and race and sports. Three theoretical frameworks anchor the course, which I will hereafter call "Seminar in Critical Race Studies": (1) the College Board's Advanced Placement (AP) Capstone curriculum, (2) Critical Race Theory (CRT), and (3) Freirean critical pedagogy (FP).

Advanced Placement Capstone Framework

First launched in 2014 at 17 high schools worldwide, AP Capstone is advertised as a two-year program designed to prepare students in "independent research, collaborative teamwork, and communication skills" (College Board, 2016). For students who are accustomed to always being shown the solution to a problem and expected to memorize it, the mission of the program is to train students in four proficiency areas: (1) Research: how to properly locate primary documents and scholarly secondary sources; (2) Reading Comprehension: how to critically evaluate the line of reasoning in those texts as well as to identify the bias within each source; (3) Writing: how to write thesis-driven reports that synthesizes ideas from a variety of voices and identifies a gap in previous research; and (4) Presentation: how to engage an audience through oral and multimedia performance. AP Capstone gives teachers a pedagogical framework to help students "develop, practice, and hone their critical and creative thinking skills" as issues in American society are problematized. The AP Capstone framework (2016), otherwise known as QUEST, is as such:

1. Question and Explore: In this initial stage of research, students explore a topic. As preliminary research is conducted, students are expected to come up with questions "that spark one's curiosity, leading to an investigation that challenges and expands the boundaries of one's current knowledge" (College Board, 2016). This is also a step

     where students acquire a collection of sources for their respective research topics.

2. Understand and Analyze: In the second stage of research, students begin to summarize into his or her own words the individual sources and contextualize an author's line of reasoning. This is the step that students brood over the central arguments of each source.

3. Evaluate Multiple Perspectives: In stage three, students compare and contrast various points of view on a chosen topic by concentrating their research in ongoing debate over an issue. The students must include counterarguments in their textual constellation.

4. Synthesize Ideas: Students are expected to fuse the ideas of varying sources with one's own in hopes that a new understanding of the topic surfaces.

5. Team, Transform, and Transmit: In the final stage, students are able to work with a team to "combine personal strengths and talents with those of others" to create a presentation that is capable of connecting with an audience (College Board, 2016). This stage is about "transmitting" an individual or group's ideas to an audience.

The five QUEST skills have made my classroom a space for developing critical and creative thinking skills as students learn how to find appropriate academic sources, identify an author's reasoning while generating one's own claims, and stand confidently in front of large audiences while defending an original idea (College Board, 2016). Moreover, students obtain skills needed to negotiate the relationships between text, context, and subtext as they evaluate sources.

AP Capstone is based on two yearlong Advance Placement courses: AP Seminar during the first year and AP Research during the second year. Students that pass end of year exams in both courses and pass four additional Advanced Placement exams in any subject with a score of three or higher are awarded an AP Capstone diploma.

The first year AP Seminar course is not designed to be subject-specific. Teachers, instead, are expected to prioritize the QUEST skills. According to the College Board, teachers may choose one theme, multiple themes, or a compendium of topics that "allow for deep interdisciplinary exploration" in which students enhance skills in "research, analysis, evidence-based arguments, collaboration, writing, and presenting" (College Board, 2018). Students enrolled in AP Seminar explore any given topic through several academic lenses, not limited to the following: (1) cultural and social, (2) artistic and philosophical, (3) political and historical, (4) environmental, (5) economic, (6) scientific, (7) futuristic, and (8) ethical.

Gap High School incorporated the AP Capstone program in the 2017 fall semester. When selected by the administration to teach the first-year seminar course, I jumped at the chance to make my course's theme a critical study of race in America. While Seminar in Critical Race Studies is an Advanced Placement course, not everyone enrolled in the class is expected to take the end of year AP exam. In other words, my class is open to non–AP students as well.

Seminar in Critical Race Studies is divided into two parts. The first semester is spent using the theme of critical race studies to teach AP Capstone's QUEST skills. Students then spend the second semester performing AP Seminar testing requirements, which entail two thesis defenses (one in group and one individual) and an end-of-course written exam. The first semester begins with an introductory unit on critical race studies, open-ended problem-posing pedagogy, and AP Capstone standards. All successive units concentrate on topics related to Whiteness studies, Asian American studies, African American studies, Latinx studies, Jewish American studies, Islamic American studies, and Native American studies (course specifics, including pacing, pedagogy, and objectivity are discussed in Chapter 5). The AP Capstone framework is important because it provides an additional incentive for students that contemplate enrolling in the class. While some register for the course on account of partaking in cross-racial dialogues, others join in hopes of learning skills that will help them research, write, and present. This approach also increases the academic worth of Seminar in Critical Race Studies as students obtain much needed skills to perform well on state standardized tests, the SAT, and college application essays. The way that Seminar in Critical Race Studies is designed affords students a well-balanced education that uses tax dollars wisely as I offer opportunities to practice important professional skills such as teamwork and communication while remaining proactive in providing opportunities for students to engage with one another about their own heritage and the heritage of all other communities that exist in the United States.

Critical Race Theory in Social Studies

If there is room in education to work in Critical Race Theory, it is in the social studies curriculum. History tends to be the only social studies course that touches on America's various racialized groups at every end of the curriculum. There are ample opportunities for historians to discuss historical as well as contemporary injustices. And still, students in those classrooms are offered a cursory history of marginalized groups where race is scarcely a configuration in the construction of the nation. Students graduate from high school having never reckoned with the fact that the United States was founded as a slave state and built on stolen land. They never learn that America was also founded on addiction to rum, tobacco and sugar; but it is today that addiction is criminalized, particularly in Communities of Color, where 75 to 90 percent of drug offenders are sent to prison (Small, 2001; Khan-Cullors and bandele, 2018). Sadly, the erasure of race is not only a matter of curriculum. The silence is compounded by what education pedagogical theorist Gloria Ladson-Billings (2003) calls "societal curriculum," an absence of non-dominant cultural representation that "operates within and beyond the school and classroom." Ladson-Billings says students observe this hidden societal curriculum every time they "turn on the evening news and see people of color as menacing" or when they see "people who look like them occupy the lowest skilled jobs in the school-janitors, cafeteria workers, instructional aids." Her point, which is reinforced in the work of critical race theorist Derald Wing Sue (2015), is that social markers such as peer groups and the mass media reinforce the culturally insensitive curriculum learned in school. Sue contends that the hidden curriculum manifests itself in a "master narrative," wherein White Americans tell themselves stories that reinforce democratic tropes: that they are "good, moral, and fair"; that "allows them to live in a world of false deception"; that propagates White racial innocence, "perpetuates the racial status quo"; that blinds them from the "inequities that exist for people of color"; and "justifies inaction on their part." For this reason, teachers would benefit their students by adopting courses on Critical Race Theory, which fundamentally challenges one-dimensional notions of implicit bias, meritocracy, colorblindness, and the absence of institutional racism, while exposing the abounding power of White privilege and, in Sue's terms, "the denial of individual racism" (Sue, 2015; Eddo-Lodge, 2017). I contend if the education system is supposed to prepare students for a multicultural world they should have experience grappling with race issues before having to navigate in a racially complex society. Whereas, if educators send students into predominantly White settings where the values of the majorative system of Whiteness prevail, should students not have to wrestle with these ideas somewhere?

As a relatively new theoretical approach in the Humanities classroom, Critical Race Theory dates back to 1987 when a team of legal scholars, led by Derrick Bell, Jr., Alan Freeman, Kimberle Crenshaw, Jean Stefancic, Patricia Williams, and Richard Delgado, met at the Critical Legal Studies Conference outside Madison, Wisconsin, to discuss ideas drawn from the civil rights and Black power movements and the ethnic studies programs that came around after the Black student disruptions of the late 1960s (Delgado and Stefancic, 2017). With interests in critically assessing the intersection of race and law, these legal scholars created an academic field that uses the law to redress racial injustices. While the field began as a movement to examine racism in laws and courts, it has grown to include cross-disciplinary methods and comprises of intersectional issues related, but not limited, to LGBTQ+, Latinx, women, ethnic studies, American studies, and Educational theorists. Critical Race Theory (CRT), as it came to be known, aims to foster a racial enlightenment in America; that racism is, according to the late legal scholar Derrick Bell (1993, 2017), "permanent" in American society. Bell argued "that [racism] is not an aberration" but a fixture of White supremacy that is maintained perpetually in the dominant culture. This frame of mind sees racial oppression ingrained into the foundation of America's institutions, including the public education system. The field holds that race is a social invention, wherein skin color has nothing to do with higher-order traits in humans, such as personality, intelligence, and moral behavior. Underpinning the work of critical race theorists is the continuous questioning of legal means that surround the equal protection doctrine of the 14th Amendment, false claims of race neutrality and fairness, and the importance in reforming power relations. Like Bell, CRT cofounder, Richard Delgado (2017) calls this approach "legal indeterminacy"—"the idea that not every legal case has one correct outcome," arguing instead that jurisprudence played an integral role in substantiating the racial caste, and legal decisions can be overturned in the future.

The aftermath of the ruling in *Brown v. Topeka Board of Education* is one explanation of CRT's approach to academia. CRT theory suggests that following *Brown,* African American communities were damaged not because of the integration of Black and White children, but that Black schools and, by association, the occupations of Black educators were eliminated. Bell (1976; 1980) contended the Supreme Court in 1954 would have been better off enforcing the "equal" aspect than repealing the "separate" part of the 1896 *Plessy v. Ferguson* "separate but equal" doctrine used by Thurgood Marshall to obtain a unanimous decision in *Brown.* The absence of culturally relevant freedom pedagogy is part and parcel of desegregation as African Americans post–*Brown* lost the ability to shape their children's education (Peller, 1990). According to Education researcher Vanessa Siddle Walker (2000, 2018), author of several books tackling the history of equity in education, including *Their Highest Potential: An African American School Community in the Segregated South*, about 38,000 African American teachers and administrators lost jobs in the first 11 years following *Brown.* A *USA Today* report published on the 50th anniversary of the *Brown* decision showed that the number of Black students then enrolled in preservice teacher programs was already in rapid decline. At the turn of the millennium, just six years after *Brown's* golden anniversary, 84 percent of public school teachers were White while 16 percent were Teachers of Color. Of that number, just eight percent were African American (Toppo, 2004; Geiger, 2018). The lack of teacher diversity heading into the 2020s has compounded the problem of unequal access to educational resources and, in turn, a widening opportunity gap as well as a sustained culture of providing non-dominant students an education that appears alien to the communities from which they arrive (Constantine and Sue, 2006). The National Center for Education Statistics (2018) reported that White teachers make up almost half (45 percent) of the teachers in schools comprised of 90 percent Students of Color. By comparison, in schools with a White student population at 90 percent or higher, White educators make up 98 percent of the faculty. Not only does the lack of Black teachers hurt Black students—a point once argued by W.E.B. Du Bois (1935) in "Does the Negro Need Separate Schools?," in which he claimed that Students of Color receive greater levels of attention, respect, advice, opportunity, and education when a teacher that looks like them is standing in the front of the classroom—but White students also suffer from not having a Person of Color as an authority figure in the classroom.

Even if most scholars today agree with Bell's assertion that desegregation damaged the cognitive development of Black students and forced into unemployment tens of thousands of Black educators, they would surely not deny that some Black children have benefited from going to school with White children. Of course, it is commonplace that not everyone agrees that it is fair to lambast the 1954 Supreme Court decision as not having the impact on improving schools that is so-often revered in American history and culture. Author of *Children of the Dream: Why School Integration Works*, Rucker Johnson pushes back against the argument that public school desegregation was a failed experiment. Johnson (2019) calls Bell's assertion "defeatism," claiming that school desegregation has always benefited Students of Color along with White students. "*Brown* did not overturn everything overnight," Johnson contends, but after tracking students "over an extended period of time" and in school districts that adhered to court-ordered integration versus school districts that remained segregated only does it become easy "to see the [positive] impact of the *Brown* decision" (Johnson, 2019). Using the Panel Study of Income Dynamics (PSID), which has surveyed 18,000 Americans since 1968, a period spanning 50 years and three generations since *Brown*, Johnson argues *Brown's* success is shown "in the way integration affected access to school resources," such as after school programs, class sizes, and school facilities. The PSID data shows an increase in per-pupil spending by 22.5 percent and reduction in average class sizes experienced by Black students since 1968. He also credits desegregation for integrating the teacher workforce, though without acknowledging either the disparity between White teachers and Teachers of Color or the student-led movements of the late 1960s and early 1970s that led to greater curricular changes and faculty diversity at integrated schools. The National Center of Education Statistics

(NCES) offers a similar perspective on school desegregation. According to the NCES (2018), the Black and White high school graduation rate at present is nearly the same: 88 percent for Whites, 76 percent for African Americans. This is a significant shift in a positive direction since the generation of students immediately following *Brown*, when the graduation rate for Whites was near 50 percent while African Americans graduated from high school at a lowly rate of 23 percent. In 2016, the Century Foundation (2016), a nonpartisan think tank that works for various causes concerning inequity and inclusion, issued a report backing Johnson's claim and reinforced the new data disseminated by the NCES. While ignoring both the Teacher of Color deficiency in addition to the nonexistence of culturally responsive curriculum, the Century Foundation's study showed that socioeconomically and racially diverse schools improve students' cognitive and social development. The report illuminated several encouraging outcomes of desegregation: that diverse schools have a reduced opportunity gap between White and Black students, 30 percent more growth in state standardized test scores, lower dropout rates, increased likelihood for students to go onto college, and classroom environments that promote critical thinking and problem-solving skills. Moreover, integrated schools enable cross-cultural dialogue that ultimately is more beneficial for society. According to the Century Foundation, these schools reduce racial biases by confronting stereotypes. They also enhance leadership and teamwork skills.

While persuasive, Johnson's thesis and the Century Foundation's 2016 report are problematic simply because there exists very few racially integrated schools in America that go beyond placing White students and Students of Color in the same building, let alone the same classroom. In the same National Center on Education Statistics (2018) report previously mentioned, 66 percent of America's schools are racially segregated (segregated schools are defined as schools where less than 40 percent of the students are White). More than 70 percent of African American students attend those segregated schools (Stancil, 2018). Bell's racial realism theory, along with Du Bois's 1935 query, cast a spotlight on the dueling definitions of schools that are desegregated versus schools that can be considered integrated. There is a judicial component to desegregated schools existing exclusively in the South following the *Brown* ruling. Therefore, concluding on one hand that desegregation was an involuntary enterprise forced by court order upon White segregationists for a generation; and, two, school segregation due to residential racial zoning practices enabled northern school districts to ignore the Supreme Court's *Brown I* and *II* rulings. Desegregation, therefore, maintains the racial status quo that existed before 1954, according to Nikole Hannah-Jones (2018), award-winning investigative journalists whose work concentrates on school re-segregation in contemporary America, by means of ensuring that White students "receive an inordinate amount of resources" while only a handful of Students of Color join their White counterparts in class. Whereas, integrated schools encompass culturally relevant curricula, equal access to advanced placement courses and gifted programs, and culturally responsive teaching; as well as diverse teaching and administrative staffs.

Bell, Hannah-Jones, and other critical race theorists suggest that law-makers gave up on the dream of integration within a generation of *Brown v. Board*. The failure of *Brown's* promise is the biggest indication of plausibility for Bell's assertion on the permanence of racism. According to Hannah-Jones, integrating schools is "civil rights made personal," as her almost two decades spent covering the topic has illustrated that the biggest obstacle to achieving school integration is "lack of will." While White families can live lives away from People of Color in a backyard pool or a neighborhood restaurant, the school exists as a place where parents can "no longer control" who their children come in contact with. She explains, "it is my child away from me in a building where I don't even see what's happening with my child.... It's so personal that's why we have made the least progress" in public school integration.

Data exists to confirm Hannah-Jones's case. The U.S. Commission on Civil Rights reported 33 percent of African American and Latinx students attend schools that are hyper-segregated, or what the Civil Rights Project classifies as schools where 90 percent or more of all students are of a darker hue and 75 percent of the student body is low-income. A shockingly high portion of America's 1,700 school districts (40 percent) fit the classification of hyper-segregation (Orfield et al., 2014). A U.S. Department of Education report from 2011 showed 40 percent of African American students attend high-poverty schools, compared to six percent of the White population. The report indicated, "As racial segregation in schools increases, so does the concentration of poverty" due to historical racial inequities, which is largely a result of economic and educational disadvantages generated from residential segregation dating back to first half of the 20th century (Jordan, 2014).

Since Critical Race Theory argues that racism is a normal and undying certainty, it would come as no surprise that other than debating the failure of public school desegregation, the most contentious example that might come up in a race studies class today is the value of dark lives. The Black Lives Matter movement is a nonviolent endeavor that adheres to the tenets of the Black Panther Party's intercommunalism, or racial solidarity. However, the movement's relationship with the framework of Black pride has brought allegations of reverse racism. CRT would argue against this accusation, claiming that Black intercommunalism is not a racist movement. It is a deep philosophical contestation that challenges notions of post-racialism, of which scholars suggest is a misunderstanding easily imagined since America no longer has actual laws that divide the races into disproportionate societies and because

Barack Obama was twice elected president of the United States. Critical Race Theory, however, claims that race really does matter in American culture; thus propelling any conversation about race beyond old notions of integrationism and colorblindness.

The work of Beverly Daniel Tatum (1997, 2017), author of *Why Are All the Black Kids Sitting Together in the Cafeteria?: And Other Conversations About Race*, reinforces CRT's notion that racism is a natural aspect of human interaction. She compares America's permanent race problem to the "smog" that people inhale. Tatum writes, "Sometimes [racism] is so thick it is visible, other times it is less apparent, but always, day in and day out, we are breathing it." Notwithstanding the landmark legislations of 1964 and 1965 that effectively granted full citizenship including suffrage rights to African Americans, and despite the election of President Obama, America is still not fully equal and is certainly not fully integrated. Thus, movements like Black Lives Matter exist to raise awareness about unequal social arrangements in addition to institutionalized inequity in the criminal justice system. Additionally, Black Lives Matter and CRT endorse the notion that Whites will never support efforts to improve the lives of people of non-dominant races unless it is in their interest to do so. This concept, which Bell (2003) calls "Interest Convergence" theory, is sustained by academics like Tatum, who upholds the belief that although the laws have changed, America's institutional authority has remained influenced by White supremacy. Believing in the permanence of racism does not mean social justice advocates should accept racism or to become passive spectators in the contemporary struggle for inclusion and equity. Rather Bell would say to work to mitigate the harms that the White supremacist system will bring while enjoying good moments knowing they will last just a short time (Bell, 1993, 2018).

Colloquially put, CRT debunks theories of colorblindness, meritocracy, and classism (Eddo-Lodge, 2017). The absence of Jim Crow and residential discrimination laws makes it easy for people to dismiss race. It emboldens some Whites to shut down the debate with charges that we have attained post racialism; Oscar victories by Actors and Directors of Color, and Oprah's media, entertainment, and business empire mean that the American dream is possible for everyone. Though Jim Crow laws no longer exist, CRT maintains that systemic racism supersedes class when dealing with routine issues. In *Critical Race Theory: An Introduction*, Richard Delgado and Jean Stefancic (2017) and several university researchers reinforce CRT's position that race trumps class. For example, African Americans and Latinxs are refused loans and jobs at greater rates than poor Whites. According to information gathered under the federal Home Mortgage Disclosure Act, 27.4 percent of African American applicants and 19.2 percent of Latinx applicants are denied mortgages, compared to about 11 percent of White applicants. Additionally, wealthy African Americans are pulled over by police officers more often than poor Whites, as indicated by a *Washington Post* report showing Black drivers are about 30 percent "more likely than whites" to be pulled over. Data on other topics shows that the majorative system of Whiteness prevails over dark-skin children as early as preschool. A team of Yale University researchers and the U.S. Department of Education's Office of Civil Rights issued similar reports indicating African American children make up 50 percent of suspension in preschools, and are suspended at a rate of 3.6 times their White counterparts in preschool despite accounting for just 18 percent of preschoolers nation-wide (Malik, 2017; Rock, 2017). When examining all age groups, Students of Color are three times more likely than White students to be suspended. African American students make up 16 percent of the nation's K-12 enrollment but 27 percent of students referred to law enforcement (NPR, 2014; U.S. Department of Education Office for Civil Rights, 2014). In each instance, skin color, not class, is the determining factor.

The disparity can also be seen in the disproportionate dark-skin prison population, shorter life expectancy of People of Color, inferior medical care given to racially minoritized people, and the fact that those representing non-dominant cultures occupy more menial jobs than do Whites. Even the way government has habitually decided who meets the criteria as a refugee says everything about how America has historically placed race ahead of class. The word "refugee" is often used when referring to individuals most Americans want to care for, while disparaging and dehumanizing terms like "alien" and "criminal" are commonly reserved for people who are darker hued immigrants. For instance, a study conducted by five researchers from Tufts University revealed a troubling fact about how the media reported on Hurricane Katrina. After analyzing almost 3,000 stories, the Tufts University report presented an uneven tendency to associate African Americans in New Orleans with looting and violence, while Whites were described as "refugees" and "evacuees" (Sommers, 2006). The driving force for this seemingly endless way of describing People of Color has been the threat that Black and Brown foreigners would disrupt the American way of life. Devaluating language is commonly used about refugees from Mexico, El Salvador, the Democratic Republic of Congo, Syria, and other countries Donald Trump deemed shitholes, meanwhile hardly a word is said about Nordic, Russian, Ukrainian immigrants as well as those from the Global North that enter the United States.

Drawing from Critical Race Theory's many tools can guide teachers and students toward implementing social justice causes into daily curriculum. Using the CRT model, I have constructed a course that deconstructs objects in American culture in an attempt to analyze the racial implications and offer solutions to improve the standard of living for all citizens. This critical approach is essential for spotlighting both obvious and latent oppressive structures within both a students' school environment and that of the country. Since privilege is granted to those who make up the dominant culture, there is little incentive for Whites to change the legal, political, economic, and educational systems. With this in mind, Bell's (1993, 2004) "interest convergence covenant" is buttressed by the work of Delgado and Stefancic (2000). My Seminar in Critical Race Studies, however, is a medium where students can critique those interests. In what Delgado and Stefancic describe as the "voices-of-color" thesis, texts and stories told by and about marginalized groups (African, First Nation, Asian, Latinx, Islamic, and Jewish) combined with the works of great thinkers that make up the decolonial epistemology like Frederick Douglass, W.E.B. Du Bois, Frantz Fanon, James Baldwin, Cesar Chavez, bell hooks, Michel Foucault, Stuart Hall, and Antonio Gramsci will communicate with White students who have been unaware of their own privileges, prejudices, and stereotypes.

Freirean Critical Pedagogy

The classroom is a safe space where students can engage in conversations about touchy subjects in a structured and productive way. For K-12 students, however, those discussions are fleeting opportunities that come in the middle of a teacher's lecture or during a day designated for debate. Students deserve enduring dialogues about race to develop cognitive abilities that make one a critical thinker. Students are worthy of opportunities to obtain a comprehensive and nuanced understanding of the problems that plague their lives. As the late Brazilian education philosopher Paulo Freire (1970, 2018) believed, "No one is born fully-formed: it is through self-experience in the world that we become what we are."

As noted by critical educational scholar Isaac Gottesman (2016), critical pedagogical praxis is a product of social movements dating before Freire's time. And yet Freire's critical, or problem-posing, teaching style has made him, in Gottesman's words, a "mainstay" in the field of education. Near the end of the decolonial era and after the American civil rights movement, Freire developed a teaching style to jettison a culture of obedience that customarily prevails among oppressed persons commonly forced to comply and conform to the majorative culture. According to biographer Moacir Gadotti (2014), Freire was a critical pedagogue known for "improving the living conditions of marginalized populations" by linking decolonial freedom struggles in Africa, Asia, and South America with his unconventional educational pedagogy. Influenced by 20th-century revolutionary figures, such as Vladimir Lenin, Antonio Gramsci, and Che Guevara, Freire developed his approach to decolonial education theory while teaching literacy to rural Brazilians near Sao Paulo in the 1950s and 1960s (Gottesman, 2016; Sue, 2015; Freire, 1970). He encouraged his students to think critically about their living conditions and the social institutions around them. Repulsed by the oppressed learning environment, he devised a pedagogy based on student-teacher dialogue and problem solving. According to Nicholas B. Lundholm (2011) of the *Arizona Law Review*, Freire's model "recognized that both the student and the teacher were holders of knowledge"; Freire believed this new method of removing power from the instructor would awaken his students to the roots of their social conditions and respond accordingly with social activism. For pressing his case for the world's oppressed people, Freire is often criticized by some on the right as an instigator of anti-government insurrection.

Freire's pedagogical theory can be summarized as such: students share the power with the teacher in a democratized environment where students learn about the world by listening to one another as individual truths are spoken. In a Freirean-styled classroom, teachers and students learn together. The teacher has created an environment wherein the construction of knowledge is more democratic and efficient for learning. Everyone in the room is an active participant in what Freire (1970) calls "dialogics," a style of teaching that awakens students to systemic forms of oppression through the use of cooperative and open-ended discussions organized around deconstructions of society at large in the form of problem-posing instruction geared toward problem-solving. This "awakening," or as Freire calls it "*conscientization*," is the development of a critical consciousness requiring that a student locate himself or herself within a racist, sexist, and heterosexist hierarchical structure that he or she can now begin to dismantle.

Freire spoke more specifically to freeing the colonized mind; a break from the traditional "banking" approach to education, wherein students are considered empty bank accounts to where, in Lundholm's (2011) words, the "teacher stands in front of the classroom and authoritatively" deposits information. The banking system of education operates on the assumption that a student's ability to memorize and regurgitate information at a later date is representative of gaining knowledge. Freirean pedagogy rejects the banking concept for, as Freire (1970, 2018) wrote in his seminal book, *Pedagogy of the Oppressed*, the "passive role [regularly] imposed on" the student suppresses cognitive development. The banking model, he argued, is capable of minimizing or annulling "the students' creative power." Learning environments that manipulates thinking or limits opportunity to think critically, "serve the interests of the oppressor," Freire maintained, "who care neither to have the world revealed nor to see it transformed." In a word, Freirean pedagogy rebukes the traditional teaching method that contains "contradictions about reality."

Freirean pedagogues and critical race theorists like Shirley Mthethwa-Sommers (2014) see traditional education as "perpetuat[ing] inequities and social injustices" in the curriculum and school culture that also "exist in society." Very much like SNCC's freedom schools and the Black Panthers' intercommunal schools, Freirean critical teaching method of using problem-based, open-ended, and solution-oriented dialogues through interdisciplinary and multicultural lenses strive to free students of mundane and monocultural processes of learning. It shows young men and young women that there is nothing wrong in seeing the world in their own way. After all, it was Freire who reasoned, "Liberating education [for students] consists in acts of cognition, not transferals of information." While I have found essay exams based on my lectures beneficial to the high school and college students I have taught, I believe for students to become free agents in the world that banking approaches to education should be outweighed by classrooms grounded in Freirean critical problem-posing techniques.

In a well-intentioned yet mythical post-racial perception of American society, the act of engaging in Freirean pedagogy is a culture shock to K-12 teachers as it is certainly a different teaching method than what they had been taught in preservice college training. Additionally, the decision to introduce a radical pedagogical style into the classroom is unnerving because it calls for a critical understanding of the curriculum. Douglas J. Simpson and Sally Mc-Millan (2008), two university professors from Texas Tech, asked, "Is it time to shelve Paulo Freire?" in the *Journal of Thought,* a publication devoted to reflective examination of problems in the field of education. Likewise, Comparative and International Relations expert Jeannie Grussendorf (2012) contends that when students and/or the teacher is accustomed to the banking concept, Freirean approaches to learning can be "disconcerting." In addition to unfamiliarity and distress that problem-posing concept of education places upon students and teachers, she writes in "Teaching Peace When Students Don't Know (About) War," that when students lack the contextual understanding of institutional forms of discrimination, the experience will be "frustrating and possibly off-putting rather than engaging." Despite the criticism, by moving from a banking to a critical dialogic approach allows students and teachers to engage more freely with texts and personal experiences that will awaken White students to hegemonic systems of domination while simultaneously differentiating pedagogical practices to teach diverse groups of students. The instructor's job is to ask students a variety of questions during a class period, which sequentially requires the educator to possess the ability to produce improvised questions to students that will regularly offer unanticipated insight to the dialogue.

A protégé of Freire's, Gloria Jean Watkins, better known as bell hooks (1994), offers a sharp estimation on the power of Freirean methods: while radical shifts to teaching style might initially be viewed as "potentially disruptive of the atmosphere of seriousness assumed to be essential to the learning process" owing to its unfamiliarity, hooks says Freirean-style dialogics generate "excitement" that will "co-exist with and even stimulate serious intellectual and/or academic engagement." She affirmed that the way to produce excitement among students that are accustomed to traditional banking practices is to "insist that everyone's presence is acknowledged"; to ensure that everyone's opinion is genuinely valued; that the teacher ensures that every student contributes to the dialogue and that those contributions are reinforced by the teacher's affirmations. Excitement, hooks believes, "is generated through collective effort." She adds, quite appropriately, that "transformative pedagogy [is] rooted in a respect for multiculturalism." True to Freirean methods, hooks argues, the teacher abdicates his or her role as "the-one-who-teaches," only to become "jointly responsible" for creating a learning environment "in which all grow." Indeed, when engaging in this method of instruction, Freire justified, "no one teaches another, nor is anyone self-taught. People teach each other, mediated by the world." The product of this type of instruction, Henry Giroux (2011) claims, is a "critically engaged and socially responsible citizenry" (MacPherson, 2015).

Conclusion

Gap High School exists as a space where a course that combines AP Capstone curriculum with Critical Race Theory and Freirean problem-posing pedagogy can be tested. In ways large and small, the school contains a dynamic much like those colleges of the 1960s where racial discontent rested ominously beneath the surface both in the form of non-dominant student anxiety along with White faculty and White student insecurities. It is this dynamic that led me to construct Seminar in Critical Race Studies at Gap High School. It is constructed to deal directly with identity development and cultural competence. Additionally, the course is built to provide each student with research, composition, and presentation skills through an evaluation of decolonial texts and counter-texts. The particulars of the class, including conversations and specific activities will be detailed in the forthcoming chapters.

5

The Course

Seminar in Critical Race Studies

Introduction

Gap High School is divided into four academic levels: Career Prep, which primes students for the workforce after high school; College Prep, which is designed to prepare students to read and write at or above grade level and attend post-secondary education after graduation; Honors, which is made up of accelerated courses intended for students that succeed in College Prep courses and desire an even more demanding challenge; and Advanced Placement (AP), which is the most academically rigorous program, designed for students that want to take the College Board's end-of-year exam. Students that take AP classes but do not take the AP exam receive Honors credit. Several of Gap's College Prep, Honors, and AP students take advantage of the school district's early enrollment program with local colleges, including Millersville University, Harrisburg Area Community College's Lancaster branch, and Thaddeus Stevens College of Technology. Often referred to as "dual enrollment," students simultaneously complete their senior year of high school while also taking 100-level and 200-level courses at a college. Students receive honors level credit for a 100-level class and AP level credit for a 200-level class. Gap students also have the opportunity to enroll in the Career and Technology Center (CTC) program, which gives students six credits in vocational on-the-job training (Gap School District, 2018). The school district's high school has recently gained an admirable reputation for its academic success. There was a string of three consecutive years (2015–2017) that the *U.S. News & World Report* ranked Gap High School the No.-1 high school in Lancaster County, and 35th ranked school in the Commonwealth of Pennsylvania. The high school's national ranking is 1,049 out of 28,000 public schools in all 50 states and the District of Columbia. The report's estimates are determined from test results in reading and math for all students.

Also considered in the calculation are ethnic subgroups and economically disadvantaged students as well as graduation rates and the number of students taking and passing college-level courses vis-à-vis dual enrollment with local colleges and AP exams.

As stated in Chapter 4, not every student that enrolls in Seminar in Critical Race Studies is an AP or Honors student. Since I am the only teacher in the building that teaches the course, I want every student to join who desires an education in critical race studies. As it turns out, Seminar in Critical Race Studies has become a diverse space that matches the demography of the school district. In the three years that the course has run, 23.8 percent of the students in the class have been African American, Asian American, and Latinx; it is a figure that nearly matches the total enrollment of Students of Color in Gap School District (26.3 percent). Female students have made up 65.96 percent of those in the class. This number exceeds the total number of women in the school district (52 percent). Additionally, three students that have taken Seminar in Critical Race Studies, or .05 percent, have self-identified as LGBTQ+. Though there are no racial or ethnic affinity groups at the high school, students in December 2018 were permitted to form a Gay-Straight Alliance club. With this data in mind, I offer a descriptive analysis of Seminar in Critical Race Studies in this chapter.

Writing the Curriculum

Preparing objectives for Seminar in Critical Race Studies was an easy task since I must adhere to AP Capstone's QUEST curriculum. The objective of AP Capstone's first year seminar is to teach students how to engage "both collaboratively and individually, in cross-curricular conversations and research that explores real world topics from multiple perspectives." Students in the class must "analyze and evaluate information with accuracy and precision to effectively write and present evidence-based arguments" (College Board, 2016). In addition to Capstone's goals, I wrote my own objectives for the course. I want students to use the QUEST framework to discuss topics related to race, ethnicity, and gender in the United States while practicing reading and analyzing academic articles, research studies, literary texts, speeches, podcasts, interviews, personal accounts, film, graphic novels, and works of art. Students spend a semester digging through a variety of primary and secondary sources, novels, peer-reviewed articles, and more as they learn how to synthesize the ideas conveyed by multiple authors.

During the first semester, students sharpen skills in research, reading analysis, critical thinking, writing, and presentation using texts about race in America. It is during these initial months that students participate in critical dialogues about the texts. As John Dewey (1915) once said, "Give the pupils something to do, not something to learn; and the doing is of such a nature as to demand thinking; learning naturally results." In the spirit of Dewey's progressive approach to education, critical dialogues are our multifaceted open-ended discussions where we focus on themes found within a text; identify personal connections with the text; discuss solutions for the worldly issues found in the text; and evaluate the author's style, structure and prose. During these critical dialogues that students become empowered to critique race conditions in their personal experiences as they pertain to the assigned reading. Everything performed and measured in class lead students to two thesis projects that are defended during the spring semester.

To prepare students for the thesis defenses, I divide the course into 11 thematic units that engage students in narratives and counter-narratives about many of the racial and ethnic groups in America as well as gender identity. I designed and titled the following units in a way that meets the interdisciplinary standards of AP Capstone: (1) Introduction to Critical Race Studies and Problem-Posing Pedagogy, (2) Whiteness Studies: A Deconstruction of White Supremacy, including Race Making, the Melting Pot Myth, White Privilege, Colorism, and Color-Blindness, (3) Asian American Studies: A Social Analysis of Dueling Asian American Stereotypes, (4) African American Studies: A Historical Survey of Interest Convergence Theory, (5) Latinx Studies: A Cultural Examination of Racial Scripts, from Gregorio Cortez to the roots of Hip Hop, (6) Jewish American Studies: Cuisine, Politics, and Other Cultural Aspects of the Americanization of Jews since World War I, (7) Islamic American Studies: A Philosophical Assessment of Edward Said's "Orientalism" and Jack Shaheen's "Arabland" in Popular Culture, (8) Native American Studies: The Politics of the Vanishing American and a Content Analysis of the American Indian Movement in the Media, (9) Gender Studies: Toxic Masculinity in Film, Hip Hop, and Sports, (10) Team Project: The Team Thesis Defense, (11) Individual Project: A High School Level Dissertation Defense. Each unit's subtitle uses either a Capstone buzzword (history, social, culture, ethics, economics, politics) or reference (bias, survey) related to the curriculum's academic lenses discussed in Chapter 4. When the time arrives for students to submit their two theses, they must create titles and subtitles that identify their research lens and indicate the central argument of their theses. Each unit in Seminar in Critical Race Studies, then, is designed as a research model for students to sort through sources while utilizing specific research lenses.

Students then spend the second semester using the interdisciplinary methods acquired during the first semester to complete two thesis defenses about topics of personal preference. I do not make the students choose a topic related to race in America. Though thesis topics have ranged from privatizing space exploration to the flaws in America's mass transit system, most students choose research topics that fall within the theme of race, ethnicity, and gender. The first thesis project (Team Project: The Team Thesis Defense) is a collaborative research based-essay and oral defense. Students can form groups no smaller than three members and no larger than five members. Members of a group agree on a topic then create a single research question from which each member chooses a research lens for investigation. Each member then writes his or her own 1,200-word report. Differentiation in research lenses means that each group member will write a unique report. After paper submission, groups prepare a presentation that combines each member's research. Group presentations are capped at 10 minutes with follow-up questions that are untimed. While every student receives his or her own grade on the written report, everyone in the group receives the same presentation grade. The way oral defense presentations are graded amplifies stress because each student is responsible for one another's success or failure.

The second thesis (Individual Project: A High School Level Dissertation Defense) is developed individually. Again, students can choose any topic of interest. This time, however, they may use one-to-four academic lenses to write the 2,000-word paper. While preparing for the team presentation is much more difficult to manage since the work of many people has to be blended together; in this case, planning the presentation for the individual thesis defense is much easier. It is the presentation itself that is more stressful for many students who are forced for the first time in their lives to know a subject well enough to prepare and present an eight-minute speech. This presentation concludes with the student fielding oral defense questions.

Students submit both thesis papers to me through turnitin.com. The oral defenses are filmed, which also adds to the students' anxiety. I have found anxiety tends to boost the students' performance on these tasks.

Classroom Policies

What follows illustrates my approach to classroom management. I share my classroom management strategies in the event it may be useful, though of course, all educators make independent choices based on school culture and policies.

On the first day of the semester, the students and I discuss the classroom rules and procedures. Students understand the daily expectation is that they must arrive on time and ready to learn. Though most days are spent in critical dialogue, students are required to have their notebooks on their desks with any additional texts assigned for the day. Students are encouraged to write down notes based on what their peers contribute to the conversation. The most strictly enforced rule is that students must be respectful while I or a classmate is talking by not rolling eyes, interrupting, laughing, or goading. Everyone is expected to participate in all in-class activities. No one may complete work for another class while in Seminar in Critical Race Studies. In congruence with school policy, electronic devices may not be used in class without my permission. Often, however, students receive permission to use their phones instead of taking out their laptop to look something up that was introduced during discussion. I have found it better to keep laptops entirely off the desk during critical dialogues to avoid potential distractions.

There is little leeway given to students who choose not to complete an assignment. Attendance in class is also vital to one's grade. If a student knows in advance that he or she will miss a class, he or she must email me (for documentation purposes) to receive assignments and discuss due dates. In the case of an unplanned absence, students write to me during the school day to inquire on that day's lesson. As noted before, participation is expected during every class. So missing class will negatively impact grades. Students know that unless it is an emergency, no one may leave class during a critical dialogue. And I cap at four the number of students who may leave class temporarily for bathroom usage during any given period. Accordingly, students have made it a habit to use the restroom before class begins.

Students are not permitted to use profanity unless quoting from a text. Only are White students and I totally prohibited from using the N-word, even if written in a text.

AP Capstone has a strict plagiarism policy so I avoid writing my own. Students will receive a score of 0 on a particular component of an AP Capstone tasks (which doubles as a major performance measure in my grade book) if caught falsifying or fabricating information.

For the most part, the students adhere to the classroom policies. Granted, they are teenagers and many of them are as young as 15 years old. So, the mundaneness of daily routine leads a few students to test my forbearance to enforce the policies. Students realize pretty quickly that adherence to the rules makes for a more transformative experience that would not be shared in any other classroom at the high school.

Course Thesis

In 1903, social historian W.E.B. Du Bois predicted the problem of the 20th century would be the issue of the "color-line"; however, a Gallup Poll taken in the final year of the century reveals that the public felt World War II was the biggest issue of the century, followed by women's suffrage, the dropping of the atomic bomb, and the Nazi Holocaust. The passage of the 1964 Civil Rights Act came in fifth on Gallup News Service's 1999 survey of the most important events of the last century. Despite the conflicting views of the nature, structure, and importance of racial and ethnic identification, Seminar in Critical Race Studies evaluates Du Bois' assertion by examining the role that race has played in the formation of systems in the United States since the arrival of the first African in the New World in 1619. Since that moment, People of Color have been subjected as an underclass. It is because of that social isolation that America's African, Latinx, Native, Asian, Islamic, Jewish, and LGBTQ+ people have been preserved as wilderness dwellers. Molefi Asante (2003), the creator of Temple University's Ph.D. program in African American Studies in 1987, was the first to use the term "wilderness" as it relates to oppressed and indigenous people. The term in this context implies something that is unknown, alienated, and ostensibly dangerous; therefore, wilderness dwellers are rendered subhuman by the standards of Eurocentric centered norms. This begs the question: how can truth and reconciliation eliminate structural forms of racial oppression? After 350 years of slavery and over 90 years of legal and socially imposed second-class status, as well as confinement under the dictates of an institutional utilitarian means of cultural extermination, mental hijacking, and domestic colonialism, racially minoritized groups no matter how much education or money they possess have been kept in the American wilderness. To move society closer to eradicating systemic racial abuse, it is important for people to first realize that the lives of every American is structured by race; and second, to take the lead in litigating America's original sin—White supremacy in its many forms—at local, state, and federal truth and reconciliation commissions.

Course Texts

The first assignment given to Seminar in Critical Race Studies students is during the summer leading up to the start of the school year. Students must purchase one book from a provided list and read it during the summer. They must prepare an oral presentation that lasts 15 minutes, with an additional 10 minutes of discussion. Students will address the book's topic, the author's research question, central argument, supporting claims, important evidence, key terms, and comparable sources. Students put together a PowerPoint, Prezi, or Keynote presentation and create an accompanying handout that gets distributed to everyone in the class. I try to select books under 200 pages that will underpin the critical dialogues that will take place later in the semester. The books for this assignment expose students to a wide range of race and gender issues plaguing American society; also, my goal is to capture research interests, making it easier for students to select thesis topics later in the school year. Titles include those books written by, but not limited to, W.E.B. Du Bois, Richard Delgado, Linda Gordon, Tim Wise, Matt Wray, Americo Paredes, Gloria Anzaldua, Michelle Alexander, Michael Eric Dyson, Mitchell Duneier, Shelley Fisher Fishkin, Sherrilyn Ifill, Imani Perry, Patricia Turner, Choiu-Ling Yeh, Moustafa Bayoumi, Carol Spindel, Susan Ware, and Katrina Kimport. See Appendix 2 to view the summer reading assignment and the complete list of book options.

After deciding on the thematic units to include in the course, I begin to compile texts. I strive to design units that students come to see as a method for writing an extended essay, wherein we work as a class to use a specific research lens to analyze and synthesize a range of sources to produce an original study on the topic of focus. I search through digital libraries like JSTOR, EBSCO, and SSRN to find scholarly articles in the public domain. I also scour the internet to find podcasts, works of art, songs, and media articles for our use. I work with Gap High School's librarian to purchase the right to use an array of documentaries. In addition to the summer reading book, students must read a graphic novel (Voloj and Ahlering, *Ghetto Brother*) based on a historical event and a short book of fiction (Chin, *Donald Duk*) during the first semester. After compiling up to 10 texts per thematic unit, I begin structuring the performance measures for students to refine research, writing, and presentation skills. I am reluctant to use texts that contain profanity; however, I see the class as a space to deconstruct America's racist structures and, by association, violent past. Vulgarity, particularly the N-word, is part of that racist and violent history. If a text were bordering on overdoing gratuitous language, then I found a different source to use. For example, I ruled out of the "Toxic Masculinity in Film, Hip Hop, and Sports" unit the academic article, "Tupac Shakur: Understanding the Identity Formation of Hyper-Masculinity of Popular Hip-Hop Artist" because its author, Derek Iwamoto, included the F-word too many times throughout the piece and wrote of the artists' misogyny a bit much for high school students. Additionally, I was hoping to screen either *The Mask You Live In* or *Miss Representation* documentaries in the same unit because both contain powerful messages regarding cultural expectations placed upon adolescent and teenage boys and girls. Although both received ratings appropriate for 13 years old and 15 years old by Common Sense Media, respectively, I decided to exclude both from the curriculum for sexual innuendo. I thought each film possessed an excess of unnecessary foul language and vivid references to pornography to be shown without parental consent. Recommended texts for each unit are shown in figure 5.1.

Figure 5.1—Recommended Course Texts

Unit	Texts
Introduction to Critical Race Studies and Problem-Posing Pedagogy	Du Bois, *The Souls of Black Folks* (introduction) *All additional texts in this unit are comprised of students' summer reading assignment. See Appendix 2.
Whiteness Studies: A Deconstruction of White Supremacy, including Race Making, the Melting Pot Myth, White Privilege, Colorism, and Color-Blindness	1. *Race: The Power of an Illusion*, Part 2 (film) 2. Nina Jablonksi, "Skin Color Is an Illusion" (Ted Talk) 3. James Baldwin, "On Being White … and Other Lies" 4. David Reich, "How Genetics Is Changing Our Understanding of 'Race'" (media) 5. U.S. Census, "Standards on Race and Ethnicity" (government document) 6. Carl Campbell Brigham, *A Study of American Intelligence* (book introduction) 7. WatchtheYard, "Paper Bag Test: Letter from 1928 Addresses Black Fraternity and Sorority Colorism at Howard University" (media) 8. Allyson Hobbs, "The Chosen Exile of Racial Passing" (Ted Talk) 9. Pew Research Data, "The Changing Categories the U.S. Has Used to Measure Race" (empirical data) 10. Deborah Post, "Cultural Inversion and the One-Drop Rule" (peer reviewed article) 11. Allyson Hobbs, "I'm Not the Nanny: Multiracial Families and Colorism" (media) 12. Monnica T. Williams, "Is Being Colorblind Just Another Form of Racism?" (media) 13. Ta-Nehisi Coates, "The Good, Racist People" (media) 14. Ralph Ellison, "What American Would Be Like Without Blacks" (primary) 15. Robin DiAngelo, *Deconstructing White Privilege with Dr. Robin DiAngelo* (film) 16. Jennifer Harvey, *Raising White Kids* (Introduction) 17. Peggy McIntosh, "Unpacking the Invisible Knapsack" (essay) 18. Kyle Korver, "Privileged" (media) 19. Tim Wise, *White Like Me: Race, Racism, and White Privilege in America* (Film) 20. Dennis Prager, "The Fallacy of White Privilege" (media) 21. Tal Fortgang, "Why I'll Never Apologize for My White Male Privilege" (media) 22. Vincent Harinam and Rob Henderson, "Why White Privilege Is Wrong—Part 1." (media) 23. Diversity in the Classroom, UCLA Diversity & Faculty Development, "Tool: Recognizing Microaggressions and the Messages They Send."

Unit	Texts
Asian American Studies: A Social Analysis of Dueling Asian American Stereotypes	1. Maxwell Leung, "Jeremy Lin's Model Minority Problem." (peer reviewed article) 2. Bob H. Suzuki, "Asian Americans as the: 'Model Minority': Outdoing Whites? Or Media Hype?" (peer reviewed article) 3. William Pettersen, "Success Story, Japanese-American Style" (primary source) 4. Teaching While White, "The Myth of the Model Minority" (podcast) 5. "Summary of Georgia's New Registration Law, 1958" (primary source) 6. "Statement of United States Citizen of Japanese Ancestry" (primary source) 7. *American Pastime* (film) 8. *Other: Mixed Race in America*, "I'm Not a Jap, I'm Half Jap" (podcast) 9. *Donald Duk* (novel)
African American Studies: A Historical Survey of Interest Convergence Theory	1. Derrick A. Bell, *Space Traders* (film) 2. Malcolm Gladwell, "Miss Buchanan's Period of Adjustment," *Revisionist History Podcast*, July 27, 2017 3. Terry Gross and Rod Rothstein, "A 'Forgotten History' of How the U.S. Government Segregated America," *NPR Podcast*, May 3, 2017. 4. Andrew Buckser, "Lynching as a Ritual in the American South" (peer reviewed article) 5. Billie Holiday, "Strange Fruit" (song) 6. Nina Simone, "Strange Fruit" (song) 7. Racial Justice Group, "Lynching in America" (website) 8. James Weldon Johnson, "Lift Every Voice" (song) 9. Martin Luther King, Jr., "Letter from Birmingham Jail" (primary source) 10. *Loving* (film) 11. Peter Wallenstein, "The Right to Marry: Loving v. Virginia" (peer reviewed article) 12. Frantz Fanon, "An Introduction to Frantz Fanon's *Black Skin, White Mask* and *The Wretched of the Earth*" (film) 13. James Baldwin, *James Baldwin Debates William F. Buckley* (film) 14. James Baldwin, *James Baldwin and America's "racial problem"* (film) 15. Bureau of Justice Statistics, Arrest-related deaths (empirical data) 16. David French, "The Numbers Are In: Black Lives Matter Is Wrong About Police" (media)

Unit	Texts
African American Studies: A Historical Survey of Interest Convergence Theory (*cont.*)	17. Ta-Nehisi Coates, "Civil Rights Protest Have Never Been Popular" (media) 18. Mapping Police Violence (empirical data) 19. Heather MacDonald, *The War on Cops* (introduction) 20. Mazin Sidahmed, "Critics Denounce Black Lives Matter Platform Accusing Israel of Genocide" (media) 21. Nate Parker, *AmeriCAN* (film) 22. Gallup News, "Americans' Respect for Police Surges" (empirical data) 23. Gallup News, "Americans' Worries About Race Relations at Record High" (empirical data) 24. Tes One, "Stand Your Ground" (art) 25. Nikkolas Smith, "MLK in a Hoodie" (art) 26. Daye Jack ft. Killer Mike, "Hands Up" (song) 27. Caleb Paul, "Thin Blue Line" (song) 28. Garrett Bradford, "I Back the Blue" (song) 29. Joe Budden, "Freedom Freestyle" (song) 30. J. Cole, "Be Free" (song) 31. Robert Cohen, "Black Lives Matter: A Movement in Photos" (photo) 32. Tim Wise, "On Kaitlin Bennett grad picture with gun" (tweet) 33. Clint Smith, *How to Raise a Black Son in America* (film) 34. Newspapers.com–*Philadelphia Inquirer* (2015–present) and *Los Angeles Times* (2015–present)
Latinx Studies: A Cultural Examination of Racial Scripts from Gregorio Cortez to the roots of Hip Hop	1. Julian Voloj and Claudia Ahlering, *Ghetto Brother: Warrior to Peacemaker* (graphic novel) 2. *Flyin' Cut Sleeves* (film) 3. Natalia Molina, *How Race Is Made in America: Immigration, Citizenship, and the Historical Power of Racial Scripts* (introduction) 4. Barack Obama, DREAM Speech (policy speech) 5. Jan Brewer, "Speech after Signing House Bill 1070" (policy speech) 6. Donald J. Trump Presidential Campaign, "Immigration Reform That Will Make America Great" (policy agenda) 7. The Opportunity Agenda, "Immigrants and Immigration: A Guide for Entertainment Professionals" (empirical data) 8. The Opportunity Agenda, "Immigration Representation on Television" (empirical data) 9. The Opportunity Agenda, "Immigrant Character Representation" (empirical data)

Unit	Texts
Latinx Studies: A Cultural Examination of Racial Scripts from Gregorio Cortez to the roots of Hip Hop (*cont.*)	10. The Opportunity Agenda, "Power of Pop: Media Analysis of Immigrant Representation in Popular TV Shows" (empirical data) 11. Grandmaster Flash and the Furious Five, "The Message" (song) 12. Sugar Hill Gang, "Rappers Delight" (song) 13. Kurtis Blow, "The Breaks" (song) 14. Afrika Bambaataa, "Planet Rock" (song)
Jewish American Studies: Cuisine, Politics, and Other Cultural Aspects of the Americanization of Jews since World War I	1. Hasia Diner, "The Global History of Jewish Food." YouTube. University of Gastronomic Sciences, June 23, 2014 (lecture) 2. Samuel C. Heilman, *Portrait of American Jews: The Last Half of the 20th Century* (book chapter) 3. Rachel Gross. 2014. "Field Trip to the Kosher Kitchen: Religion and Politics in the University Ding Hall." *Transformations: The Journal of Inclusive Scholarship and Pedagogy* (peer reviewed article) 4. Judith Friedlander. 1986. "Jewish Cooking in the American melting-pot." *Revuen francaise d'etudes americaines.* (peer reviewed article) 5. Leonard Dinnerstein. 1979. "The US Army and the Jews: Policies Toward the Displaced Persons After World War II." *American Jewish History* (peer reviewed article) 6. Bob Dylan, "With God on Our Side" (song) 7. Henry Fore. Feb. 12, 1921. "The Jewish Aspect of the 'Movie' Problem." *The Dearborn Independent* (peer reviewed article) 8. Linda Schwab and Todd Mealy, *Displaced: Surviving the Holocaust and the Road to a New Beginning* (book chapter) 9. Edward Morrissey, "Nothing about 'blood and soil' is American." *The Week* (media) 10. Eitan Chitayat, "The Blogs, Eitan Chitayat" (website) 11. Jewish Forward Film Project. 1988. *The Forward: From Immigrants to Americans.* Los Angeles, CA: Direct Cinema Ltd. (film) 12. Elliot Oring. Oct. 1983. "The People of the Joke: On the Conceptualization of a Jewish Humor." *Western Folklore* (peer reviewed article).
Islamic American Studies: A Philosophical Assessment of Edward Said's "Orientalism" and Jack Shaheen's "Arabland" in Popular Culture	1. Edward Said, *Orientalism* (introduction) 2. Middle East Policy Council, "Barring Muslims Would Spell a U.S. Economic Disaster" (policy council) 3. Univ. of Freiburg Dept. of International Economic Policy, "The Determinants of Islamophobia—An Empirical Analysis of the Swiss Minaret Referendum"

Unit	Texts
Islamic American Studies: A Philosophical Assessment of Edward Said's "Orientalism" and Jack Shaheen's "Arabland" in Popular Culture (*cont.*)	4. Jehanzeb Dar, "Holy Islamophobia Batman!" (peer reviewed article) 5. Jack Shaheen, *Reel Bad Arabs* (film) 6. Jack Shaheen, Introduction to *Reel Bad Arabs* (book chapter) 7. Aladdin, "Arabian Nights" (song) 8. Moustafa Bayoumi, "NAFSA Worldview with Moustafa Bayoumi" (interview) 9. Khaled A. Beydoun, "The Rise of American Islamophobia" (lecture) 10. Renee Montagne, NPR, "Filmmakers Shatter Arab Stereotypes in Hollywood" (podcast) 11. Naif Al-Mutawa, "The 99 Comics: Islamic Superheroes alongside Marvel" (Ted Talk)
Native American Studies: The Politics of the Vanishing American and a Content Analysis of the American Indian Movement in the Media	1. Brian W. Dippie, *The Vanishing American: White Attitudes and U.S. Indian Policy* (introduction) 2. DocsTeach, American Indians: Primary Sources and Ready-to-Use Teaching Activities (website) 3. *In Whose Honor?* (film) 4. Cornel D. Pewewardy, "Playing Indian at Halftime" (peer reviewed article) 5. Aaron Huey, "America's Native Prisoners of War" (Ted Talk) 6. Paul Lukas, "Tribe Supports Native American Mascots" (media) 7. Britni De La Cretaz, "MLB Commissioner, Cleveland, Discuss 'Offensive' Logo" (media)
Gender Studies: Toxic Masculinity in Film, Hip Hop, and Sports	1. Kara Keeling, "A Homegrown Revolutionary?: Tupac Shakur and the Legacy of the Black Panther Party" (peer reviewed article) 2. Tupac Shakur, "Panther Power" (song) 3. Audre Lord, "The Uses of Anger" 4. Ann M. Savage, *Women's Rights* (introduction) 5. Rashida Jones, "Why Is Everyone Getting Naked" (media) 6. *Cheers.* Season 1, Episode 16, "The Boys at the Bar" (film) 7. John Lennon. "Woman Is the Nigger of the World" (song) 8. Warren Farrell, "The Myth of Male Power" (Introduction) 9. Walt Hickey, "The Dollar-and-Cents Case Against Hollywood's Exclusion of Women" (media) 10. Mark Brown, "British Cinema's Gender Imbalance Worse in 2017 than 1913, says BFI Study" (media) 11. Zorana Micic, "Female Interactions on Film" (dissertation)

Unit	Texts
Gender Studies: Toxic Masculinity in Film, Hip Hop, and Sports (*cont.*)	12. Neda Ulaby, "The Bechdel Rule, Defining Pop-Culture Character" (podcast) 13. Dorothy L. Hurley, "Seeing White: Children of Color and the Disney Fairy Tale Princess" (peer reviewed article)
Bonus Unit: Screening and Discussion on the original *Planet of the Apes* series	1. Eric Greene, *Planet of the Apes as American Myth: Race and Politics in the Films and Television Series* (introduction) 2. Planet of the Apes Series, Movies 1–5 (film) 3. Randall L. Kennedy, "Who Can Say N-word? And Other Considerations" (peer reviewed article) 4. Ericka J. Fisher, "The N-Word: Reducing Verbal Pollution in Schools" (peer reviewed article) 5. Justin Chang, NPR, "'War for the Planet of the Apes' Offers a Masterful Vision of Humanity's Many Forms" (podcast) 6. Martin Luther King, Jr., "Beyond Vietnam" Speech, April 4, 1967 7. Clayborne Carson, "Watts" Chapter 27 in *The Autobiography of Martin Luther King, Jr.* 8. Mario Savio, "Sit In Address at the Steps of Sproul House" 9. Ralph Ellison, "What America Would Be Like Without Blacks" 10. Vox, "Lighter Skinned Black and Hispanic People Look Smarter"

The Pedagogy–Critical Dialogues

For more than two decades, a growing body of scholarship has focused on progressive education. This literature has offered educators pedagogical ideas ranging from how to connect with students through technology to paperless classrooms to strategies for higher-level thinking. One of the more popular pedagogues is John Collins (2007), creator of a "Writing Across the Curriculum Model" that offers five types of writing assignments (1. Capture Ideas, 2. Respond Correctly, 3. Edit for Focus Correction Area, 4. Peer Edit for Focus Correction Areas, and 5. Publishable Quality Writing) that help students develop "essential writing and thinking skills." K-12 educators use his book *The Collins Writing Program: Improving Student Performance Through Writing and Thinking Across the Curriculum* widely across the United States. Perhaps the biggest influence of Collins' work is the tool practiced by teachers to help students identify "target areas of improvement" called Focus Correction Areas (FCA). The FCAs are supposed to mitigate anxiety within students who feel overwhelmed by having to think about too many writing standards. Instead, students can concentrate on improving only a handful of skills at any one time. "Over the course of the school year," Collins asserts, "students master numerous FCAs, resulting in significant improvement in their [overall] writing abilities." His writing program has now become official procedure in thousands of school districts throughout the United States, including the Gap School District. Collins Writing is a good district policy as it relates to improving writing skills in our students. However, teachers using only Collins will fail to train students as critical thinkers.

With the pressure to get students proficient in writing so they can pass standardized tests, what obstacles do teachers face when attempting to create a culture of higher-level thinking? A student's aversion to school is not the same as his or her aversion to learning. So while students want to learn, they often struggle to succeed because of an existing disconnect with the systems or guidelines a school has in place. Cofounder of the Center for Health Equity and Urban Science Education at Teachers College, Columbia University, Christopher Emdin (2016) offers teachers "Reality Pedagogy," a method that improves student interest in school by connecting them with their home-lives and lived environment by "focus[ing] on the cultural understandings of students within a particular social space." Emdin asks his students to bring to class "artifacts" representing who they are and where they come from, providing that the objects relate to the lesson. He believes, "When students can physically see and examine artifacts both in the classroom and in their home communities, the divides between the school world and their real lives are broken down." Emdin's pedagogical framework, which centers most on White teachers who educate Students of Color at urban schools, also calls on teachers to become familiar with the community in which they work. He argues that teachers should know the "social spaces"—community centers, basketball courts, churches, housing projects, businesses, and hangouts—their students often patronized. The result will be a marrying of classroom content with the context of students' life experiences. Students will then be more interested and better engaged in daily lesson plans.

Like Emdin's Reality Pedagogy, Django Paris, author of several books about training teachers on cultural relevancy, including *Culturally Sustaining Pedagogies: Teaching and Learning for Justice in a Changing World*, claims that progressive education's best foot forward is for schools to assess its curricula, identifying implicit and explicit microaggressions in the curriculum and teaching methods. Paris (2014, 2017) refers to the current system as "Curricularization of Racism," suggesting that curriculum and pedagogy advantage White learners, while neglecting multicultural relevance in both aspects of teaching and learning. Paris's work aspires to extinguish White priority from curricula that "blanket the country." He says the long tradition of curricularizing racism makes Whiteness "a central part of the explicit and implicit curriculum," thus maintaining White supremacy as the default. As Stokely

Carmichael and other freedom school leaders realized in the 1960s, colonized curricula is damaging to both White and Black students, as racism is implicitly perpetuated by way of books and pedagogy. Paris also disparages state education departments for not forcing schools to emphasize diversity studies. Learning in the 21st century, Paris says, should reflect the type of critical thinking that colonization tried so hard to destroy.

Linking various aspects of instruction to progressive education scholars like Collins, Emdin, and Paris can shape new educational processes. A blend of these scholars' pedagogical approaches demonstrates how writing combined with critical race studies can increase student engagement and result in a racial awakening. At the root of the scholarship undertaken by Emdin and Paris, in particular, is Paulo Freire's democratized problem-solving pedagogy, which aims to empower imagination and connect truth to power as students strive to understand freedom and justice in the world by way of text-based open-ended discussions (Darder, 2017). After considering this body of scholarship, this is where Seminar in Critical Race Studies fuses writing repetition with contextual experiences, race consciousness, and solution-oriented seminar style discussions to create the course's signature feature: our critical dialogues.

Making the classroom a democratic space where everyone feels responsible for one another's learning is central to Seminar in Critical Race Studies' success. Everything done in the course is designed to make students feel comfortable while *being* uncomfortable—which is what discussions about race are supposed to accomplish. To achieve a degree of utopia in the classroom at the beginning of class, the students and I move the desks around to form a circle. Flanked by the students, I sit in the front of the room where my podium would otherwise rest if I were teaching in a traditional setting. From my seat, I facilitate the critical dialogue.

Similar to Socratic Seminars, our critical dialogues prize inquiry over information and discussion over debate. Dialogues are based on a text (or a collection of texts) from which I ask opened-ended, thematically based questions. Within the context of the discussion, students listen closely to the comments of their peers, thinking critically for themselves. My responsibility is to help students articulate their thoughts and to give affirmation to each point that is made. I am also obligated to help students process what their peers are saying. Any time a discussion begins to letup, I pose a new question that is centered on the text or an insight previously proffered by one of the students. During the process, students learn to work cooperatively as each dialogue vets the nuances of a problem and steers everyone toward finding a solution to the issues presented in the text.

Critical dialogues also help students learn how to question one another intelligently and civilly (Israel, 2002). If troubled by what a peer said during a dialogue, or if wishing to offer an alternative perspective about a topic, students must direct all comments to me. This classroom approach prevents ugly spats that often play out among analysts and professionals appearing on corporate media's daily news broadcasts or in the comments section of social media posts. Since the democratic nature of the critical dialogue is for everyone in the room to have an equally empowered voice, students have every right to challenge the insight that I offer at any point. This method places extra pressure on the teacher to know the material covered in any given text. In other words, the instructor must be a master on the topic with the competency to surgically guide students between themes with the capability to process student comments, cite the information of the selected text, and carry on the critical dialogue through unrehearsed and improvised enquiries; otherwise the dialogue will come to an abrupt conclusion.

While greatly different from what most high school students have experienced prior to enrolling in Seminar in Critical Race Studies, the purpose of this configuration is to force everyone to look at one another, to recognize each other's existence, and to create a sense of community. Enrollment in this course has ranged from 14 students to 30 students. The circular arrangement has worked in both cases. The ideal number of students in one class is 18. Though my class of 30 students was tough to manage, we made it through. Of course, I am skeptical about class sizes being greater than 30 students, as it would likely create a problem with both the classroom's configuration and student participation in critical dialogues.

Notebook/Binder Check

All students are required to have a three-ringed binder and a notebook. In the binder, students hold all assignments, readings, and graded assignments. Notebooks are used only to keep notes. I collect both at the end of each semester for a grade of 100 points. Notebooks are assessed for content and neatness. Binders are graded for having all paperwork organized neatly into unit dividers. My hope is that students find keeping a notebook and binder is an important organizational skill that can be applied in other classes. I want them to see that the notebooks and binders will also be helpful for storing notes and printed sources retrieved during the research process.

Group Norms

Students form teams, or groups, within the first two weeks of the semester. At the moment groups are formed, students will compose a list of "group norms," or set of rules, that determine acceptable and unacceptable behavior. Groups are instructed to write down four-to-six rules that group members must abide by. They discuss and agree on a set of norms that include potential consequences if rules (and effectively trust) are broken, ranging from calling home to a parent to me intervening as an arbitrator. The accords are turned into a contract that every group member will sign. Additionally, to build team dynamics, students assign one another roles within the group. Roles include that of facilitator, recorder, timekeeper, presenter, and fact-checker. Every so often, groups rearrange roles so that each group member experiences each role.

Class Participation and Other Grades

In addition to the two required thesis defenses described earlier in this chapter, students' grades are based on a range of performance measures. Participation is a vital component for success in the course and is factored into the overall grade. I grade class participation on a weekly basis on a score out of 15. I keep a seating chart with me during every critical dialogue so that I can mark each occasion a student comments. I work a "rapid-fire" round into the dialogue once a week. The rapid-fire questions typically ask students to comment on the quality of an author's argument or to discuss an important passage found within the text. Students can neither avoid commenting during the rapid-fire activity nor can they make a comment directed at a classmate's insight until the rapid-fire session has concluded. I have differentiated the levels of participation for students into (1) Highly Effective Participant (15/15), (2) Regular Participant (14/15), (3) Occasional Participant (13/15), (4) Only an Observer (12/15), and (5) Disengaged Student (11/15). A student might receive lower than 11/15 for the weekly participation grade if he or she is caught doing work for another subject, found playing with an electronic device, or attempts to sleep during class.

Because I agree that bias exists against introverted students, and that it is never necessary to punish a student for shyness, I do strategize with quiet students to find ways (such as being the first student to comment on a reading, to pick out a passage that might resemble a contemporary or personal issue, or to script a response during the "rapid fire" portion of the discussion) to help them speak up in class. I grade students on participation because public speaking is a necessary part of the final grade, as students must perform two oral defenses of their research in front of an audience. My hope is that through class discussion, the students will become comfortable enough to speak in front of their classmates by the time their presentations begin during the spring semester.

I also grade students on curricular skill-based work. The skills are shown in Figure 5.2.

Figure 5.2—Basic Course Skills

Performance	AP Capstone QUEST Category	Skills Measured
Research Skills	Exploring	1. Developing research questions 2. Source constellation of the topic 3. Selecting research lenses (disciplines) 4. Choosing research method(s) 5. Writing a works cited/bibliography
	Analyzing Texts	1. Text rendering 2. Annotate sources 3. Identifying solutions
	Compiling Textual Constellation	1. Evaluate multiple voices and evidence 2. Counterarguments 3. Credibility of printed sources 4. Credibility of online sources
	Ongoing Debate	1. Merge the ideas of varying sources with one's own
	Teamwork	1. Team: Group norms and consequences are agreed upon, plus a system of communication (ZOOM) is established, and calendars are shared.
Writing Skills	Exploring	1. Outlining
	Analyzing Texts	1. Ellipses/omissions 2. Line of reasoning (thesis, claims, and evidence)
	Compiling Textual Constellation	1. Articulating in writing how dueling voices are evaluated 2. Drawing relevant connections between sources 3. Writing Introductions 4. Acknowledging counterarguments 5. Identifying authors' credibility in essay form
	Ongoing Debate	1. Synthesizing scholarly ideas/insight 2. Writing paragraphs in which the theses of two or more voices are connected or divorced from one another 3. Signal phrases (establishing credibility) 4. Avoiding drop-in quotes 5. Developing warrants and claims 6. Writing conclusions (solutions and implications)
	Teamwork	1. Students can work in teams to collect and compose a scholarly essay based on information about a single topic that is shared through varying research lenses. A group leader facilitates discussions. A peer-editing review of one-another's work is conducted

Performance	AP Capstone QUEST Category	Skills Measured
Presentation Skills	Exploring	1. Develop a presentation that explains the relevance of a research question in a larger context
	Analyzing Texts	1. Develop a presentation that offers detailed and plausible resolutions, while considering limitations and implications of any suggested solution
	Compiling Textual Constellation	1. Through oral presentation, draw relevant connections between sources 2. Signal phrases (establishing credibility) 3. Acknowledging counterarguments 4. Identifying authors' credibility in verbal form
	Ongoing Debate	1. Verbal articulation of synthesized insight and evidence from various points of view to support an argument 2. Draw relevant connections between sources
	Teamwork	1. Students are able to put together a team presentation that engages the audience with soft skills (eye contact, vocal variety, subtle movement, energy, and volume) and avoid non-lexical fillers. Students are able to engage the audience with multimedia that is designed for the audience's benefit. Students prove that they can clearly articulate their argument's line of reasoning and explain why sources are credible

Students must also keep a running database of annotated sources. Since the entire class is a model for how students create a thesis paper, each text is used to reinforce the course's thesis (stated earlier in this chapter). Opportunities to practice annotating sources are vital for the students' research on the two thesis defense projects.

To build confidence and comfort, students are graded on their performance in several informal and formal presentations ranging from two minutes to 20 minutes.

Conclusion

Seminar in Critical Race Studies has two objectives: one, to provide students with a balanced and thorough examination of race in America in order to make them race conscious; and, two, to teach students how to produce publishable work. Given that Gap High School operates on a block schedule, there is enough time to cover both the content and the skills only if the teacher is methodical in his or her preparation and is structurally consistent. Everything that is done in the class is oriented toward the thesis defense projects. Of vital importance are the critical dialogues, which offer students a method to hone critical thinking skills, to get comfortable speaking up in public, and to experience a blending of divergent opinions into one cohesive argument.

This course, with its race conscious lens, however, with all of its advantages, comes with gratuitous skepticism and nasty criticism. This I will detail in the two chapters that follow.

6

Those That Fight Back

Introduction

This chapter examines the struggle for a multicultural curriculum in the Tucson Unified School District, which generated considerable controversy and signified a national debate between 2006 and 2017. In 1998, Tucson Unified School District created the La Raza (Mexican American) studies program. Eight years later, the program went under attack by the Arizona Superintendent of Public Schools and members of the state legislature. Eventually, the state passed House Bill 2281, which included language banning La Raza studies. Parents and teachers sued the state for enacting a law they viewed as unconstitutional. In the summer of 2017, they won their case in Federal District Court. While the struggles in Tucson are not the same that I have experienced at Gap, this episode serves as the backdrop for my experiences dealing with problematic parents, colleagues, and students after the launch of my critical race studies class in rural Pennsylvania.

A Challenge to the Existing State of Affairs

In 1998, the Tucson Unified School District (TUSD) in Arizona implemented an ethnic studies program that included interdisciplinary departments on African American culture, Asian American culture, and the comparative and trans-border program called "La Raza Studies" (later known as Mexican American Studies). The school district's ethnic studies program helped students work toward careers in social work, counseling, international relations, creative writing, and politics. It came crashing down—momentarily—in 2011 when the Arizona State Legislature enacted House Bill (HB) 2281, giving the Arizona State Superintendent of Public Instruction the authority to withhold funding from the Tucson Unified School District (TUSD) if it refused to stop teaching La Raza Studies, the only department in the Ethnic

Studies' program that attracted adversaries for its curriculum. Supporters of HB 2281 saw La Raza Studies as a non-traditional education program that combined radical teaching styles with a politically divisive curriculum.

The attack on TUSD's La Raza Studies curricular program began on April 3, 2006, when long-time labor activist Dolores Huerta, with a reputation dating back to the 1960s of organizing Latinx communities in pursuit of social justice, told an audience at Tucson High Magnet School, "Republicans hate Latinos." The remark put school officials in the spotlight as Fox News's Bill O'Reilly insisted on his show *The O'Reilly Factor* that TUSD Superintendent Roger Pfeuffer subscribe to Huerta's statement (Scarpinato, 2006; Fischer, 2006). Later that month, the House Select Committee on Government Operations, Performance, and Waste conducted a partisan investigation into Huerta's TUSD speech and found that her comments about Republicans represented "hate speech." A month later, Margaret Garcia Dugan (2006), Deputy Superintendent of Public Instruction in Arizona, spoke to an assembly of students at the same school as a countermeasure to Huerta's politically charged comment. Days before Dugan's address, the students requested a question and answer session with the deputy superintendent. Dugan, a 30-year veteran in public education and supporter of the 2000 ballot initiative Proposition 203, which required schools to teach in English only and created a segregated experience for Arizona's English Learners for long durations of the school day, declined the request (Scarpinato, 2006). Angry over the refusal to take questions, it took just seven minutes into her speech before about 50 students stood in silence with their mouths duct taped, their backs turned, and their fists in the air to protest what they believed to be an attempt to frighten students away from taking an interest in social justice causes. The student demonstration was aimed at "individuals who think that we don't know what we're talking about," said one of the student protesters (Commings, 2006). Soon after, Dugan's boss, Tom Horne, Arizona's Superintendent of Public Instruction, who was in attendance, believing La Raza Studies' teachers had instigated this "rude" behavior of a "small minority," launched an unrelenting counterattack on TUSD's La Raza Studies program. Horne's campaign to discredit the La Raza Studies program would endure through 2017.

The Ethnic Studies Department materialized as an antidote to fix an otherwise culturally irrelevant curriculum that abetted other institutional problems in the Tucson Unified School District that had seen high dropout rates, mounting disciplinary infractions, and poor state-administered standardized test scores among Mexican American students (Sparks, 2002; Acosta, 2011). The La Raza curriculum was the department's most popular program as Mexican American students made up 60 percent of the school district's 53,000-student population. At its peak in 2011, about 1,300 students in eight high schools and middle schools were enrolled in La Raza Studies.

Although enrollment in the course load was on a voluntary basis and was open to every student in the district, approximately 90 percent of the enrollees in the program were Latinx teens (*Gonzales v. Douglass*, 2017). Proponents of the program hoped culturally relevant curricula would capture the interests of its at-risk Mexican American students, making learning more interesting, and in turn lead to lower dropout rates, lower discipline rates, increased attendance rates, and higher test scores. According to curriculum objectives, the concept of the program was to help Mexican American students see "themselves or their family or their community" in their studies as well as expose the district's White, African American, Asian American, and First Nation pupils to the history and culture of Latinx people. Court documents later show, as it pertains to the legality of the program, La Raza Studies aimed to "close the historic gap in academic achievement between Mexican-American and white students in Tucson." A University of Arizona professor Nolan Cabrera (2011; 2014), who published a study on the effectiveness of the La Raza Studies program in the *American Educational Research Association Journal,* testified "there is an empirically demonstrated, significant, and positive relationship between taking [La Raza] classes and increased academic achievement-measured by increased high school graduation rates and increased AIMS test passing rates for all students who took the courses, but in particular for Mexican American students in TUSD."

The school board and TUSD faculty were correct. The graduation rate of Tucson's Mexican American students enrolled in La Raza Studies averaged 93 percent between 2005 (the year before the movement to ban the program began) and 2011 (the year House Bill 2281 passed the legislature to terminate the program). Another apropos to the program, Mexican American La Raza students scored higher on Arizona's standardized tests than Mexican American students in Tucson who did not participate in the program. Sean Arce, former director of the La Raza Studies Department, told board members in 2010 that 97.5 percent of Mexican American students participating in La Raza Studies between 2005 and 2010 graduated from TUSD. This is a remarkable number when measured up against the 44 percent of Mexican American students that graduated nationally during the same duration of time (Arce, 2010; Lundholm, 2011). Arce credited the increase in academic proficiency to the curriculum. The La Raza Studies Department's objective was "to bring content about Chicanos/Latinos and their cultural groups from the margin to the center of the curriculum." The department offered courses in history, literature, government, and art to students in kindergarten through 12th grade. Teachers were certain to create classes that met Arizona's state standards, which necessitated curriculum covering the history, literature, and culture of Mexican Americans and other Latinx ethnic groups. The classes in La Raza Studies were "American History: Mexican American Perspectives"; "English:

Latino Literature"; "American Government: Social Justice Education Project"; "Chicano Art"; and one course for middle schoolers titled "Chicano Studies." Each high school class was research-based, designed as college preparatory courses, and accordingly used books and articles "regarded as canonical in the fields of Ethnic studies and Mexican American Studies" (*Gonzalez v. Douglass*, 2017).

But in 2006, after Huerta's "Republicans hate Latinos" comment, the program's enemies took aim at the La Raza Studies curriculum and its teachers despite empirical data buttressing the program's success. Among the grievances that topped the list was not that the program was a financial burden imposed on Tucson taxpayers or that the program was a failure; rather, opponents reviled the use of Paulo Friere's *Pedagogy of the Oppressed*, which references the works of Karl Marx, Vladimir Lenin, Mao Zedong, and Che Guevara. Even more disturbing to the department's opponents was how instruction in La Raza Studies employed Freirean pedagogy, prioritizing democratized dialogues over traditional banking models detested by Freire. According to legal historian Nicholas B. Lundholm (2011), during a classroom exercise called "My History," students answered "seemingly simple questions" about their personal lives, family history, and their views about the community. Students were encouraged to talk about how they saw the world and what might come of their future. Questions included "Why do you believe this?"; "Where did that belief come from?"; "Who does that belief benefit?"; "Who are we?"; "Why do we do these things?"; "What is our identity?"; and "How was our identity constructed?" This form of questioning meant to guide students into recognizing that personal stories are a legitimate part in the making of America; thus, teachers helped students acquire a greater appreciation for their own cultural identity and value in the construction of the United States.

The pedagogy utilized in La Raza Studies resembled the origin story of Friere's problem-posing dialogues in rural Brazil (discussed in Chapter 4). Like the peasants of Brazil, students in TUSD were encouraged to think critically about their living conditions and the social structures around them. They were taught not to fatalistically blame themselves for their social circumstances or to accept society as it currently existed. In the spirit of Freire, La Raza students took a greater interest in their own education, which carried over into a critical examination of lived experiences. The students in Tucson were trained similar to how the Mississippi students were during the summer of 1964: they learned to become active participants in the American democratic project. Students in Tucson were taught like those in the intercommunal schools of 1973: they learned *how* to think, not *what* to think. This resultant rejection of the traditional banking model unquestionably challenged the normative educational culture in Arizona, which the students had deemed oppressive. While this challenge to the existing state of affairs hardly bothered educators or parents in the Tucson Unified School District, for many elected officials and the Arizona State Superintendent of Education, La Raza's unfamiliar approach to education was too much to stomach.

The men who spearheaded the takedown of La Raza Studies were then Arizona State Superintendent of Education, Tom Horne, who would later announce his candidacy for the seat of Arizona's Auditor General, and Arizona state legislator Steve Montenegro, who chaired the Arizona House Education Committee. The biggest talking point perpetuated by Horne and Montenegro was that La Raza Studies was fundamentally "anti–American" and "seditionist." The men argued that the program turned students into "angry radicals" (Lundhom, 2011). The problem that Horne and Montenegro faced at the start of their campaign was that under Arizona law, the only authority that possessed the power to develop or end curriculum was local school boards. Horne's state superintendent office was powerless to dictate policy in the Tucson Unified School District. Both men, but Horne in particular, would spend the next four years blitzing the media circuit in an attempt to rally the public around issues of anti-immigration and anti–La Raza to compel the TUSD school board to capitulate or to force Arizona legislators to pass legislation giving Horne's office the power to abolish the La Raza Studies program. While often omitting on air the important detail that La Raza Studies was both successful and open for all students regardless of race, ethnicity, or gender, Horne debated the likes of Michael Eric Dyson and Marc Lamont Hill on PBS, CNN, MSNBC, and several statewide news networks claiming Tucson's Ethnic Studies program, "divides students up by race." His talking points centered on accusing teachers of teaching "a separatist agenda, anti–Western Culture … using ethnic solidarity as their vehicle" (Hengler, 2010). Horne also penned multiple open letters to the citizens of Arizona in Tucson's *Arizona Daily Star* and Phoenix's *Arizona Republic* depicting La Raza teachers as "anti–American communists" that utilize classrooms as training centers for soldiers in an impending race war. While most of his editorials appeared in Arizona newspapers when Horne was still the superintendent of Arizona schools, one column written as the state's attorney general in 2012 accused La Raza teachers of conditioning their student into "becoming angry, distrustful of teachers, negative toward Western civilization and the U.S., and disrespectful of authority of non–Latinos." (Horne, 2007; Horne, 2008; Horne, 2012; Ethnic Studies Law, 2010). Even a former La Raza teacher, John Ward, who taught in the program until 2002, supported Horne's efforts saying the program was designed to "create the next generation of ethnic radicals" (*PBS News Hour*, 2010). Despite the betrayal of one of the program's teachers, the faculty and students in the La Raza Studies Department never relented. Not a single class halted during Horne's campaign. And it appeared the public was behind the school district, as constituents did not vote anyone off the school board for supporting the department.

Things statewide changed quickly, however, when Republican Jan Brewer replaced Democrat Janet Napolitano as Arizona governor on January 21, 2009, after Napolitano accepted the job as Secretary of Homeland Security under President Barack Obama. The new governor charged first with a sweeping undocumented immigrant immigration policy known as Senate Bill 1070. In the eyes of its opponents, SB 1070 encouraged racial profiling as federal immigration laws were barred from intervening after an Arizona immigration official conducted a "lawful stop, detention, or arrest" of a suspected undocumented immigrant. It was during the debate over SB 1070 that Representative Montenegro introduced Horne's anti–La Raza Studies House Bill 2281 to the House Education Committee. Horne was very involved in writing the bill and in lobbying for its ratification. In speeches before Montenegro's House Education Committee and before the Senate Education Accountability and Reform Committee chaired by then-senator John Huppenthal, Horne blamed La Raza Studies teachers for promoting "ethnic chauvinism" and denounced the use of works by Paulo Freire, whom he described as a "well-known Brazilian communist." Horne likened TUSD's entire ethnic studies curriculum to segregation: "Raza studies for the Raza kids, Native American studies for the Native American kids, [and] oriental studies for the oriental kids," was "just like the Old South" (Arizona State Senate Immigration Research Committee, 2010).

La Raza students and faculty obtained an opportunity to testify before both Houses of the Arizona legislature and make a case to the public in the columns of various Arizona newspapers that the program did not promote the overthrow of America or the separation of the races. Senior Director for Ethnic Studies at TUSD Augustine F. Romero (2008) claimed all programs in the Ethnic Studies Department were "anti-racist projects [and] are an instrument of equity through which the students are able to have a more inclusive and meaningful educational experience." Romero argued their program helped students "develop a critical socio-cultural identity that helps them develop a new and/or a deeper sense of purpose [to] make a better place for all people." The program, he argued, was life changing. Romero explained, "The overwhelmingly vast majority of our students have said that our pedagogy, our curriculum and the way we authentically and respectfully interact with [students] and their parents not only help develop identity, purpose and hope, [the courses] also help them develop an academic identity wherein they develop a belief that they can be academically successful." Romero closed, "All in all, this means that we help nurture students who do better in school, who believe that our world can be a better place and who are committed to work that must be done to create that better place."

After listening to the TUSD representatives, Senator Huppenthal agreed to audit La Raza's Latino literature class. Even then, it was not enough to put an end to Horne's campaign. Huppenthal would later claim that after a review of the curriculum, the "materials repeatedly emphasized the importance of building Hispanic nationalism and unity in the face of assimilation and oppression" (*Gonzalez v. Douglass*, 2017; Lundholm, 2011). It would take just three more months, but with a final push from Huppenthal, who had by then declared his candidacy for Horne's superintendent seat and who contended that the program "planted evil ideas in kids' minds," the beginning of the end of La Raza Studies at TUSD could not be stopped.

It was true that the La Raza teachers had students questioning for the first time the legal and educational systems that controlled their lives. In one exercise called "Four Tables," students received a word or phrase related to an oppressive hierarchy. Words like "hegemony," "subordinate group," "dominant group," "colonization," "inequality of language theory," "racism," "oppression," "fatalism," "privilege," and "resistance" were given to students who were told to define, list associated words, and draw a picture representing it. In an article published by the *Arizona Law Review* titled "Cutting Class: Why Arizona's Ethnic Studies Ban Won't Ban Ethnic Studies," legal historian Nicholas B. Lundholm defended the exercise, claiming that word associations and pictures "helps students place the word or phrase into the context of their own life experiences" (Lundholm, 2011). Though teachers designed many classroom activities in a way to get the students to think critically about the world, stories about such lesson plans continued to threaten a small number of people in positions of authority. One member of the Arizona General Assembly, John Kavanagh, was heard uttering, "If you want a different culture then fine, go back to that culture. But this is America" (*Gonzalez vs. Douglass*, 2017).

On May 11, 2010, Governor Brewer signed the Horne, Montenegro, and Huppenthal House Bill 2281 into law, stating that Tucson schools

shall not include in its program of instruction any courses or classes that include any of the following:

(1) Promote the overthrow of the United States
(2) Promote resentment toward a race or class of people
(3) Are designed primarily for pupils of a particular ethnic group
(4) Advocate ethnic solidarity instead of the treatment of pupils as individuals.

Horne issued a statement from his superintendent's office declaring January 1, 2011, the date the statute would become effective. Failure to comply with the law by eliminating the La Raza Studies curriculum would result in a forfeiture of 10 percent of Tucson Unified School District's budget. Horne also issued a threat to the Asian American, African American, and Native American programs, alleging that they, too, "could be found in violation under criterion three" of HB 2281, prohibiting "courses designed primarily for pupils of a particular ethnic group" (*Gonzalez v. Douglass,* 2017). Horne left office for his first and only term as Arizona's Attorney General before acting on eliminating those programs. When Huppenthal replaced Horne as Arizona's Superintendent of Public Instruction on January 3, 2011, a second and more thorough audit of the La Raza Studies curriculum commenced. Though Huppenthal's decision allowed the program to run through the 2010–11 school year, it meant that auditors would have time to conduct classroom visits, review of La Raza course texts and lesson plans. In addition, auditors ran focus group interviews and conducted a survey. At the conclusion of the 2011 spring semester, Huppenthal ordered TUSD to terminate the La Raza Studies program. The penalty for any further delay was the withholding of $15 million in state funding for education. La Raza Studies appeared to be over.

Was La Raza Studies a Trojan horse for an ethnic overthrow of the United States government? History has indicated no. In his timely piece for the *Arizona Law Review,* Lundholm explains that nothing in the La Raza Studies curriculum "authoritatively tells students that they are currently oppressed" and that they should overthrow any local, state, or federal government. There was no indication that La Raza courses were designed primarily for Mexican American students—even a look at the races of students who took the classes would not be an indication of racial exclusion. Moreover, La Raza courses did not teach "ethnic solidarity," as suggested in the language of House Bill 2281 (Lundholm, 2011). In short, since the *Pedagogy of the Oppressed* and other supplemental texts told students their ethnic group has been *historically* oppressed rather than suggesting to students they *are currently* oppressed, those who wanted to save La Raza Studies had a case to make against the state.

A group of teachers along with two students promptly sued the state of Arizona for enacting a law they viewed as "not for a legitimate educational purpose, but for an invidious discriminatory racial purpose, and a politically partisan purpose" (United States District Court of Arizona, 2017). The plaintiffs questioned whether the law violated the 1st and 14th Amendments by preventing their right to intellectual free speech and equal protection under the law. Over the course of six years the case would make its way up to the U.S. District Court for the District of Arizona, the federal court in the Ninth Circuit Court of Appeals where Judge A. Wallace Tashima would issue in August 2017 a final judgment on La Raza Studies' legality. Stating in *Gonzalez v. Douglas, Arizona Superintendent of Public Instruction* (2017; Gassen, 2017) that Horne and Huppenthal "were motivated by a desire to advance a political agenda by capitalizing on race-based fears," Judge Tashima ruled House Bill 2281's ban on La Raza Studies in Arizona public schools was unconstitutional because it was racially motivated (violation of the 14th Amendment) and a political prop (violation of the 1st Amendment) for those seeking elected office.

During *Gonzalez v. Douglass* (2017), the plaintiffs offered evidence that showed Horne, Huppenthal, and other government officials acted with "racial animus" in their attacks against the La Raza program. During and after the effort to ban La Raza Studies succeeded, Huppenthal made several blog posts conveying racial hostility toward Mexican Americans generally. On December 14, 2010, posting under a pseudonym, Huppenthal commented, "No Spanish radio stations, no Spanish billboards, no Spanish TV stations, no Spanish newspapers. This is America, speak English" (*Gonzalez v. Douglass*, 2017). Within 24 hours he posted, "The rejection of American values and embracement of the values of Mexico in La Raza classrooms is the rejection of success and embracement of failure." The following day he posted a third comment: "I don't mind them selling Mexican food as long as the menus are mostly in English." Then in January 2011, after the enforcement of HB 2281, Huppenthal (*Gonzalez v. Douglass*, 2017) gloated: "La Raza … [is] shorthand for classroom studies that depict America's founding fathers as racists, poisoning students' attitudes towards America." In October of that year, he posted, "The Mexican-American Studies classes use the exact same technique that Hitler used in his rise to power. In Hitler's case it was the Sudetenland. In the Mexican-American Studies case, it's Aztlan"; a reference to the area of the Southwest that includes Texas, New Mexico and Arizona, the land Mexico lost to the United States as a result of the Mexican War. Then on March 8, 2012, he posted one more pejorative comment, "MAS = KKK in a different color." Judge Tashima ruled that since Huppenthal's blog posts were made weeks before and soon after HB 2281 went into effect, and that he wrote under two pseudonyms, Falcon9 and Thucydides (if he believed nothing was inappropriate with his posts, he would have used his real name), and that he voted on the bill, they are indicative of his state-of-mind during the time period (Acuña, 2017).

The judge also considered Horne's attacks on a single academic program used in a single Arizona school district. Judge Tashima said, "This is probative of discriminatory intent, as [Horne's] own evidence showed that it is unusual to address a perceived problem with one school program on a statewide, rather than a local, basis." The Court relied on the actions of these two men, as well as statements made by several other lawmakers, which included the repetitive used of "Raza," "un–American," "radical," "communist," and "Aztlan"; these words were racial mischaracterizations, or coded dog whistles, that Tashima considered "demonstrat[ing] discriminatory intent." In a derisively sarcastic tone, the Judge declared, "In Huppenthal's own words, the term 'Raza' became 'shorthand for … communicating with Republican primary voters in the Tucson community.'" Given the prosecutor's 14th Amendment equal protection claim, the Court found evidence in Huppenthal's anonymous blog posts that he harbored racial animus toward Mexican Americans. Circumstantial evidence corroborated that Horne and other actors held the same anti–Mexican American views, causing a heated attack on the faculty teaching in the La Raza program. Likewise, the Judge ruled that the 1st Amendment guarantees students the right to "receive information and ideas, a right that applies in the context of school curriculum design" (*Gonzalez v. Douglass, 2017*; Gassen, 2017).

While people celebrated the U.S. District Court's ruling across almost the entire country, Huppenthal, who had since stepped down as superintendent of Arizona schools, pilloried both Judge Tashima and the Tucson Unified School District in Tucson's *Arizona Daily Star*. In a 600-word piece—half of which exculpated himself—Huppenthal (2017) condemned Tashima's ruling in an effort to spook the state's White masses; he evoked his time-honored argument that La Raza teachers indoctrinate students to "hate whites." He called the curriculum "a skinhead philosophy." Diana Douglas, Huppenthal's successor as Superintendent of Public Instruction in Arizona, also issued a statement claiming that although she was not directly contesting Tashima's ruling, she disagreed that the entire HB 2281 needed struck down. To Douglas, the first two provisions of the House Bill forbidding classes that both encourage the overthrow of the United States government and that teach resentment toward a race or class of people "just sound like common sense" (Fischer, 2017).

On the contrary, educators up and down California were motived by the U.S. District Court's ruling. Lawmakers have been debating in Sacramento since 2016 to implement a statewide curriculum guide for schools wishing to offer ethnic studies courses. Some educators in the state have already taken action before the state settles on the curricular blueprint, which hopes to provide educators course outlines, units, classroom activities, and a glossary of terms (Gewertz, 2019). Educators in Los Angeles, San Diego, San Bernardino, and Ventura fought with relative success for ethnic studies programs in their respective school districts. Some schools require it to graduate; others offer it as an elective. In San Francisco, which played host to an ethnic studies summit in 2017, three middle schools created extensive ethnic studies curricula for students as young as sixth grade (Waxman, 2017; Weissert, 2018). In Texas, a state with the second-largest Latinx student population behind California, the Board of Education approved the creation of a statewide academic standard for ethnic studies, which was the name agreed upon as a political compromise with skeptical state education officials that argued calling it Mexican American Studies would alienate other racial and ethnic groups. Within two years of *Gonzalez v. Douglass*, over 100 school districts in the Lone Star State offered ethnic studies courses (Phippen, 2015).

There is an important lesson about committing to race conscious pedagogy in juxtaposing of the battle for ethnic studies in Tucson, Arizona, and the implementation of ethnic studies in local school districts: there is a very real emotional price to be paid when performing racial equity work in schools. That price is usually paid in suffering through vitriolic insults as well as racist and politically incentivized counterattacks. In school districts that are predominantly White, or school districts in which administrative leadership is largely White, there will likely be a form of pushback against new and unfamiliar curricula that challenges traditional boundaries about how race is studied in public schools. In a culture where Whites are dominant, it is common for White people to get defensive when racial oppression and White supremacy are deconstructed in a classroom. When race comes up in school, it is likely that a teacher will encounter a White parent that reacts defensively and may also escalate the conflict beyond the confines of the classroom. The incident often goes directly to the principal or the office of the superintendent. Occasionally, a parent will choose to use a social media platform to engage in slanderous rhetoric against the teacher. In either case, the well-intentioned teacher must endure the trauma of that assault. As this chapter has demonstrated, challenges to Race Conscious Pedagogy are widespread, common, and persistent.

It is important to see that many of the stakeholders involved in fighting for the La Raza Studies program were teachers, parents, and Students of Color. Their stake in the fight against legislators and educational leaders concentrated on self-worth and cultural relevance—issues either not understood or willfully ignored by the program's adversaries. Seminar in Critical Race Studies has faced such challenges by stakeholders in the Gap School District that I will detail in the following chapter. Nonetheless, I must situate myself as a White male educator with inherited privileges that Teachers of Color, Students of Color, and Parents of Color were not afforded in Tucson.

7

"The most brutal, and the most determined resistance"

The Backlash to Race Conscious Classrooms

Introductory Note: This chapter details some of the backlash experience at Gap High School to the existence of Seminar in Critical Race Studies.

On Christmas Eve in 2015, philosopher George Yancy (2018) caught many well-intentioned White Americans off guard when the *New York Times* published his Op Ed titled "Dear White America." Not addressing the individual Alt-Righter or card-carrying member of the Ku Klux Klan, Yancy instead challenged progressives and White liberals for avoiding courageous conversations about race. He dared his readers to let go of their "white innocence" in America's pervasive anti–Black sentiment that has been integral to White identity (Yancy, 2015). When asked later to explain the meaning of "Dear White America," Yancy said he aimed to expose "deep roots of American white supremacy and subtle ways in which so many white people go about their daily lives oblivious to the gravity and violence of white racism." Granted, his labeling all White persons racist who do not proactively resist institutionalized racist policies was eye-opening. Nevertheless, his point that there is no neutrality when it comes to racism is correct. Occasions in my life when I have challenged White colleagues for acting on their predispositions, the kneejerk reaction has been a defensive posture, falling back on implausible declarations to confirm themselves as anything but a racist: "How dare you call me a racist," "I don't see color," or "Race has nothing to do with my behavior." White readers responded to Yancy with angry, profanity-laced denunciations ranging from death threats to comments calling him a "pavement ape" that needed to "go back to Africa" (Yancy, 2018).

Yancy certainly shoulders what James Baldwin described as "go[ing] for

118

broke." In Baldwinian context, the mantra, which might be familiar to some as the all-or-nothing rallying cry of the 442nd Infantry Regiment made up of second-generation Japanese American soldiers in the fight against the Nazis during the Second World War, refers to the tempestuous nature by which Whiteness will inevitably retaliate against anyone that challenges racial indifference, racist policies, or colorblind attitudes. In *The Price of the Ticket: Collected Nonfiction*, Baldwin (1985) forewarns, "[Y]ou must understand that in the attempt to correct so many generations of bad faith and cruelty, when it is operating not only in the classroom but in society, you will meet the most fantastic, the most brutal, and the most determined resistance. There is no point in pretending that this won't happen." That stern warning gives weight and meaning behind the commitment to use any given platform (in Yancy's case, the classroom and the columns of *The New York Times*) to educate White Americans about the hazardous effects of racial apathy, which fosters racial stress among Black Americans while enabling a sense of superiority in the White community.

The truth, Yancy says, "can hurt, stun, unsettle, and unnerve." Speaking truth to why and how White people stay silent on matters of race is a moral and lifesaving imperative. The potential of receiving an aggressive form of backlash, like the type Professor Yancy received after his 2015 *New York Times* column, should not deter one from speaking about matters of race; neither should it dissuade teachers that want to make race studies an integral, almost daily, part of the curriculum. As seen in the unforgiving attacks on the ethnic studies instructors in the Tucson Unified School District, Yancy is not alone when facing down defenders of the racial status quo, even when those defenders are White liberals. Award-winning historian Ibram X. Kendi (2016, 2019) would call those well-meaning Whites targeted in Yancy's Op Ed "assimilationists" who try "to have it both ways" in racial discourse but nevertheless become hypersensitive when challenged on the racist idea that African, Latinx, Asian, and Native Americans must conform to White Eurocentric values. Being "not racist" is not the same as being "antiracist," argues the founder of the Antiracist Research and Policy Center at Boston University. So when challenged on "racist passivity," Kendi explains, well-intended, though frankly unconstructive, Whites counter with statements of self-exoneration such as "I'm not a racist because I have Black friends," or hurl vile personal insults like the comments Yancy received after his Christmas Eve 2015 Op Ed.

In 2018, Robin DiAngelo wrote *White Fragility: Why It's So Hard for White People to Talk About Racism* to explain the ways White people "insulate" themselves from race-based stress. She claims Whites are protected from encountering racial discomfort through social institutions and cultural representations that include the media, advertising, and school curriculum.

According to DiAngelo (2018), White navigation around the fringes of racial discomfort is due to one's "familiar ways of perceiving, interpreting, and responding to the social cues around him or her." Thus, she argues that White people are socialized into a comfortable disposition that produces deep-seated thoughts and perceptions about the world. Those who grow up with a White worldview and a White frame of reference deeply entrench themselves in ideologies of colorblindness and meritocracy that makes one feel he or she is beyond the need to admit how racist America actually is; thus, he or she will possess a simplistic perception of the world as a lived environment where race matters little and in which all are treated equally.

Whether one sees it as Yancy's "backlash," Kendi's "assimilationist" theory, or DiAngelo's "white fragility," this is what happened to me at Gap High School not long after the launch of Seminar in Critical Race Studies in the fall of 2017. The course began just ten days after the racially motivated violence in Charlottesville, Virginia, that resulted in the death of 32-year-old Heather Heyer and injured about 20 other social justice activists. I received a phone call from Jeff Hawkes, a local journalist, three days after the school year started. He obtained permission from my superintendent to contact me for a story he was writing on how local public school teachers broach the topic of race with their students. Most area school districts refused Hawkes access to its teachers. This fact made our conversation more comprehensive and exhaustive, as I considered I had a lot of insight to add to his story. More practically, I had just created the race studies seminar and I wanted to share with him my experiences. Hawkes was not aware that I taught such a class. So when I brought it up in our conversation, his interest peaked and accordingly asked if he could visit to see what a race studies class looks like at a predominantly White high school in rural Lancaster County, Pennsylvania. Hawkes also wanted to interview some of my students and to bring a photographer along to document the trip. A few days after his 90-minute visit to my seminar, Hawkes' article (2017) appeared on the front page of the local newspaper with solemn approbation from readers. In fact, Hawkes' article was picked up by the Associated Press and distributed throughout the United States. It read as follows:

> In the era of Charlottesville and Kaepernick, some Lancaster County
> Educators look to address race in the classroom.
> Jeff Hawkes, Staff Writer, *Lancaster Newspaper*, September 10, 2017.
>
> Tim Hermansen is a white sophomore in a predominantly white high school with little in common with W.E.B. Du Bois, a civil rights pioneer and influential African-American voice who died 39 years before the [Gap] student was even born.
> But on the second day of school, Hermansen was in Room 307 for his advanced placement history class when teacher Todd Mealy lived up to his reputation and tackled race head-on, opening the young man's eyes.

Teaching about race isn't a priority at most schools here and around the country, and some educators say that's a problem if high school graduates are going to find their way in a multicultural world.

Today, Charlottesville and Colin Kaepernick are the flashpoints of America's volatile race relations, controversies on many students' radars. Underlying the eruptions is a fractured society's simmering unease with difference. Race, ethnicity and income to a large extent set the markers for where people live, work, socialize, worship and attend school.

But schools are a special case. They are run by the dominant white culture, especially in Lancaster County, but they're also in a position to try to heal the divide.

Mealy, 38, takes that responsibility seriously, as his second-day-of-school presentation on race dynamics suggests.

Mealy, who is white, his lean, athletic build clad in business casual, talked about Du Bois and his penetrating lament that being black in America means "always looking at one's self through the eyes of others."

They're not dusty words from a by-gone era to Mealy, but a powerful truth helping to explain the lives of minorities in America today.

But how to get his class of mostly white, suburban, middle-class teens to relate to the concepts of alienation and double consciousness he wanted to drive home?

Mealy told stories of times when he was the only white person in a crowd, recalling the self-consciousness he felt on an inter-city bus trip in China and at the movies in Detroit.

For a moment, at least, Mealy had the teens stepping into the shoes of the other, their white blindness beginning to dissolve.

"I was sitting there in the classroom, and it was like, Wow!" Hermansen, 15, said. "It just hadn't really been presented to me in that kind of way."

Mealy's seminar—new this year—on race, ethnicity and gender was offered only because he took the initiative.

He's concerned schools are shirking a "moral obligation" to teach the legacy of white supremacy and privilege.

The need is huge, he said, pointing to Pennsylvania receiving a grade of "F" in the Southern Poverty Law Center's look at how well states teach the civil rights movement.

Mealy began teaching the seminar to two classes of 15 students each after [Gap] High School principal … gave him the green light.

But for the rest of the 1,800 students, race relations isn't a focus, mostly coming up "indirectly," [Gap's principal] said.

"We don't have a set curriculum" on race, he said. Instead, the school stresses collaboration and people skills that employers value.

"It's difficult when you have students of different races and start to talk about one race over another," [Gap's principal] said. "How do you deal with that as a teacher? How do you not create that environment where it's awkward?"

Professors at Millersville University's College of Education and Human Services agree teaching about race can be fraught, but say it's no excuse for tiptoeing around it.

"If we don't do this—and it's not being done—that's why we have issues that we have today in our society," said Nakeiha Primus Smith, assistant professor of educational foundations. "You have students who are not being confronted with values or perspectives that are not similar to their own."

Their unfamiliarity with cultural differences gives rise to fear, and fear, Smith said, leads to building walls.

Students training at Millersville to become teachers do get a grounding in racism, white privilege, gender and other diversity issues, the professors said.

"Race is relevant to almost every single topic we talk about," said Beth Powers, an assistant professor who specializes in early childhood education. "Research indicates that if a new teacher does not know how to be culturally competent with children, they will not be a successful teacher."

While Leslie Gates' class on Methodology and Pedagogy of Art is about educators teaching art to promote critical thinking, she said the class will discuss race all semester.

"My goal is to make sure that they have queried their soul about the issue of race, not to find an answer, but so that they invite their students into that inquiry," Gates said. "They are going to be responsible for small human beings of all shapes, sizes, colors, abilities."

Kazi Hossain, an associate professor of education, said he teaches two classes that touch on race relations and diversity, and he's heartened that today's students, even those raised in white communities, seem to be more receptive to the concepts than students were 10 or 15 years ago.

"Many say thank you for helping me think differently," Hossain said.

Erica Long, 31, said she graduated from [Gap] High School having had few opportunities to experience diversity and having no understanding of how being white gave her unearned advantages.

Her eyes were opened as a college student in the diverse setting of Pittsburgh, and now she teaches English and journalism at Solanco High School. She said she wants to advocate for race education in the district so students, many of whom have seen little of the world beyond Quarryville, aren't as naive as she was when they graduate.

"The school is dedicated to anti-bullying, making students feel safe and emphasizing kindness, but we don't mention race, class and diversity in that," Long said. "I think that's a question we should constantly ask ourselves."

Long has signed up for a training for educators on teaching anti-racism, a five-session workshop that starts September 18 and is sponsored by The Stone Independent School and Lancaster Action Now Coalition.

"Racism exists in our society. It built our society," said Nick Miron, an anti-racism educator who will lead the training. Because the issue is so entrenched and complicated, schools, like many institutions, address the issue superficially or "avoid it altogether because the change necessary is so difficult."

Miron hopes workshop participants become advocates of change.

"I do believe folks in education are well meaning and want to create a good society," he said. "If we can channel that into a very intentional and purposeful conversation about things that effect society, like racism, we can make good on the intentions we have so our impact matches our intent."

Hempfield School District and School District of Lancaster did not respond to LNP's interview requests, and Manheim Township School District declined to offer a staff member to speak about how it teaches race.

Instead, Karen Nell, Manheim Township's curriculum and instruction director, issued a statement stressing how the district tries to create "a safe, inclusive environment in our classrooms for all students at all times."

"This is particularly true when discussing timely, but highly emotional subjects, such as race relations," Nell said.

She added that "both sides" of controversial topics are explored and materials represent diverse peoples.

Miron characterized Manheim Township's statement as a "generic, feel-good response ... that is so typical of institutions that are afraid or unwilling to be real."

"To discuss racism as merely emotional and controversial, with two sides, completely negates the complex nature of racism, the structural power of it, and the trauma that is passed intergenerationally," he said.

Tim Mahoney, director of educational foundations at Millersville University, said Manheim Township's statement tries to appear "responsive to racial issues" but dodges a difficult topic.

Manheim Township employs exceptional educators, Mahoney said. "They just have not taught in places where timely, but highly emotional, subjects are talked about openly with a variety of people," he said, "so they don't know what they don't know."

One place frank discussions are starting to happen is in Mealy's [Gap] race seminar.

Students have divergent views, particularly on the racial climate in the school.

One white student told LNP race "is not a huge issue." Others disagree.

Gabby Abreu, 16, is a senior and the daughter of parents from the Dominican Republic. She said that as often as twice a week she overhears racist comments in the hall.

"I guess it's because the majority of the school is white, it makes it seem like it's kind of OK to say these things," Abreu said. "I think that's a problem."

Jane Tumanga, 17, a senior whose parents came from Kenya, said she's never felt like a target of racism but has heard classmates disparage blacks and Hispanics.

"That started happening when the (presidential) election was going on," Tumanga said. "They were like, If someone else can say it out loud, then I can, too."

The students in Mealy's class knew what they were signing up for, and they welcome being guinea pigs.

"I just think race is an uncomfortable topic," said Sameeha Hossain, 16, a junior whose parents are from Bangladesh. "But we're in a small group, so I think it's easier to talk about. I think that's the first step."

Hermansen, the student whose eyes were opened by Mealy's discussion of Du Bois, said he doesn't want to just learn about racism, but also learn how to do something about it.

"Maybe we can be the solution," he said. "It doesn't have to be somebody older than us that has to fix everything. It can be us."

Hawkes' article cast a spotlight on the Seminar in Critical Race Studies course. I fielded a call from a representative of "The Race Project, KC" based in Kansas City, Missouri. Then the *Lancaster Newspapers'* Sunday edition (2017) ran an editorial singing the class's praises. "Small group discussions, led by a teacher willing to talk about difficult topics like privilege and White supremacy, are a good first step [to teach students to think in different ways, and inspire them to venture beyond their comfort zones to seek solutions]," the editorial staff opined. "We laud Mealy for taking the initiative to create his seminar class on race, ethnicity, and gender, and [Gap] High School Principal ... for green-lighting it."

The local newspaper's commendation was shortly replaced with disparagement from groups that felt challenged on some level. Perhaps on request by a few school board members or after fielding several phone calls from concerned community members questioning my motives for creating the course, my school district's superintendent sat in on the class. I only presumed he needed to report back to someone or something about the nature of critical discussions and the curricular logistics of the course. The class he audited was about the myth of the model minority. I presented a short contextual lecture that was followed-up with a scholarly reading about NBA basketball player Jeremy Lin, an examination of William Petersen's 1966 *New York Times* article that created the model minority stereotype, and an open-ended discussion about both texts. I got the impression things were going well when the superintendent started participating in our discussion. Even then, many students in the hallway decried the course while images of the Confederate flag became more prevalent on t-shirts, sweatshirts, book bags, and belt buckles outside my classroom door. A student of one of my colleagues who taught in my classroom during my prep period drew a swastika on my wall. One of my students in an American history class I taught spent about a month drawing the Nazi emblem on his calves before entering my classroom.

Then an opinion columnist for a newspaper in Eastern Pennsylvania, the *Bucks County Courier Times*, wrote a disparaging editorial about my course. After reading Hawkes' article, JD Mullane (2017) responded with a biting piece wherein he used me as an anvil for his 800-word article that hammered a flawed point about critical race studies classes being a waste of time. He claimed since White students from White high schools will ultimately enter White careers after graduation, formal (and by insinuation informal) education about race is a futile endeavor. Here is his column:

The Unbearable Whiteness of Detectors of Disrespect
JD Mullane, *Bucks County Courier Times*, September 19, 2017

Pennsylvania public schools apparently don't talk enough about race and diversity to students, unless it's to erase race and diversity, such as Neshaminy and Council Rock North high schools' attempt to tear down their honorable Native American mascots.

The irony is that, almost without exception, the hectoring lecturers who appoint themselves detectors of racial disrespect are as white as a college sociology department, by which I mean, vanilla.

But in the Amish country borough of Millersville, a guy named Todd Mealy—"who is white" the AP adds helpfully—Is continuing the tradition of white people telling the rest of us how it is with his classroom seminar on race.

"He's concerned schools are shirking a 'moral obligation' to teach the legacy of white supremacy and privilege," the story reports.

"Teaching about race," the story reports, "isn't a priority at most schools here and around the country, and some educators say that's a problem if high school graduates are going to find their way in a multicultural world."

Lessons on race are especially necessary in Pennsylvania, the story states, because the Commonwealth received an "F" from the Southern Poverty Law Center, which evaluated how the civil rights movement is taught.

That Pennsylvania and America is more racially "diverse" and that white kids will have to adjust to this reality (under the tutelage of enlightened whites, of course) has been a progressive talking point for decades. Let's test that.

First, most of the students at [Gap] High School in Millersville, where Mealy lectures on race are, like him, white. Millersville is 92 percent white, according to the U.S. Census.

Still, the big, wide, diverse world awaits these students, so they better be prepared to be with people who aren't white.

Let's say a lot of them go on to Millersville University, a teacher's college, where all those white, right-thinking professors are concerned about racial diversity. Millersville U's student body is nearly 80 percent white. My guess is, it's [sic] faculty is vanilla, too. Well, a small, remote state university in mostly-white Pennsyltucky can't be expected to reflect the new multi-culti reality just yet. It takes time, right?

But when Millersville students land jobs in the big, wide, diverse world, that's where all the Todd "who is white" Mealy's seminar on race will come in handy.

Certainly those Millersville graduates who land work as teachers will be in a highly diverse workforce.

Nope.

More than 80 percent of college BA degrees in education were attained by whites, most of them women. Just 4 percent of teaching degrees were awarded to Latinos (or Latinas), according to the American Association of Colleges for Teacher Education.

But say the students in Todd "who is white" Mealy's classroom go off to some other fine college, like Penn State. Surely his lessons on race will come in handy, given our new reality.

Nope. PSU's main campus is nearly 70 percent white. Since I am certain Old Main is in the hands of upright progressives who believe in diversity, the lopsided lack of racial diversity on campus is some sort of oversight.

But say Mealy's white students graduate from their white colleges and land jobs in lines of work that aren't as dominated by whites as his own, say the popular tech sector. Plenty of diversity in that international field, where lessons on race will come in handy.

Nope.

Almost 70 percent of the U.S. "high tech" workforce is not only white, but male, too, according to the U.S. Equal Opportunity Employment Commission.

Well, maybe those white students will find careers in the most popular college degree—business administration. In an interconnected world, surely American corporations are diverse, especially when it comes to high-paying executive suites, where decisions on diversity are made.

Nope. White males comprise 72 percent of corporate leadership at the Fortune 500 companies, according to Forbes. CEOs, where the real power lays, are 92 percent white and male.

Well, say Mealy's students decide to become lawyers. Certainly that progressive profession is diverse. Certainly not. Almost 90 percent (90 percent!) of U.S. lawyers are white, according to the Washington Post.

OK, say Mealy's students go into the entertainment biz, to become the next big Hollywood star or late night TV comic. Diversity is entertainment's strength, right?

Nope. The majority of actors, directors, producers and anyone with power in Hollywood is white, according to a study by the University of Southern California. The Academy Awards are so white, #OscarsSoWhite has become a perennial online hashtag.

I could go on and on, from journalism to medicine, to activism, and it's white.

"Diversity is our strength" is a nice slogan, I guess, but the reality is we're still living in vanillaville.

I waited seven months before showing my students Mullane's column. It was near the end of the school year and we had reached the point in the class where students had already taken the Advanced Placement exam and were now preparing their plunge either into commencement, AP Capstone's second year AP Research course, or another academic path forward. We were in a critical dialogic circle bringing closure to what we learned about the research and writing processes over the duration of the school year when I told the students about Mullane's article. I was actually speaking more directly about how an author must balance dueling perspectives in academic writing. It came to me at that moment that I would compare how Mullane used Seminar in Critical Race Studies students and me to generate a narrative against Race Conscious Pedagogy while engaging in a written dialogue about the topic with Jeff Hawkes, the Lancaster-based writer that initiated the conversation with his original article about the course.

My students erupted once I told them of Mullane's commentary about our class. A number of students promptly grabbed cellphones from their pockets and found the article online. True to form, several others used their phones to look up Mullane's background to address his merits that would warrant his qualifications to have an editorial published criticizing race studies courses.

My students were angry and overprotective of their teacher. After allowing them time to vent, we decided that the students would write responses to Mullane. I would help send them to the *Bucks County Courier Times* for publication in the letters to the editor page. What they produced, however, was too much for the 150–200 words allotted for letters to the editor. My students decided to write unrestricted pieces that they would post in the comments section of the online version of Mullane's editorial. They composed statements such as these (the essays have been lightly edited for clarity and, for obvious reasons, hyperlinks to sources have been excluded):

Response 1:

In a country that is still in the process of nurturing open-mindedness, one would assume that most of us would encourage schools to teach our students about considering other cultures, the perspectives of others, or the way that other people think. However, it appears as if not everyone would agree to a class on *race, ethnicity, and gender* (which would, we presume, support rumination of the aforementioned characteristics), a fact that was supported extensively in an article by journalist JD Mullane. In fact, Mullane seems to be backing a different conceptual horse entirely.

In a not-so-recent article by the journalist, the spotlight of negativity was placed on Dr. Todd M. Mealy's seminar regarding race, ethnicity, and gender. Specifically, the notion that a class studying race is irrelevant in Lancaster County (dubbed "vanillaville" by Mullane) was repeated multiple times because the notion "that Pennsylvania and America is [sic] more racially 'diverse' and that white kids will have to adjust to this reality" is, according to Mullane, incorrect. In the words of the journalist, "let's test that."

First, let us view the main claim that Mullane makes: America is not diverse enough to make learning about race relevant; this is done by citing a myriad of percentages indicating that various occupations in America (from post-secondary education to show business) are dominated by whites and that learning about race would not aid students in their line of work.

This is inherently untrue. For one, the statistics cited indicated the fact that (unsurprisingly) minorities *were* the minority in most fields of work, as is to be expected. Therefore, the statistics cited were, while depressing, predictable.

In addition, the very notion that those in the minority should be ignored simply because they comprise a smaller portion of the population is unethical. Sure, 80 percent of college BA degrees in education were acquired by whites. But what about the 20 percent who were given to People of Color? Should their perspective be ignored because they are the minority? Of course not.

Mullane builds upon the previous, occupation-focused claim by declaring that "almost 90 percent of U.S. lawyers are white, according to the *Washington Post*." We're sure that this claim is correct; a majority of lawyers are undoubtedly white. However, some of their *clients* are certainly not. If one were to go to law school with the mindset that they would *only* meet white people, interactions with people of other races would be mediocre at best. Ignoring the notion that interactions with one's client, regardless of race, are perhaps even more important than communicating with one's colleagues is foolish and ignorant.

The aforementioned notions can connect to the field of medicine. While slightly under 50 percent of accepted medical school applicants are People of Color, according to the AAMC, the interactions with patients are equally, if not more, important. Indeed, the lack of training that those in the medical field have with regards to interacting with minority patients is likely one of the reasons why the gap between the medical care of whites versus minorities exists. This is undoubtedly caused by racist exchanges between doctors and minority patients.

Creating and supporting classes that address race would alleviate both the unfortunate fact that some physicians are undereducated concerning racism and the inexperience with race that lawyers often face in their line of work. What better time to build upon the idea of acceptance than early in a student's educational career, such as in a high school setting?

As a side note, the issue of the healthcare gap was the topic of one of the author's major projects in the seminar class in question. As can be seen, a *different perspective* was considered. In general, the establishment of a concrete background in race can aid in opening one's eyes to the world in order to see the inner workings of America from a different view.

Analyzing how individuals from other races view the world around them would also alleviate the discomfort some young adults have on the topic of race. The subject of race will definitely come up in a person's life. As stated before, while the majority is white, some people are not. Ignoring the fact that there are cultural differences is inherently malicious for the open-mindedness of students and their willingness to discuss racial issues in America.

Another one of Mullane's points was the notion that many [Gap] students live in "vanillaville," the journalist's apparent nickname for Millersville (which is, one must concede, *very* white, 92 percent in fact). One inherent flaw in his argument is the simple fact that not all students who go to [Gap] High School *live* in Millersville. Therefore, the location is not the only place in which students spend time. The nearest city, Lancaster, is a common spot that draws students for many different events. However, Lancaster is only 40.7 percent white. Thus, every time a student ventures into the city, there is almost no way they won't see or interact with racial minorities. A classroom based on race would better allow students to connect with the other cultures and races seen prominently in a close city.

So is it partially true that, as Mullane put it, "we're still living in vanillaville?"

Yep.

But should that result in a complete disregard for teaching that aids in opening the eyes of our students to discrimination, as today's youth will face people of another race or ethnicity at some point in their line of work? Should we ignore talking about race so that the unequal world around us stays unequal and put America's youth at a disadvantage when the considerations of another person's perspective are required?

Nope.

Response 2:

My name is Aniah "who is only half white" Washington and I will be pursuing a career in civil law. But why should I? Certainly there is no need for all races, ethnicities, and genders to be equally represented in the courtroom. I should most definitely not become part of the 30 percent of students that identify as a person-of-color. But, let's say that I did decide to continue to chase my dreams despite the clear odds I am up against. Would my efforts be meaningless? Would I just continue to live in the shadow of the privileged individuals following the same career path? I think not. I think that to assume my attitude, abilities, or ambitions are dependent on the racial diversity I encounter is foolish.

I have experienced firsthand the drastic difference in diversity outside of my hometown, but yes our population will always be predominantly white—I have not ever been told otherwise. What I have been told is that despite the underrepresentation and minority status I will always incur, I should continue to fight for my voice to be heard. A class like our race and gender seminar is exactly what I need to help strengthen my voice to speak out against the systems that continues to deny people of color equal opportunities. My seminar teacher does not teach me what to think. Rather, I have learned skills on how to develop my thinking and express my views in and outside of the classroom.

The chance to discuss my opinion about "sensitive topics" in a classroom setting was new to me. Whoever heard of such an absurd thing? Teenagers—many on the verge of starting college while others enter the workforce—having conversations about subjects that are ingrained into their everyday lives? It is insensitive to think that a course like seminar on race and gender is unnecessary, though I can see why someone that is part of the majority may think that. Everyday a white student sits in class to learn and discuss the basic parts of an American education, all through the lens of a white society. While black and brown students sit and listen to the same lessons with no attention given to their cultural histories. So why is it that when a course is finally offered to enlighten students about serious topics like race, ethnicity, gender, and sexuality there is now an issue?

I deserve my voice. I deserve the chance to talk about the issues that affect me in my classroom without fear of judgment or marginalization. Do not try and tell me that I cannot thrive in a racially and sexually unbalanced world. Do not try and tell me that there is something wrong with culturally responsive pedagogy. There is no reason why I cannot sit in a liberal arts classroom that engages in eye opening conversations. If we are talking pedagogy only, isn't this the point of humanities?

Next fall, I will attend Amherst College, a small liberal arts school in Massachusetts. I plan to double major in Law, Jurisprudence, and Social Thought as well as Black Studies. My future school is home to students from 54 countries around the world and flourishes with a student body in which 44 percent of students identify as people of color. The world is progressing and with each day becoming more diverse. We cannot afford to shelter ourselves and our students from this fact. One day we will all experience a diverse setting in some way.

Response 3:

Growing up in conservative and predominantly white Lancaster County has left me with very little exposure to those who are different to me. My parents are very conservative in their lifestyles, and see little outside the 984 square-mile area that they have settled into, known as Lancaster. They are what you refer to as the "vanilla" population. My father attended Penn State, the "white college" you cited in your work, and my mother was born in raised in this land of "vanilla" people. So, I can see why I would be the perfect target for your attack on white activists and those promoting change.

As a child, I was exposed to very little diversity in race and sexuality; not due to hate or intolerance, but simply because everyone I knew was exactly like me. In advertisements, movies, magazines, television, and all other forms of media, there was almost no representation of minorities to be exposed to. In elementary school I had only two African American classmates, and the rest of the class was white. These numbers slowly began to grow as I got older, but they were still extremely small for the size of our district. Also, there were *zero* minorities represented in teaching staff, allowing even less exposure. And unlike your naive viewpoint on the whiteness of the world, I am able to see that this is a problem in Lancaster County and the lack of minority educators and education needs to be fixed.

To be honest, I originally took AP Seminar because I thought it would look good on my transcript and prepare me for college level writing. This class, however, has turned into so much more than that. AP Seminar has allowed me to see more than just the conservative viewpoints that I am so commonly in contact with. Through this class I have taken implicit bias tests that have helped me change my mindset on judging people upon first glance. I have learned about cultural appropriation and its harming effects. I have also become highly aware of my privilege.

The most powerful takeaway from this class is the level of discussions that I now have with my amazing, accepting, loving, and conservative parents. They were not exposed to classes like AP Seminar or people like Todd "who is white" Mealy, who promote conversations about the mistreatment of others based on skin color, gender, or sexuality. Seeing my parents slowly notice how our whiteness can affect others gives me joy. Hearing my mother confront male sales assistants in stores who treat her as less because she is a woman makes me proud of the work this class has done.

All in all, JD Mullane, I would like to thank you for making me realize how much of an impact this class has had on me. Additionally, I believe that courses like AP Seminar on Race, Ethnicity, and Gender are important in our ever changing and culturally diverse world.

Response 4:

We are students at [Gap] High School currently attending the AP Seminar class mentioned in JD Mullane's article titled, "The unbearable whiteness of detectors of disrespect."

As Mr. Mullane mentioned in said article, we live "in the Amish country borough of Millersville."

Nope.

He also may have the preconceived notion that we took this class in order to prepare us for the "diverse" world he so frequently mentioned.

Nope.

In addition, Mullane stated that "a lot of" us will attend the local Millersville University.

Nope.

Unbeknownst to him, we are students who live 10 minutes from Lancaster City that have aspirations ranging from becoming an Astrophysicist to a Supreme Court Justice. This is far from Mullane's initial assumption that we would attend small colleges and do small things in his "diverse" world.

We are students with hopes and dreams beyond Lancaster County. We hope to enter a realistic world in which diversity is much more ubiquitous than in rural Pennsylvania. Just to name a few, according to StatisticAtlas, Philadelphia is just 36.6 percent white. This is much more diverse than Mullane's cherry-picked statistics would show. Following the trend of major cities, Los Angeles is 27.5 percent white. On a much larger scale, California is just 39.7 percent white. By 2042, when we are about 40 years old, experts say minority groups will outnumber the white population. We suggest that Mullane broaden his scope. Although he may not face the same issues presented in the news, we think it would be beneficial to understand why those issues exist in the first place.

Mullane's lack of research on a course he feels strong enough to write a column about is disheartening. [Gap] High School *is* a white space, but when it comes to students of color living in "Vanillaville," Mullane can be assured that does not mean that the existence of a course teaching about race and gender is pointless. The purpose of a course like our seminar existing in a white space is to teach, not only about the racial constructs that have existed and continue to exist in this country, but about the injustices revolving around intersections of race, gender, and ethnicity that lead to many of the racially charged stories that make headlines in the news today; all the while preparing students to write about and develop solutions for the world's problems.

Harley Barber, 19, was a member of the Alpha Phi sorority at the University of Alabama. She was expelled from the university for posting racist videos on social media that later went viral. She said, "We do not waste water because of the people in Syria. I love how I act like I love black people when I fucking hate niggers." Besides the lack of moral intelligence, Barber was both ignorant towards racial issues and failed to recognize the importance of humanitarianism; something Dr. Mealy's class has taught us. It takes one student at a time to stand apart from these racist episodes and to help fight the normative social influence occurring at these universities. That one student could be any of us, white and black men and women leaving Mealy's Seminar only to join the "upright progressives who believe in diversity." So yes, Dr. Todd Mealy is white. However, he is teaching us about the gruesome events of America's past, and guiding us to work towards a culture of racial equality, the lesson all Americans could benefit from. Lessons that don't cater to the white ego must be taught so it doesn't repeat itself, and maybe it takes a white teacher from "Vanillaville," "Pennsyltucky" to instill these ideals in today's racially diverse youth.

Before this class was offered at my school, minority students at [Gap] spent up to three years of their lives wondering why such a big aspect American history was not discussed in the classroom. Race issues have always existed. The lack of discussion on these topics is what leads to feelings of white innocence and the persistence of the marginalization of people of color in this country.

Even though that wasn't our main focus before taking AP Seminar, our scopes were broadened and we now can better see the strength in the diverse world that surrounds us.

Yup.

In many ways, the impressive mixture of protectiveness, resoluteness, and confidence shown in how the responses were written certainly was a mark that major headway had been made during the school year with these students. Indeed, for different reasons they saw the value in a class that taught about race and ethnicity. Some saw it as a way to learn the full truth of American history; a method of understanding why Native American mascots are offensive or those who take bold stances on social justice issues have always been disparaged in the moment yet adjudicated positively in the future. Left leaning students appreciated the opportunity to engage in structured discussions about race because the course helped to develop an appropriate vocabulary to articulate thoughts and emotions they otherwise would keep bottled up. Right leaning students found the deliberations to be a beneficial technique of improving debate points for or against various issues. There are students that I have taught who have admitted the class is the thing that motivated them to come into school. This is a point reflective of the ethnic studies program in the Tucson Unified School District; that cultural relevance tied to education leads to better attendance, improved test scores, and higher graduation rates. Every student has moved on from the class more enthusiastic about civic engagement. All of my White students have admitted that their participation in the class has enlightened them about underrepresented racial and ethnic groups in the traditional curriculum. Not to mention that a background in ethnic studies or equity work would make one more sought-after in the job market, as many businesses, school districts, institutes of higher learning, and law firms now include diversity statements or inclusivity policies in contracts. Additionally, it has become more common for college admission essays to ask students to reflect on how their ethnic background will contribute to the diversity of the college in which they are applying. For White students, even those sitting in the top of the class, who have never considered how his or her race has impacted lived experiences, this question would be impossible to answer without an intensive education on the topic.

But these were the thoughts of those that took the course. What about the students that had not? What about the parents? How does a school system get full buy-in from the community? Simply stated, some students and parents are just plain difficult to deal with. Every teacher faces at some point in their career difficult students or parents who can torment and haunt the conscious mind well after school hours. As a teacher that utilizes Race Conscious Pedagogy, I have certainly dealt with a few challenging parents that existed as nasty thorns in my side, which would otherwise take surgery to remove. For example, a father of one of my Seminar in Critical Race Studies students was a police detective in the neighboring city. While all evidence indicates that his child enjoyed the class—this student was certainly engaged in our critical dialogues, had joined me on after-school field trips to hear guest speakers, and performed well on the end-of-year exam—he began to voice his problem with the class and me once we arrived at the unit on Black Lives Matter. This parent's concern was over how law enforcement officers were going to be represented in that study. In November 2017, he emailed a request to me seeking permission to come and speak to the students. Although I had reservations about this since his child was a student in the class, I took the request to the building principal. I was advised to utilize the school's resource officer instead, as we saw it as an opportunity to provide another insightful voice on the topic. There were too many conflicts of interest to allow the parent to visit with my students. The parent went off the rails in an email once he was informed of our decision. In a display of classism, he first shamed our school resource officer for not possessing the same level of insight or training in the police force. He maintained that his title as detective gave him more awareness of the psychological components of the job in addition to more field experience. He then criticized the principal for the decision, saying he expected my boss to find an excuse to keep him out of the building. Of course, I was insulted as well for incompetence.

Meanwhile, a Gap High School student who was not enrolled in my seminar but was in my homeroom had created a parody Instagram account of me earlier in the school year. It was a sophomoric distortion of my politics, all driven by the existence of this race studies class. Near the end of the school year a meme of me appeared on the parody account with a misleading and insensitive quote about race, religion, and Donald Trump. The post claimed that I said: "Most Christians are associated with Trump and racism. In fact, Pastors are usually racist." The difficult parent of the student I had in class saw the meme and reposted it on his Facebook page. He also added to the meme his own defamatory statement in an effort to paint a distorted caricature of me to those in the school community that followed him on that social media platform. He wrote, "This man has lost his mind. I cant [*sic*] confirm this statement but there are others, some worse, that I absolutely can. This man has no business in the public education system. He brags about how he is untouchable. Education not indoctrination."

The fact that this parent—a police detective—shared an internet meme created by a teenager who I did not know instead of calling into the school to speak with me, the principal, or superintendent carried implications that he most likely knew the content on the meme was bogus; but since he took issue with the work I was doing in the district he decided to post it anyway. Indeed, this parent did so because he carried a personal grievance and wanted to discredit my character to the community I had served without reprimand for more than a decade. Though I crafted a response to this parent the night I learned about the meme, my building principal and the union president, who claimed slander and defamation law had not kept up with the ascent of social media, insisted that I let it go. I was told, however, to keep the parent's comments along with my response on record, especially since he had a previous history with the district and was not considered a credible source. The response that I filed away can be read in Appendix 1.

What was it that James Baldwin said? The most fantastic … resistance. The most brutal … resistance. The most determined … resistance. Why pretend that such attacks won't happen? Michael Eric Dyson (2018) suggests race is like religion. Conservative literalists see the country as an unadulterated society that accepts things as they are; that a person advances in this society through hard work alone; since Barack Obama, Michael Jordan, and Oprah Winfrey made it, that structural limitations are a thing of the past and institutional racism exists no longer; that those who have more (connections, wealth, privilege) have no structural advantage over those who have less. On the contrary, progressive liberals see pervasive contempt and both tacit and emboldened violence on dark bodies as the figurative cornerstone of the United States; "that bigotry adapts to whatever law is on the books," explains Dyson. For almost a decade, these two paradoxical perspectives have destructively collided over hyper-patriotism and over-policing; playing out during the national anthem on NFL gridirons and soccer pitches or the streets of such places as Ferguson, Baltimore, or Chicago. Those stuck in the middle have been summoned to act, obligated to pick a side, refusing to vacillate in its dogma. This is what transpired during the 11-year debate over La

Raza studies in Arizona. And it is what took place in my classroom in the spring of 2018.

The unhappy father who happened to be a law enforcement officer possessed a desperate need to control the narrative instead of letting my class do what it is designed to do: to offer his child an assortment of resources so that an authentic and evidence-based perspective could be formed on what is perceived by many to be America's racist policies and racist viewpoints. This was a predictable counterattack made by a taxpayer which stood in sharp contrast to the support given to an officer in his police department who was recorded on a viral video using a Taser on an unarmed Black man sitting legs crossed on a Lancaster City curb in June 2018, just weeks after the dispute over my class (Caron, 2018). In contrast, my profession faces condemning accusations from the community, as it rightfully should since it—like law enforcement— is a publicly funded vocation susceptible to critique. When the heavy hand of the law fairly comes down on educators involved in racist or sexually aggressive impropriety, teachers do not routinely condemn the detractors. It is the duty of citizens of this country to challenge impropriety and injustice equally. Herein lies the value of critical pedagogy. Two education professors and authors of numerous books, Peter McLaren and Joe L. Kincheloe (2007), subscribe to the teaching method:

> Critical pedagogy can be theoretically-based scholarship, grounded in the understanding of the origins and underpinnings of power within society and in the fabric of schooling. Critical pedagogy has the right to be angry, and to express anger, anger at the uses of power and at the injustices through the violations of human rights.... Those engaged in critical pedagogy don't need to agree with one another, rather, they need to passionately engage in the radical fire of discursive disagreement. Allowing students to realize that critique is the weft of the weave within democracy, those who espouse a critical pedagogy must constantly be alert and attuned to the context in which politics, power, and pedagogy intersect.

If my spat with this parent tells us anything, it is that Race Conscious Pedagogy—or anything related to causes of cultural competence, equity, inclusion, and antiracism—is today the most pressing issue in education. And since it is such a major concern in education, critical race studies' seriousness should be treated no differently in the community. Schools and communities must be linked together in the battle for equity in education.

Yet as the teacher, to be questioned and disparaged by cynics is the cost of committing to racial inclusivity and equity work. It may well be that a school community might not be ready for a transformational antiracist education. Rather than sweep away any racial barriers in the traditional curriculum, any level of resistance to the reshaping of pedagogy and curriculum toward cultural responsiveness and in an equitably inclusive way displays just how deeply rooted the sentiment behind those barriers remain. The frightening reality is that those who fight back against inclusivity and equity rarely speak from the woebegone lower social reaches of American society. Those are not the voices of part-time day laborers in rundown saloons. They speak as physicians, lawyers, receptionists, bank tellers, accounting clerks, fellow educators, and even police detectives that makeup America's school districts.

What do such statements tell us? A parent's defamatory assertion that misconstrues the job of a well-meaning teacher, along with a state's education secretary's hot demagogic promise to shut down a successful and flourishing ethnic studies program, exposes the weight of the rapid demographic shift now changing the traditional landscape of the American public educational system. The Pew Research Center (Krogstad and Fry, 2014) already shows that Students of Color outnumber White students in the nation's public schools. In 1997, 63 percent of public school students were White. That number fell to 49 percent by 2016. Projections indicate that by 2022 Whites will be outnumbered 54.7 percent to 45.3 percent (Geiger, 2018; Paris, 2016). This is why pedagogic and curricular changes are already underway. The days of educational policy and instructive practices centered on White, middle-class, monocultures, and monolingual norms are gone with the wind.

Arguably, the most difficult part of equity work is curtailing the negative voices that obstruct progress. Championing equity in education is not impossible despite encumbered critics within the faculty, the community, and some of the most important stakeholders in the school district. If there is one thing I have learned since launching Seminar in Critical Race Studies in 2017, the way to prevail over dissenting colleagues and taxpayers is to engage with the most influential persons among them. What leaders in the community do those uncooperative voices admire? Can equity workers bring those leaders into the zone of discomfort? Much of the battle is convincing the critics to collaborate on the equity mission. The way to convert suspecting individuals to the equity mission is to make the issue personal for them (see my story about my sister in Chapter 1). While explanations of institutional racism or accounts about overt acts of racism in the classroom might not resonate, convincing a critic to think about the hardships overcome by a disabled relative or to reflect on a sexist policy that victimized a daughter will strike at the heart. Once accomplished over a series of sustained conversations, it will become likely that many of the other dissenters will turn the corner.

The pace of demographic change is happening faster than anyone in my school district anticipated. While three out of four students are White, the race, class, and political dynamic at Gap High School offers an interesting environment to formally and informally engage with students about hegemonic systems. As this chapter has demonstrated, I justifiably prepared myself to deal with virulent attacks from taxpayers in the school district.

But not everything about Race Conscious Pedagogy is as bad as the last two chapters make it sound. The high level of learning that occurs in the classroom outweighs the trauma inflicted by critics. Those criticisms have helped me obtain deeper insight into how to better construct Seminar in Critical Race Studies in a way that utilizes rigorous interrogative techniques while allowing the students to develop analytical skills through group discussion and examination of a variety of peer reviewed in addition to anecdotal narratives and counter-narratives. This structure has resulted in several special moments and remarkable conversations that I will discuss in the following chapter.

8

Putting Students in
Uncomfortable Situations

Introduction

Students arrive on the first day of class having already read different books about various topics related to race and ethnic studies. Several of the pupils in Seminar in Critical Race Studies make a habit of sprinting to me in a panic before the bell has rung to ask questions about the summer reading assignment, being as they are scheduled to begin oral presentations on the third day of school. Not surprised by their query, I assure the students that as long as they follow the instructions sent to them over the summer, they should have no reason to be concerned about their performance. In addition to offering a thorough analysis of the summer reading text, students' presentations include a handout and a multimedia presentation to help their peers follow along. The students are also informed that I will give my own presentation on W.E.B. Du Bois's *The Souls of Black Folk* before anyone is scheduled to give a presentation. The predictable sense of ambiguity that I witness on the first day of school is typically not an indication of future exchanges between my students and me. Throughout the school year, the students' uncertainty about assignments and class discussions typically wanes. As their confidence improves each week, so does the level of discourse about controversial topics related critical race studies.

This chapter details only three of those discussions. With just a few days left in the school year, I survey the Seminar in Critical Race Studies students to discover what they considered to be the most meaningful critical dialogues and how those discussions shaped students' engagement with various texts during the duration of the school year. The consensus is as follows: (1) the discussion on practical applications of Du Bois's double consciousness theory, (2) the dialogue about the legal and social construction of race, and (3) the debate over the validity of the Black Lives Matter movement. The class discussions on those three topics are illustrated in this chapter. Unfortunately, there is no space to include everything the students and I examine throughout the school year. Refer to figures 1.2 and 1.3 in Chapter 5 to see a detailed reading list and skills taught in the course. I designed this chapter as a primer for navigating discussions on topics that make high school students uncomfortable. It should prove a worthwhile learning experience to engage with students across a spectrum of critical race studies topics.

Foundational Text for Seminar in Critical Race Studies W.E.B. Du Bois's The Souls of Black Folk

On the second day of school, I perform a mock presentation for the students by discussing Du Bois's *The Souls of Black Folk* (1903). Before I begin, each student is issued a handout with notes about Du Bois's biography, comparable texts, thematic concepts found in *The Souls of Black Folk*, and a chapter-by-chapter summary. Many of the notes also appear in the multimedia presentation that I prepared for the students to follow along. I have chosen this book as the introductory text for the course because of how Du Bois speaks about a psychological condition he called "double consciousness." While this concept of Black biculturalism or, in his words, "twoness," was proffered at a time when Lynch Law haunted the Black consciousness at every end of the country, there is very little debate over whether it is still among the foremost subjects in critical race studies, as racially minoritized groups in the 21st-century struggle to juggle identity with socially imposed norms. During the summer preceding the start of class, each Seminar in Critical Race Studies student selects one book to read that would span the content of the course. Strategically, I offer works under 200 pages by authors that resemble the themes found in *The Souls of Black Folk* (see Appendix 2). The books include Gloria Anzaldua's *La Frontiera/Borderlands*, Paul Gilroy's *The Black Atlantic*, James Baldwin's *The Fire Next Time*, Kim Park Nelson's *Invisible Asians*, Carol Spindel's *Dancing at Halftime*, Samuel C. Heilman's *Portrait of American Jews*, and two books by Moustafa Bayoumi: *This Muslim American Life* and *How Does It Feel to Be a Problem?*. In my presentation, I address some, but not all, of those books. It is my way of showing students how a list of sources, or what I call a "textual constellation" (a pattern of books with theses situated around the main argument of one foundational text), metastasize around one author's thesis. So while I strive to connect Du Bois' theory of double consciousness to the works of Baldwin and Gilroy—which focus on the Black experience in the Atlantic world—my aim is to get the students to see similar themes in the lives of Latinxs, Native Americans, Asian Americans, Jewish

Americans, and Arab Americans in the theories presented in the books by Anzaldua, Spindel, Nelson, Heilman, and Bayoumi. Here is the introduction to my opening lecture:

"Between me and the other world there is ever an unasked question: unasked by some through feelings of delicacy; by others through the difficulty of rightly framing it. All, nevertheless, flutter round it. They approach me in a half-hesitant sort of way, eye me curiously or compassionately, and then, instead of saying directly, How does it feel to be a problem? they say, I know an excellent colored man in my town?" The writer of these words is W.E.B. Du Bois (1903) and the "unasked question" is an endless query about what it means to be of African descent in America. Du Bois issued this question long before the undoing of legal segregation, during a time when lynching and other forms of racial violence that can be considered terrorism afflicted the daily lives of African American people. For the man born into an integrated community in Great Barrington and became a Harvard trained sociologist, owing to his skin color, could not avoid the harsh reality of being Black in America no matter the relative privilege he was born into. In his probing question: "How does it feel to be a problem?," Du Bois exposes the melancholic sense, a life of conflicting identities—a double consciousness—caused by racial inequality.

For the next 20 minutes I want us to explore Du Bois' psychological critique of the barriers between racial and ethnic groups through the concept he called "double consciousness." Du Bois first introduced the concept of "double consciousness" in his 1897 *Atlantic Monthly* article, "Strivings of the Negro People." Double consciousness is, however, more popularly known for Du Bois' profound reincarnation in the introductory chapter of *The Souls of Black Folk*. Writing in 1903, Du Bois insisted that racial dilemmas exist as a curse among the marginalized people of America. His thesis of double consciousness speaks to the struggles of the African American community haunted by slavery, Jim Crowism, and socially accepted forms of racial oppression. Double consciousness exists, in Du Bois's point of view, as a blessing and a curse. While dividing Blacks from Whites through a sense of second-sightedness that patently escapes the White majority, living life behind a veil offers African Americans a unique insight into the meaning of freedom that is misunderstood by the ruling majority, or their White counterparts.

The Souls of Black Folk examines the progress of African Americans since emancipation, namely the obstacles to progress and the possibilities for future progress in the 20th century. In it, Du Bois exposes the material causes of racism at the turn of the century and explains the effects that racism has had on Black identity by arguing, ultimately, that due to institutional racism and the failed Reconstruction promise of post-racialism, the political and economic gap between Whites and Blacks had actually widened since the abolition of slavery. Arguably the beginning point of the civil rights movement in the 20th century, Du Bois' book, like Rachel Carson's *Silent Spring* (1963), Betty Freidan's *The Feminine Mystique* (1963) and Michelle Alexander's *The New Jim Crow* (2010) would do in future years, launched a nationwide civil rights movement that eventually led to the defeat of legal discrimination in the United States.

Beginning in 1897, Du Bois started writing about double consciousness as a way to describe the perpetual mental state of confusion and alienation felt by African American people. In constructing the concept of double consciousness, Du Bois was able to redefine three centuries of interactions between White and Black people. This psychoanalytical notion explains the divergent feelings, a double-sighted mental state that forces African Americans to neither reject America nor live life too vociferously wherein they challenge the status quo. Du Bois's passage deserves uninterrupted prose.

"It is a peculiar sensation, this double-consciousness, this sense of always looking at one's self through the eyes of others, of measuring one's soul by the tape of a world that looks on in amused contempt and pity. One ever feels his two-ness, an American, a Negro; two souls, two thoughts, two unreconciled strivings; two warring ideals in one dark body, whose dogged strength alone keeps it from being torn asunder. The history of the American Negro is the history of this strife—this longing to attain self-conscious manhood, to merge his double self into a better and truer self. In this merging he wishes neither of the older selves to be lost. He does not wish to Africanize America, for America has too much to teach the world and Africa. He wouldn't bleach his Negro blood in a flood of White Americanism, for he knows that Negro blood has a message for the world. He simply wishes to make it possible for a man to be both a Negro and an American without being cursed and spit upon by his fellows, without having the doors of opportunity closed roughly in his face" (Du Bois, 1903).

Double consciousness is the active awareness of two conflicting identities that cannot be entirely merged together. The first identity is seeing the world through the eyes of an African American. The second conscious is observed as African Americans looking at themselves through the eyes of White Americans. It is a *split identity* overcome with a sense of estrangement as one tries to be both American and African in a White dominated society that historically suppresses the Black population as a subclass with limited chances at freedom, social mobility, or the development of a culture. Wary though Du Bois was of what's now known as "stereotype threat," a self-fulfilling prophecy, of interracial dependence and submission to an attitude of inferiority, his concept of double consciousness enabled him to offer solutions for a community struggling to find a place in modern America. When written in 1903, *The Souls of Black Folk* touched on serious racial problems that plagued the American and democratic promise that "all men are created equal."

Contextually speaking, while overtly addressing the failed promises of emancipation and equality with the collapse of Reconstruction and the implementation of the so-called Jim Crow laws, Du Bois hints that America's racial problems aren't isolated to the country's soil. Just years earlier, the United States had defeated Spain in a war that won the country annexed territory and colonized "brown and black" people in the Philippines, Guam, Cuba, and Puerto Rico. It is important, then, to see the African American civil rights struggle as interconnected with any fight for freedom by indigenous Black and Brown people worldwide. To help in the Pan-African fight, Du Bois called for the development of an intellectual infrastructure within the African American population. He charged Black intellectuals to become the best of the best. Consigned with duties to lead the reform movement for civil rights and social equality, his "Talented Tenth" would be made in Du Bois's image: college educated, analytical, and learned.[1]

Du Bois's psychosomatic theory of double consciousness had a lasting influence on future intellectuals such as the Black British critic of American Studies Paul Gilroy,

---

1. Du Bois., 73–76.

and writers James Baldwin and Ralph Ellison. To Gilroy, comparing the experiences of African people living America, the Caribbean, and Europe best discloses notions about Black identity and double consciousness. Gilroy (1993) writes about this transnational examination of Black identity in an interdisciplinary book titled *The Black Atlantic: Modernity and Double Consciousness*. The transatlantic slave trade, he contends, was the leading institution that enabled the West to establish economic, scientific, and cultural hegemony over African people on three continents of the Atlantic world. Gilroy's indicting insight sees the United States as a unique phenomenon that had manufactured systems of social control. African people were brought to America, where they make up the minority. This stands in contrast to colonized places of Africa where indigenous people were forced to live under the ruling thumb of the European minority. In America, African people have always considered themselves alienated persons that (1) aren't indigenous to the land they inhabit, and (2) can only trace their heritage back to the slave ship. The physical distance between mother country and the colonized people was not the issue. Rather, the social, political and economic disadvantages created by slavery, and the unremorseful stripping away of African culture in the form of lost surnames, language and religion amounted to a domestic form of colonialism and a unique variation of double consciousness. Forged during the crucible of the Atlantic slave trade, the world's African people now "stand between [at least] two great cultural assemblages," Gilroy argues, while adding an homage to Du Bois's concept of twoness: "Striving to be both European and Black requires some specific forms of double consciousness."

Double consciousness is an inconspicuous reality. As a possible resolution, Gilroy advances the image of a ship in motion across the space between Europe, Africa, America, and the Caribbean. Describing a ship sailing across the Atlantic Ocean, Gilroy implies that the image explains the diasporic transportation of culture throughout the Atlantic region. He concludes, "ships immediately focus attention on the middle passage, on the various projects for redemptive return to an African homeland, on the circulation of ideas and activists as well as the movement of key cultural and political artifacts: tracts, books, gramophone records, and choirs" (Gilroy, 1993). As Gilroy's book shows, any notions of double consciousness must be grounded in intercontinental, or pan-African, roots. African customs made the journey. They mixed with European traditions. It produced something unique in America. "[T]his inside/outside relationship should be recognized as a more powerful, more complex, and more contested element in the historical, social, and cultural memory of our glorious nation than has previously been supposed," he writes conclusively. It is wrong to write only about the establishment of African roots in America. What does European imperial conquest tell us about the development of double consciousness? How did the slave trade and arrival in America contribute to the intensification of a split identity? Gilroy's use of the ship, therefore, "remains perhaps the most important conduit of Pan-African communication."

As Gilroy shows, Africans in America and Africans in Europe are not poles apart in terms of culture. This sense of Pan-Africanism binds people of African descent in all places of the Atlantic world. To think that African Americans have a pure culture that is uniquely American is wrong. African American culture is an intermixture of Europe and Africa. For this reason, double consciousness is a psychological state that affects dark people throughout Gilroy's "Black Atlantic." Here exists a fusion of global Afrocentrism that is not purely African or American or Caribbean or European. We see in the "Black Atlantic" a hybrid mix of Black culture. Gilroy (1993) states, "I want to develop the suggestion that cultural historians could take the Atlantic as one sin-gle, complex unit of analysis in their discussions of the modern world and use it to produce an explicitly transnational and intercultural perspective."

Then there is James Baldwin, who once wrote, "Someone, someday, should do a study in depth of the role of the American Negro in the mind and life of Europe" (Gilroy, 1993). This assertion is a compliment to Gilroy's thesis of the Black Atlantic. Baldwin had left his Harlem home at the age of 24 to live as an expatriate in Paris for most of his adult life. On both sides of the Atlantic Ocean, Baldwin was able to craft his own form of double consciousness. Some of his notions about the topic are penned in *The Fire Next Time*. Baldwin sees the perpetuation of double consciousness a product of colonialism and the preservation of White supremacy after the decision in *Brown v. Topeka Board of Education*. Like Gilroy, Baldwin (1962) claims African Americans are unique because of diasporic slavery forced Africans to the United States. "The American Negro is a unique creation; he has no counterpart anywhere," wrote Baldwin. But it is not so much Baldwin's discourse about colonialism in *The Fire Next Time* that he espouses counter-narratives to Du Bois's double consciousness or Gilroy's Black Atlantic. In fact, Baldwin writes candidly that White Americans must talk honestly about racial justice. It was Baldwin's comment in a short essay "White Man's Guilt" (1965) that appeared in Ebony magazine where he exposes his own vulnerability, admitting the color of his skin functions "as a most disagreeable mirror." Nearly 60 years after the publication of Du Bois's *The Souls of Black Folk*, Baldwin offers a challenge to White Americans to see themselves through two lenses, to consider themselves the racialized "Other." He closes *The Fire Next Time* with an impassioned plea: "If we-and now I mean the relatively conscious Whites and the rel-atively conscious Blacks, who must, like lovers, insist on, or create, the consciousness of the others-do not falter in our duty now, we may be able, handful that we are, to end the racial nightmare, and achieve our country, and change the history" (Baldwin, 1962).

After the presentation, which spans 20 to 30 minutes, many of the stu-dents can register the authenticity of their summer reading texts by draw-ing distinctions between Du Bois's "double consciousness" and Anzaldua's "border consciousness theory" in Latinx culture as well as Bayoumi's Mus-lim American post–9/11 problem theory. For the first time in my students' lives—especially for White students—there is a realization that any close reading of double consciousness reveals resonant issues with other racial and ethnic groups in America. Though penned at a time when very few Lat-inxs lived in the United States, and while America's indigenous population was driven to near extinction by way of government policy, and during a period when most Asians inhabited parts along the West Coast, and while less than a percent of the population were Arab Muslims, Du Bois's claim that "one dark body" facing "warring ideals" is likewise applicable to any non–Western European person living within systematic subjugation in the United States. Twoness has always remained a valid lived sensation for Peo-ple of Color at any time of the nation's history. The books by Anzaldua, Nel-son, Spindel, Heilman, and Bayoumi tackle the interconnected racial and ethnic experiences called the "matrix of domination" by feminist sociologist Patricia Hill Collins (1990). These works move students away from limiting their train of thought on only race or only gender or only sexuality or only between Black and White to identify in-group as well as interracial inequities. "Intersectionality" is the analytical term critical race theorist Kimberle Crenshaw created in 1989 to describe these multiple markers of identity.

Though my presentation might come across as a bit heavy for high schoolers commencing a course in which they will engage in a year-long conversation about race, they are generally capable of connecting Du Bois's theory to their own lives and to their summer reading books. After listening to the lecture, Brian, one of the many White students in the course, asked: "So, if you're White, you don't wake up in the morning thinking about being White. But if you're a minority, you do? I can say I have never left my house before school thinking about my existence as a White person, and how that might impact my day."

To which Peter, who is Congolese, responded, "Exactly. Because everywhere you go it will be a White atmosphere. This school. The shopping mall. A party." He explained further: "As a black person at this school, I am often the only black kid in a classroom or at a party. I'm not as uncomfortable as I used to be having been in the district for many years, but it still feels different because I am often wondering what the others think of me."

"Wow," Brian said as he bounced his hands off his forehead in a gesture that suggested his mind had just exploded. "Granted, not very much, but I have found myself in that situation before. I never thought of it like that, though. I was just uncomfortable. I remember thinking to myself, so how do I act? Do I act in a certain way to fit in? Or do I get defensive and act in a way that might bring harm to me? I felt to myself, can I act in a way that no one sees me?"

In Brian's case, he, too, felt a sense of powerlessness during those few instances where he was the outsider. Brian's uneasiness when forced into a situation that made him think about his racial identity created a sensation that few White people ever experience. For White individuals unlike Brian who have never attempted to reflect on his or her own experiences or who have never been forced to think about the ways Whites and Blacks experience race and racism differently, they carry racial indifference while simultaneously embracing presumptions about the varying degrees of life experiences. Professor Crystal Fleming (2019) writes in *How Can I Be Less Stupid About Race* that 99 percent of the population has never formally studied race, and accordingly acquire a "cesspool of silly ideas, half-truths, and ridiculous misconceptions" about their racial counterparts. Popular culture, mass media, and political discourse, she argues, uphold White supremacist beliefs while shaping racial fallacies, racial scripts, and stereotypes. On the second day of the school year, Brian was challenged to examine the moments in his life when he felt alienated by his surroundings, including a degree of introspection about how he might have been stereotyped and how he felt insecure when he questioned what other people were thinking about him. Moreover, Brian was forced to deepen his racial sensibilities by thinking about how his lack of interaction with People of Color shaped his presumptions of his racial counterparts.

But what about every other White student at Gap that never thought about his or her own racial identity? What about those who avoid deep reflection on how racial scripts are both shaped and imposed upon individuals representing non-dominant cultures? Brian and his White peers are not an anomaly. A July 2015 CBS News/*New York Times* (Dutton, De Pinto, Salvanto, and Backus, 2015) survey reported that Whites have far less daily interaction with People of Color than People of Color have with Whites. At an astounding rate of 79 percent, White Americans admitted that few or none of the people in their community are People of Color. Moreover, 70 percent of Whites reported that they regularly come into contact with either few or no People of Color when they go out in public. The CBS News/*New York Times* report revealed the workplace is a similar experience. Over 80 percent of Whites admitted to coming into contact with either few or no Colleagues of Color. On the contrary, Workers of Color claim they work with Whites colleagues all the time.

Conversation about the students' summer reading books is only a first step toward engaging my Seminar in Critical Race Studies students in uncomfortable conversations about a broader system and structure of racism. It also allows for an appropriate transition from racial awareness into the next topic: the social construction of race.

The "Civility Myth" and the Making of Race

Serena Williams lost the women's singles tennis championship at the 2018 U.S. Open in dramatic fashion. Her defeat came in straight sets at the hands of Japan's Naomi Osaka. The fact that Williams lost one game by penalty was not why Osaka won; in fact, it seemed quite apparent that the 20-year-old was going to defeat her tennis idol in straight sets. Osaka's solid performance frustrated Williams to a point that the 23-time winner of Major singles titles appeared to act "uncivil." Williams' uncharacteristic display began when chair umpire Carlos Ramos gave the 36-year-old American a point deduction for smashing her racket. Moments later, after going down four games to three games in the second set, Williams was issued a game penalty by Ramos for allegedly taking a pointer from her coach, Patrick Rodrigue, making the score 5-to-3. Williams became defensive, claiming, "I don't cheat to win. I'd rather lose." Believing the game penalty was due to her consistent complaints between games, an emotional Williams called Ramos a "thief" and a "liar." When she made the match 5 to 4 in straight serves, she spent the time between services in tears. Six serves later, Osaka won the match 2–0 (6–2, 6–4).

The image of arguably tennis's most dominant player pointing her finger at Ramos inside Arthur Ashe Stadium demanding an apology was one of the ugliest episodes in the history of the U.S. Open; at least, that is how the talking heads, including ESPN's Steven A. Smith and tennis great Roger Federer portrayed it. The Grand Slam Committee later issued Williams fines amounting to $17,000 and two years of probation for three code violations. The conditions of the probation stated that if she were penalized once more during the probationary window, the fine would increase to $175,000 and Williams would be prohibited from participating in the subsequent U.S. Open.

I use footage of the Osaka-Williams match as the attention grabber for leading my students into an examination of how the notion of civility—as reflected in how the media and other members of the sports world responded to Williams' behavior—is commonly used as a method of separating non-dominant cultural groups from dominant cultural groups. Additionally, during the unit's introduction, the students read James Baldwin's "On Being White.... And Other Lies" to think about how and why race exists as a social construction, rather than an element of genetics or biology. If the video of the U.S. Open and the Baldwin treatise were the only texts in the lesson, the students in Seminar in Critical Race Studies would hardly have anything to contribute once we engaged in a critical dialogue. Marrying the social construction of race with the myth of civility is a complicated exercise that necessitates historical, political, economic, scientific, social, and philosophical points of view to understand. To prepare 15- to 18-year-olds that have never seen race as an invention to preserve a caste system for the critical dialogue, I provide students five additional sources and a short lecture on the topic and ask that they develop an outline for a hypothetical 1,200-word paper. Students must use either the reaction to the Osaka-Williams match or Baldwin's "On Being White.... And Other Lies" as a hook, write a thesis statement, include three supporting claims, and use two of the five texts as evidence per claim. Students then spend two days in class and two evenings at home scrutinizing Nina Jablonski's 2009 TED Talk "Skin Color Is an Illusion"; the U.S. Census "Standards on Race and Ethnicity," which explains how the Census Bureau classifies races in the United States; National Public Radio correspondent Karen Grigsby Bates's "When Civility Is Used as a Cudgel Against People of Color," which ran as part of a special series titled "Civility Wars" in March 2019; and one episode of the three-part documentary "The Power of an Illusion, Part 2." The counterargument offered to students is the introduction to the 1922 book *A Study of American Intelligence* by eugenicist Carl Campbell Brigham. I interrupt the students' investigation of the topic with a brief contextual lecture in which I offer a research question: "Why is the concept of 'civility' associated with the construction of race?" The presentation allows me to speak on five myths about race: (1) that some races are physically superior to others, (2) that some races are mentally superior to others, (3) that each race has a distinct culture that is genetically transmitted along with physical traits, (4) that race determines behavior of individuals, and (5) that racial mixing lowers biological quality. Students are not allowed to make comments or ask questions during the presentation except if they need me to repeat something. I tell them to take notes and make a list of questions that should be referenced during their research on the topic. I also encourage them to bring up questions later in critical dialogue.

The students view the 15-minute clip of the Osaka-Williams match on the first day of the activity. I do provide some context by telling everyone that the succeeding two days would be spent interrogating the difference between race and ethnicity, and how each have been treated in the creation of a racial hierarchy. It is easy to imagine that the only thing in that moment the students get out of the video is that Serena Williams is African American and Naomi Osaka is a mixed raced Japanese-Haitian representing Japan. They are told that although no formal discussion on the video will occur until the critical dialogue, the notes they kept should be used to weigh in on any insight gathered by the additional texts. I am always confident the students will figure out how to incorporate the video into class discussion and their outlines once they read or watch the supplemental texts. The outlines are due on the third day of the lesson.

When the time arrives for students to submit their outlines and participate in the discussion, I begin the critical dialogue with a cluster of questions that picks up on the short lecture on the myths of race I gave the previous day. Students are told they can respond to any or all of the following questions:

> If African Americans have higher rates of tuberculosis, infant mortality, sickle-cell anemia, but whites have higher rates of cancer and heart disease, is it true that some races are physically superior to others?
>
> Would you agree that not everyone has the same home life, social class background, quality of education, and health? Are we to believe IQ tests are a good indication that some races have mental superiority over others?
>
> Is it true that each inbred population has a unique culture that can't be transmitted to other races?
>
> If you were to think about the worst behaved students at [Gap], would you say race determines behavior?
>
> Is it fair to say that racial mixing lowers biological quality?

The students patiently waited for me to ask all five questions. As soon as the opportunity presented itself, one of the more vocal students in the class, a sophomore named Erica, stated: "For the first question, a particular group will appear to be strong in some respects but weak in others. Isn't achievement based on lived experiences and what is available in lived circumstances?"

To which Jake responded: "I think Erica has a point. When I drive around the city, I see park after park, basketball court after basketball court. I don't see any advertisements for free golf courses or accessible music instruments."

A junior named Charity took the conversation in a different direction. "I did some research over the summer on infant mortality. Sometimes doctors don't take some patients seriously with prenatal health care. I've read that Black women aren't taken seriously at times when they complain about pain or whatever because they are considered weaker, I guess, so their concerns aren't properly looked into." Her remark, which has since been corroborated by a Pew Research Center survey (Funk et al., 2019) showing 70 percent of African Americans and 63 percent of Latinxs believe medical misconduct by doctors is a big problem, moved the group toward reflecting on implicit biases held by doctors and nurses in the medical field.

One of Charity's friends reacted to her insight. A sophomore named Nguyen recalled, "My mom who is a nurse at Lancaster General [Hospital] told me once that White patients have refused to be treated by one of their doctors, who happens to be Indian."

Brionne, an African American student, entered the conversation by referencing her summer reading book, Michael Eric Dyson's *Was Bill Cosby Right?: Or Has the Black Middle Class Lost Its Mind?*: "In regards to what Charity was saying about the doctors, in the book I read over the summer, Michael Eric Dyson said there were more deaths of Black women going into labor than White women. When a Black person is seen by a doctor without health insurance they are not taken as seriously as a [White] patient with insurance."

"I get that," Charity replied. "There are certain jobs available to White people that offer health care benefits that a lot of Black people don't have access to. Even if a Person of Color has a good resume, the White applicant might have the right connections and references, and would therefore win the job."

After pulling out her notes, kept tidy at the front of her three-ringed binder, Brionne informed us, "Blacks lag behind Whites in employer-sponsored health care by 71 percent. Less than 40 percent of Blacks have private pension plans, but 46 percent of Whites do. This was a long time ago—2002 and 2003—but Dyson said 2 in 5 young Black people had no health insurance."

"In the book I read this summer," began Katie, a new student to the conversation, "the author [Tim Wise's *White Like Me*] boarded a plane that was going to be flown by two Black pilots. It was the first time he'd ever seen Black pilots and he was reluctant at first to get in his seat. Then he told himself, 'I had to remind myself that they are just as qualified as any White pilot to fly a plane.' He even admitted that he knew of White pilots that had been pulled off planes before liftoff because they were drunk. Wise conceded that he had been wired like all Whites to question the competence of Black pilots because they were Black."

When discussing racial biases in the medical and aviation fields lost its spirit, I refocused the students on the original comments offered by Erica and Jake. I said, "According to Erica's original comment pertaining to what opportunities exist for folks that live in the suburbs versus those in the city, I want to ask something about sports: how is the White quarterback compared to the Black quarterback?"

The class's football expert, a sophomore named Landon, started to explain his opinion on how White versus Black quarterbacks are contrasted: "Well, Tom Brady is described as accurate, a precision passer..." he started to say before getting interrupted by a peer.

Jaylen finished Landon's answer: "Well, Cam Newton is described as more athletic than Tom Brady. I see where you're getting at. Tom Brady is described as intelligent. There is an implicit nature of sports commentary. I have never heard [White and Black] quarterbacks described any other way."

Jaylen is a relatively tall, lean African American senior with a quiet demeanor. His peers know him as a track and field sprinter. He typically says very little; on this day, however, he felt comfortable enough to share both his insight on Black and White professional athletes as well as how his family has worked to overcome biases that are a result of racial scripts.

> I don't know if this is related to what we are saying here, but my older brother has struggled to find a job after college. His name is Samar. The people hiring him are not comfortable with the name Samar and draw conclusions once they see that name on a resume. I mean, I know there are people that don't have as good of a resume as my brother, but they get jobs.

Amanda responded by offering a few questions of her own: "Why not keep the names off the resume so implicit bias doesn't influence who the hiring committee calls in for an interview. How would putting a name on a resume illustrate the experience that a person has? Wouldn't you need to talk to the person to see what kind of experience they have?" The class engaged with Amanda's questions for a few minutes before falling silent. The hush caused students to either look down at their desks or put their eyes on me hoping I could offer further insight into Amanda's queries, which asked all of us to address implicit bias in hiring practices.

ME: "A few years ago, a trend by many organizations and companies was to remove the names of all job applicants. It is believed by some that this colorevasive approach into hiring helps People of Color attain job interviews. If there is no name, there can't be unconscious biases. But let me ask you this question, 'Is this type of Human Resource screening the right thing to do when choosing job applicants? On one hand, it can certainly elude the search committee's implicit bias. In contrast, it doesn't ensure that the pool of interviewees will be diverse. I want you to think of our school district, where there is only one African American teacher and just four total Teachers of Color in the entire district. Would the colorevasive approach be the best solution to fix our district's Teacher of Color shortage problem? In a racially stratified society where chances to accumulate resume credentials skews toward White males, in particular, can we settle on moving in the direction of colorevasive resumes? Did any of the texts you looked at the last 48 hours offer insight into what might be the best solution?'"

ERICA: "I don't recall one specific thing mentioned by any of the sources; however, what I gather, particularly from the Baldwin article, is that there has to be some kind of understanding that minority candidates more often [than Whites] come from a background that didn't allow them to accrue connections and on-the-job experiences specifically out of a lack of opportunity. So putting the name back on the resume makes it fairer for companies to guarantee a diverse group of candidates be interviewed."

I was pleased that Erica could at least reference one of the texts used in research (Baldwin) when offering the class a solution to our school district's hiring disparity. But it was time to refocus the discussion since we arrived at a point where the students were dependent upon me to fill in gaps. We were also navigating along the fringes of the topic of race as a social construct. So I subtly moved the class's focus toward the unit's opening texts: the 2018 U.S. Open tennis match between Williams and Osaka and Baldwin's essay, "On Being White.... and Other Lies."

Whether they agreed or not, I was testing the students on their ability to argue for or against the notion that race is a social invention, as all of the documents fixed on the point that the construction of race was driven by, first European, and later, American policies. I asked them to think about the "Race: The Power of Illusion" documentary when the narrator claims that both the institution of slavery and treatment of Native American people preceded the construction of racial categories in America. So when the races were created—white, black, red, yellow, and brown—they were created to reinforce certain policies and to keep darker groups subservient to the White ruling class.

Another conversation started: Assuming that the students learned about the myth of the American melting pot in their U.S. History class (full disclosure, many of these students had me as their United States History teacher in previous years), I asked, "How does the idea of the American 'melting pot' shape beliefs about race and civility?"

ERICA: "Well, every ethnic group is supposed to have blended into a single American culture."

ME: "Did or does that actually happen?" To this question, most of the students shook their heads side to side indicating no. "Then, what was the reason to come up with this illusion that America is a place where ethnic groups can live side-by-side without disagreements?"

CHARITY: "It forces people to conform."

ME: "Conform or to assimilate into what?"

CHARITY: "White values, I guess."

After looking for a new student to respond, Brian raised his hand and said: "If you refused to assimilate to white values, you'll be treated as un–American."

ME: "Take a look at the Baldwin article. There is a line in the second-to-last paragraph that reads: 'We—who were not Black before we got here either, who were defined as Black by the slave trade…. If we had not survived [the slave trade], and triumphed there would not be a Black American alive.' Then he closes the essay, 'It is a terrible paradox, but those who believed that they could control and define Black people divested themselves of the power to control and define themselves.' What is he saying?"

A junior named Tyler figured it out: "So if you take a look at the merging of all these various European ethnicities into a single race being White, there is a racial caste system formed that maintains White supremacy."

ME: "I wonder if the rest of you see it like Tyler. As you think about what he just said, and as you were reading Baldwin and as you looked over the other sources, especially the Jablonski Ted Talk, can you explain the blending of African ethnicities into a single Black race?"

SADIYA: "The Baldwin passage has me thinking about an argument I have had with other students over slavery. They were arguing that, 'Why was slavery so bad if Africans were selling other Africans into slavery?' You know, they were trying to justify white people selling black people as slaves. I didn't agree with them, but I couldn't defend my position."

ME: "So what are you thinking now?"

SADIYA: "The way you've laid out all of the readings, and from what everyone is saying today, I'm starting to see that Africans were not one racial group at the time of the slave trade. Meaning, African tribes were different groups rather than one race of people."

ME: "Or ethnicities."

SADIYA: "Yeah. So it wasn't like Black Africans were selling their own Black Africans to Europeans. They were selling a prisoner of a different ethnicity or of a different cultural group. To Africans in the 1500s or 1600s, they did not consider themselves a race of Black people like we all think today."

Sadiya is a one of the higher achieving students in the junior class. Though not overly talkative in class, and while it was not uncommon for her to give a profound insight during random stages of our critical dialogues, this contribution was particularly remarkable. Her insight created an opportunity for me to speak a little on the theoretical formula that produced racial classifications: the divine "curse" theory (belief that the descendants of Noah's son, Ham, would become slaves), the eugenics movement in the late 19th and early 20th centuries, and polygenesis (belief that multiple creation stories occurred). I then asked her peers to respond to another question: "Did anyone pay particular attention to the times when the words 'civilized' and 'uncivilized' were either used or implied in the texts?"

AMANDA: "To piggy back on what Sadiya said, I think within America, in theory, 'civilized' is connected to religion; and religion is connected to morals. If you are Christian, then you have Christian morals that the majority supports and so you are therefore 'civilized.' If you are not Christian—like African slaves sold in the slave trade—or are not at all religious, it can be possible that you can [still] have morals, but people don't see something backing up your morals. So it's in question and therefore you're not 'civilized.' This idea also amounts to the justification of creating and then enslaving a certain group."

ME: "So if you don't conform to White, Christian, heterosexual, values, you are thus not part of the American melting pot. Then what happens? Why has American society continuously found ways to label darker groups uncivilized before and after slavery?"

TYLER: "As Amanda said, well, one of the misconceptions of race is behavior. Civilized would be good behavior. So when we associate one person with bad behavior, the entire race becomes characterized as uncivilized. Like the [Karen Grigsby Bates] NPR podcast said, 'civility is used to contain nonconformists, or, in this context, people of color.'"

ME: "Yes, the text claims higher expectations for civility are imposed upon racialized groups. We are talking about racial scripts. This is a term I would like you all to know. Racial scripts are patterns or narratives about racialized groups that have been passed down generationally, and thus link people across various times and spaces although members of the racial group never meet. Scripts perpetuate stereotypes that are applied to entire racial, ethnic, or gender groups rather than looking at people as individuals. That is what Tyler is getting at. We have racial scripts that describe the Asian American as erudite. The Latinx as criminal. The Native American as once savages and now substance abusive. You go through life and you watch movies or the 6 o'clock news and these racial scripts get reinforced and seared into your brain. Meanwhile, you reach teenage years and these presumptions have never been challenged."

SADIYA: "Some people are afraid about what they don't really know about yet. They look for one thing [wrong] that one person of a different racial group does and they tend to stereotype the entire group. It makes it easier to understand the minority group better."

EMMA: "Discerning who is civilized and uncivilized could help with constructing racial hierarchies, and who is in power and who makes the laws."

ME: "So, Sadiya is saying that one person comes to represent an entire race and Emma is speaking about justification. If you see a group out there you're deeming as uncivilized, that justifies the actions you do to them; it validates the

American government taking land away from Native Americans because they aren't Christian. It rationalizes the enslavement of African people because they aren't Christian. It justifies giving longer prison sentences to darker hued people because the racial script is that they are prone to violence. True or not, believing that they are prone to violence creates a false presumption in the White conscience. Thus, it is easier to issue out a longer sentence to Black people for the same crime committed by a White person."

WILLOW: "I feel like in a lot of instances people already believe stereotypes and they don't need evidence. Or they witnessed only one person do something wrong, and that serves as the only evidence for calling an entire group uncivilized."

ERICA: "The Founders said that 'all men are created equal,' but they didn't consider African Americans to be men, so they would use that as a way to restrict their rights [when writing laws]."

ME: "One of the things I also asked you to think about is the term 'Other.' How does the racial hierarchy make it easy to 'Other' someone? Is it another way of calling someone 'uncivilized?' I think that what Erica and Willow are saying here is about misinterpreting the other person's culture. And if you don't understand the culture of another group of individuals, you think your way [of life] is better. You can be part of a sports program at one school but transfer to a new school and think the way it was done at your previous school was better. And yet you go to that new school and your team wins as many games if not more. You're not used to that, you're not comfortable with how things are done. And if you can identify that with racialized groups as well or with non–Christians as well, then you say 'Well, their religion is not as good as mine. They won't be saved. They are inferior.' You have just 'Othered' them. In that sense, we don't need legislation to keep different religions, or races, or genders apart, but it can be the accepted form of discrimination in a society."

BRIONNE: "There are stereotypes of Black women that I have endured. When we [Black women] decide to express ourselves we are portrayed as angry."

ME: "So what are you getting at here?"

BRIONNE: "I am getting at that, even when people are wealthy and popular, such as Serena Williams…"

ME: "Keep going!"

BRIONNE: "…they are still viewed as uncivilized. When she decided to defend herself at the U.S. Open, there were people that painted her as uncivilized. There was even a political cartoon that caricaturized her like a gorilla."

The critical dialogue did not end there. I referred the students to Kimberle Crenshaw's scholarship on Intersectionality as a way to get them to think about overlapping methods of oppression as it pertained to how Serena Williams was treated by the public after the 2018 U.S. Open. The students brought up the disparity of how many times Williams had been drug tested versus other professional tennis players. They cited examples when male tennis professionals were not punished when acting in a similar manner. Some commented on how the girls are commonly talked over by boys in the school during club meetings or student council. Brionne brought up the time in 2014 when Stanford graduate and member of the NFL's Seattle Seahawks Richard

Sherman, who is African American, was called a thug by football analysts after an emotional post-game interview in a victory over the San Francisco 49ers. "Sherman said getting called a 'thug' was another way of being called the N-word," she said. "He was deemed uncivilized in that moment, but Trump wasn't when he called NFL players SOBs."

Mark, a new voice in the dialogue, but known to his peers as a sports enthusiast (he is the shooting guard on the high school's basketball team) said, "Let me be devil's advocate. Williams' coach admitted on ESPN that he was coaching Serena during the match. Now, he said every coach does it..."

Michelle, a member of the school's girls' tennis and basketball teams, interrupted him. "It is so rare to see coaching violations, especially in big matchups like this one."

> MARK: "Yeah, but she didn't handle this well. She has a habit of complaining when she's down a set. In this case, she certainly overreacted."
>
> MICHELLE: "I don't think she overreacted. I read that Serena's sister, Venus, had a similar interaction with that same judge a year ago."
>
> MARK: "Sure. What I am saying is that she shouldn't have been penalized. I just wanted her to let it go."
>
> ME: "Just a moment ago, we had two students, both athletes that I'm sure have been in competitive, high-intense situations before, debate over what Serena should or shouldn't have done. So, if you were writing a paper on race and sports or about race and the myth of civility, what solution would you offer in your conclusion?"
>
> AMANDA: "My first thought is directed to the media coverage. My takeaway from this debate is that there needs to be more diverse representation in sports journalism. Black writers likely see what happened differently than White sports columnists. And I am sure Black female columnist see what happened to Serena differently than everyone else. This would be my solution."
>
> ME: "This is a good start. But let me ask one final question: I'd like to come up with a formula that explains why it is important to understand the dimensions behind constructing racial categories. You finish this sentence: 'racial categories plus civil expectations/behavioral norms equals what?'"

Several students gave vague answers before Brionne responded in a word: "Privilege." To this answer, I referred students to Peggy McIntosh's 1988 article "Unpacking the Invisible Knapsack," which served as a primer for a future discussion and writing assignment on the existence or nonexistence of White privilege.

What was most pleasing is that the students collectively determined that behaviors are not genetically inherited traits. They agreed that behaviors are demeanors nurtured by social settings, policies, and popular culture. This is an important notion to bear in mind, as the next topic of conversation spotlights the varying attitudes about the Movement for Black Lives.

Nate Parker's AmeriCAN, Black Lives Matter and Implicit Bias

After the Thanksgiving holiday, Seminar in Critical Race Studies students are ready to study texts and engage in critical dialogues related to excessive police violence and Black Lives Matter, the most contentious topic examined during the school year. But it is not controversial in the way most might think. Students are genuinely ready for the conversation and surprisingly comfortable. Rather, the administration and parents have expressed the most concern about how the topic will be presented by me (as discussed in Chapter 7). In terms of duration, the Black Lives Matter lesson plan is the longest. I title the lesson "Dispute Over Etymology: Black Lives Matter, Blue Lives Matter, and All Lives Matter." The students spend four days in groups examining up to 30 sources that represent a vast array of perspectives and through a compendium of academic lenses, which include historical, political, aesthetic, cultural, and psychological examinations of newspaper articles, mainstream media coverage, music, artwork, polling data, poetry, film, book chapters, and comprehensive websites. The recommended sources, which the list can be seen in its entirety in figure 5.1 in Chapter 5, also strike a balance between the points of view in favor and opposed to Black Lives Matter. In their respective groups, students use the online newspaper archive Newspapers.com to conduct a content analysis of how the Movement for Black Lives was covered in two newspapers, *The Philadelphia Inquirer* and *The Los Angeles Times*, between 2015 and 2019, by using a coded metric that evaluates article length, voices used in the article, headline insinuation, and language that indicates either sympathy for or disapproval of #BLM protests. Then students synthesize their data with the knowledge gained from the 30 additional sources to develop an eight- to 10-minute group presentation that offers a research question, thesis statement, three supporting claims, one counterargument, one international perspective on #BLM, and solutions for the issue.

To provide students context beyond what they already know about the topic, I make a short presentation on Eddie S. Glaude Jr.'s *Democracy in Black: How Race Still Enslaves the American Soul* (2016). More specifically, I speak on Glaude's notion of the "value gap," the devaluing of Black lives that is entrenched within American values and systems, to help students reflect upon their presumptions about the Black Lives Matter movement. The thesis that I present to the students is that the disparity between the values placed on White lives versus the values placed on Black lives is not only seen through how police monitor Black communities or how White people speak to Black people, but through the differences between physical environments (size of houses, availability of open fields to play on, unkempt public parks, under-funded schools, cracked roads, condemned buildings). I share with students a personal story about my best friends from childhood. Shakka and Senica were twin brothers that lived along the border between a deprived part of Harrisburg called Allison Hill and my neighborhood, a wealthy part of the city called Bellevue Park. Near their childhood home is Reservoir Park, a place where I played in a summer basketball league with my older brother, Tommy, and our friends. My brother and I were the only White players in the basketball league. Each time I visited Shakka's and Senica's house, and each evening I had a basketball game at the park, I saw firsthand that the value placed on this community was not the same as where I lived. While Tommy and I played our basketball games, our younger sister, Crissy, who was forced by our parents to watch, passed the time by walking around the park collecting empty marijuana dime bags from the ground. She was too young to know what they were; but to the rest of us, experiences like this made everyone in my family think about our own lived experiences versus those whose social arrangements were devalued. I understood as a teenager that the community where my friends lived was not valued the same.

To get the class ready to engage in an open-ended critical dialogue, I ask, "What evidence exists today that might suggest Black lives aren't as valued as White lives?" The students reflect on Glaude's value gap theory. Glaude (2016) tells us to look at the double-digit unemployment rate among African Americans and to consider the mass incarceration disproportion between Whites and Blacks. He explains that social welfare was once a valued program by White Americans during the 1930s and 1940s; however, after African Americans became the face of welfare under Lyndon Johnson's "Great Society" in the 1960s, it is now a stigmatized program wherein Whites complain that welfare allows darker hued people to pull money away from honest taxpayers.

The class then screens the 15-minute short film *AmeriCAN* (2014) directed by actor Nate Parker. Be warned, what follows contains spoilers. I suggest that the film (found on YouTube) be viewed before reading any further. Packed into 15 minutes and in just three acts, *AmeriCAN* follows LAPD officer Jim Mitchell for one night while working the beat in inner city Los Angeles. The film opens with the Mitchell family at dinner. The family matriarch is talking about ice-creamed sandwiches and telling jokes to Bryce, the younger of two boys. Justin, the oldest son, engages with the family patriarch and film's main character, Jim, who is assigned to duty later that night, about whether he can go over to his friend's house after dinner.

Jim is asked by his son, "Can I go out tonight?"

Jim probes, "Out where?"

"I don't know. We'll figure it out when we get in the car," Justin replies.

Jim: "We who?"

"Me and JB," says Justin. Nobody reveals it at the moment, but viewers discover later that JB is African American and lives in the Black neighborhood that Jim is assigned to patrol.

"No," Jim says.

Justin later storms away after his father scolds him for texting at the dinner table.

The scene cuts to Justin's bedroom, where the teenager is playing a violent video game. Jim interrupts his son, and the two engage in a heart to heart. Jim tells his son, "I'm trying to keep you away from bad situations."

Justin replies: "So, JB is fine to hang out here, but if I want to go with him then…"

"I am not worried about JB. JB is a good kid," Jim assures his son. "What I'm saying is, is that I want some control over where you're at and who you are around with…. Trust me, you'll get it when you're older." The two hug it out, but not before Jim says, "You know I'm not going in [to work] with you still pissed at me. Look, we can do this the easy way or we can do this the hard way." And the two embrace. "I love you kid," Jim says to his son. "I want to keep you around."

"I know," replies Justin. "I love you too, Dad."

Later that night, when on the beat around 2:30 in the morning, Jim receives a dispatch that there has been a robbery at a liquor store. He sees four African American men in their twenties talking on a street corner. Jim's patrol car skids to a stop. He gets out and yells, "Let me see your hands. Shut your mouth. Put your hands up chest level. You know the drill." He asks further, "Are any of you on parole?" He then conducts a pat-down and asks, "Which one of you hit the liquor store on Greenleaf, huh? Don't try to play me. One of you knows something."

One of the men asks if he is under arrest and says to Jim, "Want to kiss my ass?"

The frisking yields nothing, so Jim lets the men go. At this juncture of the film, Jim sees three men in hoods walking in his direction. When their eyes meet his, the men sprint in the opposite direction. As they seek cover in a vacant parking lot, Jim pulls out his revolver and flashlight. Once a bottle clanks in the distance, the three men jump from their hiding spot. Jim then fires four shots in the direction of the noise. The slowest one in the group is shot and falls to the ground.

Men in the distance yell, "He shot him!"

"[This is a] Police matter, get back inside your house," Jim yells. "Want to go to jail, keep walking!"

The bystander yells: "I ain't going nowhere! You going to shoot me too? He didn't even have no gun!"

Feeling threatened, Jim calls for backup. But just as he arrives at the dead body on the ground, an African American teenager comes out of the darkness: "Mr. Mitchell?" the boy asks. In that moment, Jim sees that it is JB, his son's friend. Jim then turns the body over to find that he had shot his son, Justin, who had disobediently snuck out of the house.

In tears, Jim radios for an ambulance. He yells out, "Where are we? What is the address? What is the address here? Help me! Help me, please! Someone call an ambulance. Call 9–1–1! Help me!"

J-Cole's "Be Free" plays through the three remaining minutes of the film. Before the credits roll, a diverse group of men and women appear wearing hoods with American flag bandanas over their faces. Each individual pulls the bandana from his or her face, showing a range of White, Black, old, young, famous, and unknown Americans staring into the camera. Several hashtags are presented during the credits, including #AmeriCAN_Empathsize, #AmeriCAN_Heal, #AmeriCAN_Change, and #AllLivesMatter. Parker's short film released in 2014, before #AllLivesMatter became a counterpoint to #BlackLivesMatter.

More than anything, this film gets at the heart of the Black Lives Matter movement. No different than what Martin Luther King, Jr.'s followers in 1968 intended when they held signs declaring "I Am a Man," Black Lives Matter activists strive to ensure People of Color their worth as human beings. In and of itself, the movement has been successful in disrupting racial scripts and institutions that continually undervalue the lives of dark people. Parker's *AmeriCAN* does a brilliant job at giving students of all hues a resource to begin a dialogue on truths about implicit bias and problems that arise because many White Americans carry, in Robin DiAngelo's terms, "a white frame of reference": in one sense, this film allows us to think about what it feels like to be a police officer doing his or her job in impoverished communities known for having the highest rate of violence, substandard education, and high unemployment. From another point of view, the film presents a case where inhabitants of said communities endure intergenerational poverty caused by circumstances out of their control and find themselves watched over by heavily armed police forces. The critical dialogue in Seminar in Critical Race Studies about this topic allows everyone to offer insight about what Whiteness means to each individual in the context of implicit bias. The following exchange between my students and me illustrates the eagerness of young folks to share insight on this issue.

> ME: "Two things about the film: First, it is written and directed by an African American male. Second, the film is shot through the view of a White, male, middle class, police officer whose job it is to patrol the beat in a community he would otherwise never step foot in. Knowing that and considering our discussion about the value gap, what did you notice in the way Officer Mitchell

reacted in this film before he knew it had been his own son that he shot? Was Nate Parker justified in making a story with this point of view?"

JAKE: "Maybe it's because it's his son, but maybe if he shot an African American he wouldn't have been as quick to ask for someone to call an ambulance."

ME: "Was he quick to beg for someone to call for an ambulance?"

ERICA: "Well, he didn't show as much sympathy to the individual he shot until he realized it was his son."

WILLOW: "He didn't do anything up until the point he knew it was his son. And then he didn't show any emotion for what he did until he realized it was his son. It makes me think about how the police left Michael Brown's body in the middle of the street for three or four hours."

KATIE: "Before he knew it was his son, and while the crowd of bystanders— including the four African American men he patted down minutes earlier— he demanded they stay back: 'Back up! This is a police matter,' he told the onlookers. But then he realized it was his son, he cried for help. The thought by the bystanders was 'if it was one of us, you didn't care, but now that you know it's your son, you care.'"

CHARITY: "The lack of concern that police officer had was disturbing. He shot the perpetrator, but he was matter-of-fact about it. He wasn't sick about it."

ME: "Was less value placed on that life until Officer Mitchell found out it was his kid?"

AMANDA: "This doesn't answer your question directly, but at the end of the film, there is a guy wearing an #AllLivesMatter t shirt. I'm not sure if Parker was trying to have a uniting factor, but I think it would have been more in tune with the message of the rest of the film if they had people of different races wearing #BlackLivesMatter because the dad only shot a kid because he thought he was a Black hooligan that robbed a store or something. It's not like he saw a White kid in a hoodie and thought he was just as suspicious."

ME: "Just a reminder, this film was made in 2014. #AllLivesMatter became a rebuttal to #BLM in 2016."

AMANDA: "Okay, but let me finish this thought. Throughout the film, even if you tried to see from the police officer's perspective, he's still not portrayed in the best light to be cast in. Because of assumptions he made, he killed his son. So when I saw the #AllLivesMatter sweatshirt, I saw it less as uniting people. It struck me more that Nate Parker was trying to tone down the message so that it wasn't anti–White. If he put #BlackLivesMatter on his shirt, the viewers would say 'Well, it was a White kid that got shot.'"

CHARITY: "I thought back to when the police officer told his son not to go out with his friend, JB. So at the point in the film when a kid got shot, I thought it was JB, the Black friend. I was wondering what his [Officer Mitchell] reaction would have been if it was JB that he shot."

WILLOW: "Earlier in the night, when the cop drove up to the three [four] adult men smoking a cigarette on the street corner at two in the morning he said, 'You know the drill, turn around and spread your arms and legs.' I feel like that indicated his implicit bias, assuming that they were the ones who robbed the store."

ME: "A few things are on the floor here that we can discuss. One, clearly, if you're a police officer you need to use an aggressive tone when dealing with folks that need to adhere to the job you are doing. But I see your point, the assumption right away that they were involved in robbing a liquor store should be addressed. Second, our discussion about value and that shooting scene is the gripping part of the short film because he pulls the trigger four times, calls in the shooting to the police department, doesn't state that they needed an ambulance to the scene because somebody is down. He only asked for backup. He gets closer to the body, then turns the body and realizes it is his son. Then he gets on the radio and calls for an ambulance. None of that happened before he knew it was his son that he just shot. There is an implication here about value and the lack of value right away in that. All of your comments have danced around this fact. Look how many perspectives are being used to tell this story: you have the perspective of a teenage White kid, of a teenage Black kid, the perspective of a parent, you have the perspective of a police officer, and you have the perspective of adult age African American people. So there are many different points of view that are used to tell a story. So what do you think is the argument?"

ERICA: "I agree with what Amanda was saying earlier. When the kids were running away, the police officer couldn't have felt endangered because the kids were running away from him. And so if he just wanted them to stop running, why would he shoot four shots? If you want someone to stop, you don't shoot them multiple times in the back; that [action] is meant to kill."

ME: "Not too long ago in South Carolina, Walter Scott was shot in the back when running away from a police officer. He was killed by an officer of the law, and this happened in real life; which happen to be after this film was made. That was just a few years ago. That is where the psychological lens applies if you plan to write about this topic further. So police officers have the right to pull the trigger if they feel their lives are threatened. In many cases, that is what is stated. So in the case of the film, *AmeriCAN*, you have a White police officer in a setting that is dark, in an unfamiliar environment that I call the wilderness—see the class thesis on the syllabus. Just by being in that space he felt threatened. And that would be a subconscious reaction to pull the trigger even if an alleged criminal is running away. The question, however, that Erica is getting at is, 'does it excuse the decision to pull the trigger?'"

I continue further: "So, I ended my lecture earlier on the value gap with a question—and Erica's comment alluding to the death of Walter Scott in South Carolina—goes into the film: when the cop car that pulled up on those four Black individuals smoking a cigarette early in the morning, they knew exactly how they were going to be profiled; the question is, 'Is there a history behind why Colin Kaepernick takes a knee or why people march on the streets claiming Black Lives Matter? Does that just crop up out of thin air or is there a history that has led to where we are in the present day?'"

NICOLE: "This summer, I read the book *I Heard It Through the Grapevine* by Patricia Turner, who explains that there is a history of police violence toward Black people and government violence to Black people. She explores rumors and legends in African American culture to speak about the historical experience of dealing with oppression. The rumors in her book include Church's Chicken, which was rumored to be owned by the KKK and they put something in their chicken to make Black men sterile. Turner also wrote about how the government might have created AIDS; and that the government needed to test the AIDS virus before they employed it in war, so they went to Africa and spread the disease. Then they used AIDS to try to eradicate the Black race in America. She also said that Reebok is a White supremacist owned business that makes money off Black customers. Also that the KKK owned Tropical Fantasy which made a drink to make Black men sterile."

ME: "That is an excellent recollection of what is in Turner's book. But can anyone tell me why that is pertinent to this discussion?"

BRIONNE: "This distrust can be explained best knowing that rumors that exist about attacks on African Americans is not an issue that occurred in a historical isolation."

AMANDA: "I guess what you want us to see is that these rumors started from something real."

ME: "Yes! But what specifically?"

NICOLE: "The surfacing of the Tuskegee syphilis study and the cases in the '70s about hundreds of black women who were unknowingly sterilized by doctors only served to reopen these historic wounds, perpetuate anti–Black rumors, and ultimately led to Patricia Turner's effort to collect these oral texts during the 1980s."

ME: "Exactly! What else? Why would the Black and Brown populations as well as a good portion of White people see validity in the Black Lives Matter movement?"

NICOLE: "I am reading from my notes here, but Turner finds a pattern in the way rumors and legends occurred. Ingredient-based legends were linked to sterilization. Rumors that reference the government suggested AIDS, drugs—something that could be closely related to real government attacks on Black people in the form of the Tuskegee experiment or the crack epidemic that plagued the Black community. And conspiracies about sports apparel and sneakers were linked to White supremacist groups like the KKK, suggesting that Whites market products to exploit Black communities and to keep economic prosperity from potential Black business owners. Also the assassinations of Black civil rights leaders were linked to government agencies such as the CIA and FBI."

ME: "Stop, Nicole. I'm sorry to interrupt, but I want someone to deduce what she is getting at? What point is Nicole about to make?"

CHARITY: "The rumors she's talking about were actual things rooted in things that occurred in history. Rumors that the FBI created AIDS to exterminate Black people might not be real, but what is real is the Tuskegee syphilis experiment. So as a result, existing rumors originate from real things done by White people to oppress Black communities."

ME: "So Charity says Turner's book suggests that it's reasonable that People of Color view the White institutions of this country with skepticism. How can we apply that to Black Lives Matter?"

AMANDA: "There is some kind of fact that lies behind the Black resentment toward police. There is some kind of history of Black people getting attacked in some way by authorities."

ME: "Can anyone think of any examples of police violence on nonviolent Black civil rights protesters?"

ERICA: "The Selma march."

BRIONNE: "The sit-ins at lunch counters and the march in Birmingham."

AMANDA: "The Freedom Rides."

ME: "Sure, and a police sheriff was responsible for the deaths of Schwerner, Chaney, and Goodman in the 1964 Freedom Summer in Philadelphia, Mississippi. You all have figured out that there is a history behind Black cynicism toward law enforcement. So where today, people might not see any kind of police abuse happening, there is an undeniable history. And that history gets passed down. Because look, White families don't have 'the [race] talk' about how to behave when confronted by police officers. Black parents have this talk with their children. This is not part of White culture. So White people have no reason to believe dark communities are policed any different. Black families think about it. Why, because there are things that have happened historically."

I proposed one final question to get students thinking about their intensive study of Black Lives Matter: "We only have a moment, but to get everyone thinking about the resources they are going to read over the next few days, can anyone in this instance offer potential solutions for the Black Lives Matter debate?"

MARIA: "Taking something from the movie, I think we need to consider that the contemporary problem is that, in many cases, the police come from outside of Black communities to police them. The police should be from those neighborhoods. And you have the popular solutions of having police wear body cameras and go through implicit bias training."

JAKE: "That's a good point, but it's not the only solution. I plan to look into factors that might lessen the level of distrust toward cops since it does appear that the job is getting more dangerous."

ME: "You will read about Trump's executive order making attacks on law enforcers a federal crime."

JAKE: "Yes, and I will explore if there is something to learn from the violent attacks on police in Dallas and Louisiana a few years ago."

Conclusion

At this juncture, I need to explain what was happening simultaneously during our critical dialogues about double consciousness, the myth of civility, and Black Lives Matter. The Seminar in Critical Race Studies classroom became a space for sharing informed arguments without the threat of being vilified by others. Additionally, the classroom existed as a space to disclose personal wounds that healed through open-ended conversations centered on texts, rather than abstract queries. The channels (formal schooling, mass media, and peer groups) that shape individual racial perceptions over the course of a lifetime are challenged in evidence-based dialogues. The men in the class learned from the women and vice versa without any mansplaining. The White students learned from the Students of Color and vice versa without any whitesplaining. For practical purposes, when it comes to their research projects, the students discovered the importance of listening to rival narratives and points of view they were previously unfamiliar with. As Albert Einstein once said, "Education is not the learning of facts, but the training of the mind to think."

9

Moving Educators Beyond Race Conscious Pedagogy and Toward Cultural Competence

Introduction

According to a 2014 report by the U.S. Department of Education, 81.6 percent of White K-12 students attend schools where at least half the students were also White. The same report indicates that the share of White students attending predominantly White public schools is shrinking. In 1995, nearly half (48.6 percent) of White students attended schools where at least 90 percent of students were also White. By 2014, that number shrunk to 21.9 percent. There are several causal effects to consider how these numbers indicate the future experiences of White public school students. As student body demographics at schools throughout the country are changing rapidly, White students and White teachers will find that the fishbowl they have lived in for so long will crack. The lived experiences of Students of Color and other marginalized and underrepresented students will permeate the classroom one way or another. If mishandled, serious trouble could arise. Rather than avoid the elephant in the room, White educators along with White students and their parents must learn that uncomfortable race talk in the classroom leads everyone to moral and social progress, which sequentially leads to transformative and transcendent existences (for details see figure 4.1 in Chapter 4, The Race Conscious Pedagogy Framework Pyramid).

Chapters 1 through 8 of this book have been a description of one long solution for improving pedagogical and curricular equity that could ultimately lead to a racially literate society. Its target audience has been classroom teachers looking for practical methods to redesign the classroom into a space where text-based dialogues can guide teachers to the top tier of race consciousness wherein difficult but honest conversations about race issues are competently managed. This chapter, however, offers teachers, administrators, and school board members some preemptive ways to turn school buildings, and in some cases, school districts, into race conscious environments.

Race Conscious Solutions for Teachers

1) Make "Community of Inquiry" (COI) Part of the Pedagogy

Because this strategy is not new to education, many teachers might already be familiar with Communities of Inquiry (COI). The teaching method was the brainchild of John Dewey and C.S. Peirce who applied the technique mainly to scientific knowledge; early COIs were called "community of scientists," which placed a team of scientists together in a room to collaborate on scientific inquiry. Though the concept of COIs has been adapted over time and applied to many different fields, this method can be utilized in any classroom to discuss important and debatable concepts that fall within the purview of a specific subject.

Take my Seminar in Critical Race Studies and consider the controversy over excessive use of force by law enforcement officers as a lesson topic. The classroom itself is a general COI. At the start of the unit or lesson, the teacher presents the facts on policing statistics and the arguments by both sides of the issue. Students in the classroom are then divided into smaller communities of inquiry, each with carefully paired team members, a set of rules, assigned roles, and a contract to compel students to be productive. The smaller groups will engage in their own conversations and debates, then separate from one another to conduct independent research. They will convene once again in their small groups to discuss what each student discovered. In that group discussion, each student will identify the most consequential problems in policing and recommend fixes for those problems. After coming to a compromise, each small group COI will write its proposal on how to solve the problem of excessive police force. Proposals should include an introduction, discuss contextual significance on the topic, offer a set of solutions, analyze the implications and limitations of their proposed solutions, write a conclusion, and provide a works cited. Finally, the smaller groups will come together one last time as a general, entire class COI where each group will present its proposal. After debating all of the shared information, the general CIO will create a comprehensive proposal on the topic of excessive force in policing.

The Community of Inquiry concept functions as a think-tank, a brain trust that relies on diverse opinions that are amalgamated through small group discussions followed by a large group discussion with the objective of coming up with the best possible solution, or set of solutions, to a problem. The methodical process teaches students the importance of team concepts of accountability and dependability. It also shows students why diversity is the strength of any team, institution, or organization.

2) Remove Racial Abuses, Commonly Known as Microaggressions, from the Curriculum

For the first 18 years of my teaching career, one comment unendingly bothers me: "You're a teacher? You look so young. I thought you were a student." This simple slight should be taken as a compliment; that even as I have entered my 40s, and as the hair on my head has thinned, some of my colleagues and my students' parents think I look young enough to be a student. I acknowledge this might be the worst slight I have experienced in my teaching career. Others, however, are not so fortunate, as abuses based on race, ethnicity, religion, sexual orientation, gender identity, disability, and socioeconomic status frustrates those from marginalized communities several times a day. In addition to teaching, I have also coached high school football for more than 20 years. It is just as common to see microaggressions, microinsults, and microinvalidations committed against players and coaches on the practice field, inside the locker room, and in the coaches' office. I have witnessed kids subjected to being singled-out, fallen victim to inappropriate jokes, and forced to practice on religious holidays. Two other racial insults have made me cringe more over the years than the others. In one case, I have witnessed coaches call Latino players "José" because it was either easier to use a common Latin name than to remember the kid's real name or the coach was trying to get a laugh from observers. A second racial abuse commonly occurs at staff meetings when scouting upcoming opponents that happen to be made up of mostly African American players. The common analysis of predominantly Black teams is usually, "Man, they have a lot of athletes!" instead of "That is a well-coached team that excels at fundamentals." The remark typically creates a moment of resentment and frustration among the Coaches of Color in the room. Well-intentioned people not meaning to insult anyone are those who commit microaggressions in the sports arena.

The same applies to the classroom, where the teacher has just as much of a chance for creating an antagonistic space through comments, actions, and jokes. The teacher, however, is not the only agent in the classroom to engage in microaggressions; the curriculum is also a mechanism by which students can be unintentionally insulted. If unchecked, the classroom environment could become toxic and unwelcoming for students from underrepresented groups (Harwood, 2015).

Not everyone agrees that microaggressions have negative mental health consequences for non-dominant students. In fact, psychology experts have called for a moratorium on microaggression discourse until further research can be conducted to address the key domains of psychological science, including psychometrics, social cognition, cognitive-behavior therapy, behavior genetics, and personality, health, and industrial-organizational psychology. Professor of Psychology at Emory University Scott O. Lilienfeld (2017) issued a succinct rebuke of microaggressions in "Microaggressions: Strong Claims, Inadequate Evidence." Lilienfeld is known for writing on topics that debunk popular psychological claims and has regularly advocated for evidence-based methods in the field. Claiming that microaggressions are validated only by "respondents' subjective reports," he suggests that psychologists cannot verify "whether a given microaggression occurred or was merely imagined" since microaggressions are only independently substantiated. What Lilienfeld effectively argues is that the study of microaggressions violates fundamental principles of scientific methods by asking leading questions meant to produce answers that reinforce a liberal agenda. Other criticisms levied against microaggressions by Althea Nagai of the Center for Equal Opportunity along with columnists from media outlets such as *The National Review* and *The Atlantic* is that the concept has been flawed since its conception because it was originally put forth by academics. Indeed, Harvard psychiatrist and professor of education Chester Middlebrook Pierce coined the term in 1970 to give language to the mental health problems that Students of Color were experiencing at predominantly White colleges. By coming up with a name to explain what racialized students on campus were feeling in a period immediately following several campus disruptions and building occupations by Students of Color, Pierce's microaggression theory offered a reasonable explanation for the existence of implicit prejudicial and implicit aggressive motives by White students on campus. Decades later, critics now see Pierce's work as nothing more than the perpetuation of victimhood culture. Thus, detractors argue, the study of microaggressions is driven by critical race theorists who cherry-pick subjective experiences so as to coddle those offended by political incorrectness; wherein, critical race researchers are able to buoy the notion that racism is a permanent fixture in the social, cultural, political, economic, and educational institutions of America (Nagai, 2017).

Despite the criticism, it is important for educators to think deeply about the psychological toll that verbal, nonverbal, and environmental (pedagogical and curricular) expressions of prejudice have had on students of non-dominant cultures situated in White schools that perpetuate biased worldviews of superiority and inferiority (Wing Sue, 2010; Kanter et al., 2017).

Monnica T. Williams is a clinical psychologist that studies the link between racism and post-traumatic stress disorder, or what she calls "race-based traumatic stress injury" felt by Persons of Color after enduring racist-related incidents. Williams' research has linked race-based trauma to "serious psychological distress, physical health problems, depression, anxiety, binge drinking, and even disorder eating" (Williams et al., 2014). Findings from national studies indicate that African Americans have a 9.1 percent prevalence rate for post-traumatic stress disorder compared to 6.8 percent in Whites (Himle et al., 2009). Bearing this in mind, what should teachers do to help marginalized students that have been traumatized by life experiences prosper academically in the classroom? Identifying intentional and unintentional racial snubs in the curriculum in an attempt to minimize the number of subtle and tacit pokes and prods Students of Color experience during a school day is a good start.

As psychologist Derald Wing Sue (2010) suggests, since microaggressions are "unconscious manifestations" of a prejudiced worldview, teachers should strive to "make the 'invisible'" everyday demeaning abuses "visible." This can be accomplished by taking the following steps that ensure subtle racial maligning and overt racial insults are removed from the classroom: (1) Examine the curriculum to identify any material that students representing a cross section of social identities would find offensive. Consider removing any text, lecture, or activity that entails anything insensitive about race, ethnicity, religion, gender, sexual orientation, age, disability, and class. (2) Work with the guidance department to learn about the students in your classroom. It will take a bit of labor in the beginning, as you and a guidance counselor will have to create a relationship of trust and communication that respects and maximizes both of your schedules before the start of the semester. This is important, however, as you should enter the school year not assuming that the marginalized groups you will eventually discuss in the course material are not in the classroom. Awareness of your students' backgrounds has an educative effect. As you acquire knowledge on various cultural experiences that will populate your classroom, you will learn to avoid making insensitive comments. For instance, conducting a family tree assignment will likely isolate Students of Color, primarily African American students, who cannot trace their family back to a country of origin. Or to give another example, calling the game of football "soft" for its new player-safety rules fails to see that there may be students in the class that believe the word in that context suggests something disparaging about masculinity and sexuality. (3) Examine components of the curriculum where you can work in culturally responsive material. Identify texts that represent cross-cultural experiences, both historical and contemporary. Additionally, ensure that lectures utilize different cultural contexts while avoiding the use of outdated terminology and inaccurate statements about racial and ethnic groups. If you are a White teacher, do not say the N-word on any occasion; this includes refraining from reading aloud the term from a book or article (Harwood, 2015). (4) Establish guidelines for respectful classroom discussions when dealing with controversial topics. Allow non-dominant students to make a cultural connection to a lesson without discrediting the student's contribution. (5) Examine your disposition toward racial diversity and the amount of racial empathy you possess before the school year begins. Yolanda Sealey-Ruiz, Associate Professor of the Teacher's College Columbia University, calls this practice, "archaeology of the self." Sealey-Ruiz's self-reflective practice is a preemptive approach that compels teachers to think about their own identity, and how that identity might clash with those of their students. While "archaeology of the self" is a creative idea, the lack of scholarship on Sealey-Ruiz's introspective approach warrants the question: what methods can teachers utilize to extract value from critiquing one's racial misperceptions? One approach is to take implicit association tests, such as Harvard University's "Project Implicit," which offers dozens of tests online to help individuals identify hidden prejudices. Implicit association tests measure subconscious feelings about race, gender, sexuality, age, religion, and ability in order to offer a moment of reflection on how to mute the adverse actions that are stoked by unconscious presumptions. As social psychologist Jennifer L. Eberhardt (2019) says, these tests help mitigate times when "bias leaks out between the words of scripted dialogue [and into] our everyday lives" through the clutching of a purse when encountering a Black man, presuming every Asian person is from China, or believing your Black pilot is unqualified to fly a plane. The Harvard test takes measurements based on how quickly participants can associate Black and White faces with positive and negative words.

Additionally, the National Association of Multicultural Education (NAME), a non-profit organization that advocates for equity and social justice through multicultural education with national and statewide chapters, offers a four-part framework for self-reflection: (1) to become self-aware of one's own prejudices; (2) to examine the physical environment of the classroom to ensure cultural representation in the form of image posters and bulletin boards; (3) to scrutinize traditional pedagogical approaches in a way that may lead to inquiry-based, integrative, and collaborative teaching methods that will enhance learning; and (4) to explore ways to establish a relationship with families of students and the school community. NAME also encourages teachers to complete a "Sorting People" activity, which challenges teachers to separate people into racial categories (Black, White, Latinx, Asian, Native American) based on presumptuous responses to individual pictures. The activity intends to expose one's racial predispositions. Challenging yourself to think judgmentally about where you stand on certain issues can lead to a new outlook, and likely create a positive environment where every student in the room feels validated. What this also means is that you can never look to the only Student of Color in your class and expect him or her to serve as *the face of the race*, as Kerry Washington put it in her original Broadway play *American Son*, assumed to speak for all members of his or her racial group on any given topic. All of these proactive approaches to implicit association training prepare educators to, as understood by Eberhardt (2019), recognize "[b]ias, even when we are not conscious of it, [because bias] has consequences that we need to understand and mitigate. The stereotypic associations we carry in our heads can affect what we perceive, how we think, and the actions we take."

Making these changes will go a long way in transforming the classroom into a welcoming space for students of non-dominant cultures that so often find themselves in inhospitable places. According to a 2015 University of Illinois, Urbana-Champaign study, 39 percent of Students of Color arrive at predominantly White schools already feeling "uncomfortable on campus because of their race." The study, which surveyed 4,800 African American, Latinx, and Asian American college students, found more than 800 examples of racial abuses on college campuses. Moreover, 51 percent of those surveyed reported that a professor and/or peers in the classroom had stereotyped them. The report indicated that Students of Color feel "unwelcomed" in classrooms full of White students, "especially if they were the only Person of Color, or one of a few" (Harwood, 2015). Though this survey focused on non-dominant students at the collegiate level, its results certainly apply to the experiences of high school students representing non-dominant cultures as well, especially those attending majority White schools.

While most studies like the one cited above concentrate on how racial abuses impact the mental health of a victim, attention must also be paid to White aggressors that are more likely to commit a racist insult. Williams, Jonathan W. Kanter, and a team of psychologists from the American Psychological Foundation issued a report in 2017 that explored the rate at which White students from large universities in the South and Midwest ("where prejudice toward blacks is stronger than in the West or New England") self-reported their engagement in racially abusive acts (Kanter et al., 2017). The report found White students who described themselves as possessing a colorevasive worldview were "more likely to microaggress." Those same White students who claimed color-blindness admitted to holding "less favorable" and "less positive" attitudes toward African, Latinx, Asian, and Native American people. The study utilized a "Racial Feeling Thermometer" that measured White participants' attitudes toward Black and non–Black People of Color ranging from 0 degrees (extremely unfavorable) to 100 degrees (extremely favorable). Low scores on the race thermometer indicated explicit prejudice. The lowest of scores, or the most offensive comments White respondents admitted to on the race thermometer were: "You seem more intelligent than I would have thought," "I have other black friends," "White privilege doesn't really exist," "A lot of minorities are too sensitive," "All lives matter, not just black lives," and "Racism may have been a problem in the past, but it is not an important problem today." The study suggests further that White students who deliver racist invectives are more likely to possess "negative racial attitudes and explicit underlying hostility" toward African, Latinx, Asian, and Native American people. Overall, this team of psychologists believes it is possible to scientifically measure self-reported racist abuse. The report verifies claims that micro and macro racist acts (if there is such a difference) are "related to prejudice" and "situated within the science of racism." Therefore, the deliberate effort to remove racist abuse from the curriculum will also benefit White students who need to know that their behavior is under scrutiny from their darker-hued peers. A teacher functioning as an ally to students of non-dominant racial groups willing to speak up in the aftermath of a racist action like a racist joke has the capacity to be more effective on how the aggressive student behaves in the future. Exhibiting respect towards the trauma felt by non-dominant students will go a long way in developing meaningful interactions between White children and Children of Color.

3) Help Students of Color
Form Racial or Ethnic Affinity Groups

The Pew Research Center reported in 2019 that 52 percent of African Americans feel that their race or ethnicity has hurt their ability to get ahead in life (Horowitz et al., 2019). This number is disturbing, as there is not another racialized group in the United States that possesses such hopelessness about obtaining success. When it comes to feeling that race or ethnicity hinders racialized groups from succeeding, here is how other groups compared: Asian Americans 24 percent, Latinxs 24 percent, and Whites five percent. The burden of such cynicism about getting a fair deal in life weighs on African American students and other Students of Color at predominantly White K-12 schools where mainstream stereotypes and social ostracism permeates each end of the schoolhouse; where students of non-dominant racial groups are inhibited from walking the halls free from White judgment; where darker hued students are concerned about making their White peers uncomfortable; where the curriculum clashes with cultural relevance; and where non-dominant students are more likely to be disciplined through suspension or referral to law enforcement. These figures beget the question: what possibilities exist for Students of Color to obtain a sense of belonging at school without White students and White faculty feeling offended? Teachers should help students from marginalized groups form their own identity groups and find protected spaces where there can be mental healing and fellowship.

As sociologist Bonnie E. French (2017) suggests, schools that prohibit racial affinity groups "deny the reality" that identity cliques naturally materialize at each level of primary, intermediate, and secondary school. It is accurate to say that French believes most affinity groups are "unofficial," meaning they do not operate with a steering committee, weekly meetings, a budget, or faculty supervision. This is why the title of Beverly Daniel Tatum's (1997, 2017) seminal book is *Why Are All of the Black Kids Sitting Together in the Cafeteria*: because students of the same identity group tend to spend time with one another at school. Tatum says, "The developmental need to explore the meaning of one's identity with others who are engaged in a similar process manifests itself informally in school corridors and cafeterias throughout the country." Thus, for students asking themselves "Who am I?" and "How do I fit in here?" the search for personal identity occurs in the clustering by race upon entrance into seventh grade, a time when children realize that there exists a majorative White culture which sees them as a racialized "Other." Helping African, Latinx, Asian, and Native American students form racial and ethnic exclusive groups during common club time at school is not an act of abetting so-called self-segregation. As Tatum believes, affinity groups allow "Black students [to] turn to each other for the much needed support they are not likely to find anywhere else." They can also exist to help members achieve academically, since academic success is often associated with being White and there is data showing that, according to Tatum, trying to achieve in school can cause "some conflict or alienation" from intra-racial and intra-ethnic peer groups. The affinity group can establish academic norms, such as common study hall hours, tutoring assistance, tips for test preparation, and general encouragement for doing well on exams and projects instead of worrying about being attacked by their peers for "acting white."

It is natural that White educators initially struggle to grasp the importance of ethnically base affinity groups. The anxiety felt among Whites that think the request for racial or ethnic affinity groups is a form of segregation is born from a long history of racializing Black spaces, that Black people gathering together is a way to ripen hate against White people. There should be no equating of affinity groups to the way segregationist policy separated White people away from Black people, argues antiracist scholar Ibram X. Kendi (2019). Affinity groups are a means of escaping racism. If the notion that Students of Color need an identity group and safe space to gather is too difficult to understand, even after completing an "archaeology of the self" to uncover and scrutinize one's own biases, teachers should still strive to share compassion for student experiences and trust that if a Black person says he or she is dealing with racial trauma, he or she is, in fact, dealing with racial trauma. To give Students of Color a group that aids in obtaining a sense of belonging at a majority White school as well as a respite from the almost daily code switching and perpetual navigation of the White school, along with the need for a mouthpiece for social and academic advocacy, a racial or ethnic affinity group and safe space would be therapeutic for students representing racially minoritized students in your school.

To establish a culture of inclusion is arguably the capstone of educational equity work. While a school's environment might fail at providing students of non-dominant cultures the feeling that they are included in the school community at large, a classroom teacher can develop a subculture that is embracing through culturally responsive and culturally sustaining lesson planning, in student-to-teacher interactions, and by supervising extracurricular school clubs and organizations that are welcoming to all students. As seen in figure 9.1, Teacher Generated Sense of Belonging for Students of Color, a teacher can help foster a positive sense of belonging within the frame of an otherwise unwelcoming environment. The results can be lifesaving as student retention and attendance will increased. Studies show that a positive sense of belonging results in academic achievement, extracurricular engagement, and a healthy self-esteem (Davis et al., 2019; Strayhorn, 2012). Race-based affinity groups aid in creating a sense of inclusion. The job of a teacher, therefore, is to support the existence of such groups and spaces.

Teachers must also take action against negative responses from White students and White parents who see affinity groups as something discriminatory, as a reverse racist movement of Black people away from White people (Kendi, 2019). French (2017), an Assistant Professor of Sociology at Caldwell University, called the predictable White backlash to racial affinity groups the "highlight whiteness for White folks." In *Race at Predominantly White Independent Schools: The Space Between Diversity and Equity*, she writes that the greatest privilege owned by White people is "we rarely have to think about our whiteness." The existence of these groups, then, challenges that particular privilege by creating the one space not owned by Whites during the school day. Exclusion from affinity groups will enrage many White students. Though it would be nice if White parents could support racial affinity groups, the counterattacks will likely be vocal and widespread since such groups are a shot to the White supremacist nervous system. It means Whites will not have ownership over all school spaces. French provides statements on how to respond to the critics. To the student, she writes:

> [If] we had a divorced student group to support students, it wouldn't mean that they would be less involved in the life of the school. It wouldn't mean that they would hate people whose parents were together. It wouldn't mean that they would spend assemblies trying to dismantle the idea of marriage. But why would that be the same case, why would you think that would be the case? We wouldn't be sitting in a room with

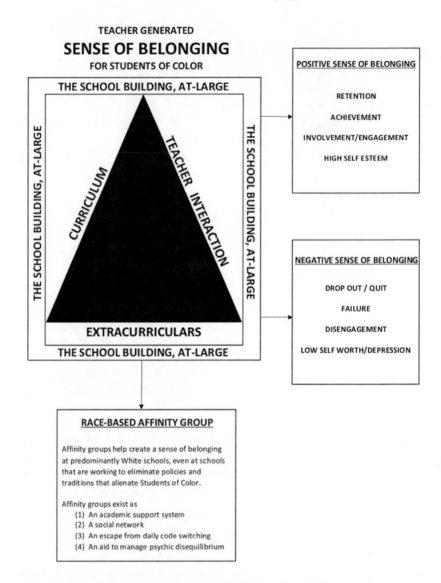

Figure 9.1—Teacher Generated Sense of Belonging for Students of Color Framework

divorced parents … [saying] "we hate married people, what are we gonna do" … we wouldn't even care.

To the parent, she writes:

Do you have a mirror at your home? Yeah. Could you imagine looking in the mirror and not seeing a reflection? What would that feel like? The term is called psychic disequilibrium. Well, you know what, we have kids who come to school every day and don't see an image of themselves. And so this is an opportunity for them to have a mirror and see an image of themselves.

Another noteworthy justification for racial and ethnic affinity groups is the shocking disparity between teachers that are White and teachers that are African, Latinx, Asian, or Native American at predominantly White schools. In 2018, the Pew Research Center study revealed that White teachers make up 98 percent of the teachers at predominantly White K-12 public schools (Geiger, 2018). Therefore, Students of Color at such schools enter those spaces with little cultural capital that is so important for navigating the "societal curriculum," as Gloria Ladson-Billings (2003) illustrates, including the absence of cultural relevant pedagogy, racial scripts perpetuated by peer groups, and a devaluating school culture. Moreover, these schools lack teachers, guidance counselors, and administrators of color that can serve as mentors. The affinity group would exist as a team of mentors, especially if upperclassmen and women can create bonds with their younger peers.

4) Conduct a District-wide Survey with the Help of Your Students

I am totally on board the data-driven culture that seeks continuous accountability to expanding access to educational opportunities, including racial and socioeconomic desegregation efforts, spending equalization, and programs designed to close the educational opportunity gap by way of increasing household spending on out-of-school learning experiences for children in preschool, sports, music and art. Collecting and using data for the purpose of holding school districts accountable will achieve results sought after by equity advocates. Indeed, owing to a requirement by the U.S. Department of Education's Office for Civil Rights, most school districts have for decades collected data on special programs, teacher diversity, Algebra and Geometry enrollment in grades 7–12, Advanced Placement exam participation; and disciplinary incidents, including violent and serious crime infractions. Data on these topics must be submitted to the Civil Rights Data Collection (CRDC) to ensure that recipients of federal funds do not discriminate on the basis of race, color, national origin, sex, and disability. The CRDC has collected data every other school year since 1968 to measure access and barriers to educational opportunity from early childhood through a student's senior year of high school. Though the CRDC has received the data biennially, few school districts across the country have felt pressured to do anything further with that data until the recent push for educational access and equity. By 2020, not only are individual school districts now using data to draw up equity plans, but also statewide school board associations are doing the same.

After witnessing the wave in statewide and district-wide equity pol-icymaking, should educators discuss how classroom teachers could apply their own data-driven analysis to rewrite curricula to become more race conscious? A survey is an appropriate tool to measure support within a school's faculty as administrators and other stakeholders strive to create a culture of race consciousness in a district. In the fall of 2018, my students in Seminar in Critical Race Studies and I received permission from the superintendent, assistant superintendent, and the high school principal to survey the Gap School District faculty to gauge the level of support for our course. The survey was timely, as the superintendent had just formed a task force to begin discussions to write the district's equity policy. The task force was interested in seeing the results. About half of the district's staff participated in our survey, which took about 10 minutes to complete. The survey's results, which showed 72 percent of participants believed that race classes should be mandatory for high school students, have come to drive district teachers to use their curriculum to speak up for social justice causes.

Race Conscious Solutions for District Administration

1) Require a Credit in Race or Diversity Studies for Graduation from High School and Place the Same Expectation on the Faculty

I realize in most cases that one class will not convince a colorevasive or racist student to become an antiracist, nor will it make any student an expert on the racial dynamics in American society. This criticism notwith-standing, waiting until college is too late for students to engage in materials and discussions about the topic. Therefore, as illustrated in Chapter 4, a race studies course will reduce ugly racist episodes that have historically prevailed at America's PWIs.

If students are required to learn about racial diversity, the faculty should undergo the same prerequisite. To paraphrase Bettina L. Love (2019), if a White teacher lacks empathy and love for his or her Students of Color, he or she cannot educate them because trauma already exists in the classroom. Formal training of faculty must possess a two-fold mission: first, educators must learn race conscious and culturally responsive educational theory as well as the history of oppressed peoples and religions; second, the faculty must be trained in how to facilitate race-based conversations (Sue, 2015). Ed-ucator Matthew Kay (2018) argues teachers must (1) learn how to distinguish between race talk deemed "meaningful and inconsequential"; (2) to establish "conversational safe spaces"; (3) to "infuse" race talk "with purpose"; and (4) be knowledgeable enough to respond instinctively to unexpected challenges. When nurtured appropriately, Kay says the classroom will become an "ecosystem" of patient and active listening where substance-filled race based conversations organically materializes. However, suppose a teacher attempts to facilitate race talk without properly preparing. In that case, the classroom can easily disintegrate into a setting for ugly spats amongst students that reflects the ad hominem shouting matches that commonly occur between political analysts on mainstream media programs (Schwartz and Ritter, 2019). But if handled well with the right combination of questions based on assigned readings and anecdotal experiences, race conversations can thrive in the classroom.

Despite some initial pushback from parents and students, it will only be a matter of time until the commitment to race consciousness becomes ingrained in the district's culture, especially after enough quantifiable data has been collected to support the merit of such courses. While the first year or two might bring foreseeable resistance from students, parents, and perhaps some teachers, a 2016 research study conducted by Thomas Dee and Emily Penner (2017) at Stanford University shows that the causal effects (reduced dropout rates and higher student performance) of Race Conscious Pedagogy helps lower achieving students as it would the highest achieving students. Dee and Penner tracked 1,405 students at several high schools in San Francisco who were automatically enrolled in ethnic studies because their eighth grade GPA was below 2.0. After tracking the students for four years, the data collected by the Stanford professors illustrates increases in the cohort's attendance by 21 percent and growth in GPA by 1.4 grade points between freshman and senior years of high school.

Similar data collected by the Division of Institutional Analytics at San Francisco State University demonstrate that college students majoring in ethnic studies graduate at approximately 20 percent the rate of non-ethnic studies majors. Though this evidence reinforces the benefits of ethnic studies at the college level, there is certain likeness for high school students that a school district's stakeholders will eventually ask for more ethnic or diversity studies. According to Kenneth Monteiro (2018) of the Cesar Chavez Institute at San Francisco State, students who took one ethnic studies class "graduated at a higher rate than students who took no Ethnic Studies classes": 77.3 percent for ethnic studies majors compared to 52.3 percent for non-ethnic studies majors. The same report indicates that students in majors other than ethnic studies but enrolled in at least one ethnic studies class graduated at "a much higher rate than their peers in their major who did not take Ethnic studies classes."

Accordingly, there will be almost complete buy-in after those early difficult years. School district officials can meet with professors from a local college to align curriculum. There are also several school districts in California and Texas that offer ethnic studies at various grade levels that can be contacted for comparative dialogue. Additionally, in Portage County, Wisconsin, Stevens Point Area Senior High, known locally as SPASH, has a graduation requirement that forces students to receive 0.5 credit in a class called American Diversity and Tolerance and 0.5 credit in another called Conflict and Resolution; amounting to 1-credit in topics associated with multicultural-related curriculum and problem-posing teaching methods (Stevens Point Area Public School District, 2012–2013).

There is another model in the Midwest. In July 2018, the Illinois General Assembly passed Public Act (PA) 100–0634, also known as House Bill 4346, mandating public elementary and high schools, as well as institutions of higher education and community colleges, write into its curriculum a Black studies unit that teaches a contours of African American history and culture. Topics include the African slave trade, slavery in America, the vestiges of slavery, as well as economic, cultural and political developments of the United States and Africa, and the socio-economic conditions that African Americans have endured in each century of American history. The legislature's mission is clearly written in the bill: "The studying of this material shall constitute an affirmation by students of their commitment to respect the dignity of all races and peoples and to forever eschew every form of discrimination in their lives and careers." The bill provides that no student can complete eighth grade or graduate from high school or college without receiving instruction in African American history.

This legislative model compensates the failure of federal and state education departments to make race consciousness an integral part of public schooling. Illinois' General Assembly leadership could be transformative for educators, as its new curriculum does two good things: challenges racial orthodoxies and acknowledges the history of racial suffering in America, which is of particular importance for White students to know. House Bill 4346 ensures that educators recognize the bitter struggles to overcome bigotry and the writing of a curriculum designed to undo centuries of structural oppression. If emulated elsewhere, this nation will take great strides forward in terms of social justice and inclusivity of race, gender, and sexuality behind new generations of racially conscious leaders.

2) Make "Diversity Attributes" District Policy

Diversity Attributes force teachers to write into curriculum diversity objectives that create classrooms where students are provided opportunities to explore ways race, ethnicity, religion, class, ability, and sexual orientation have both enriched and complicate Americans' lives. The intent of Diversity

Attributes is to ensure that teachers understand that race, ethnicity, gender, ability, class, age, and orientation is pervasive in every discipline and that courses should allow students the chance to explore issues and experiences pertaining to human relations across lines of societal and cultural differences. Teachers can accomplish this by mandating that during collaborative assignments, each group must reflect age, race, ethnic, and gender diversity. Assigned group roles should alternate after an allocated period of time. Additionally, specific lesson plans should reflect messages that all people belong to multiple cultures that influence the actions, beliefs, and interactions between one another; that value cultural difference; that provides opportunities to raise awareness; and that increases critical analysis about social responsibility.

Many colleges and universities today are encouraging professors to add Diversity Attributes to the courses they teach. For example, Dickinson College (2018) in Carlisle, Pennsylvania, prepares its faculty with "intellectual ability, ethnical grounding, intercultural understanding and the skills to work toward a just and sustainable world." The undergraduate college, which possesses an ethnic diversity that matches the national average (68.4 percent White, 32 percent People of Color) and boasts one of the highest rates of international undergraduate students, understands that its graduates will become global leaders (Dickinson, 2019). College leaders have accordingly directed its staff to implement a pedagogical policy that instructs students on how to challenge common cultural assumptions and seek "new and sustainable solutions" for the world while understanding that problems more often arise due to cultural indifference. Dickinson is not alone in endorsing a Diversity Attributes policy. For local leaders, an internet search of local colleges will likely lead to the discovery of a policy that can be implemented at the high school level.

3) Create a Cultural Competency Academy

Professional development opportunities for teachers are typically the first answer to equipping current educators with the skills needed to create a race conscious classroom. Indeed, there is a need for frequent equity training where experts teach and reteach methods and provide materials that moves a teaching staff toward cultural competence. However, instead of providing teachers one-day diversity training, create a long-term professional development program called Cultural Competency Academy (CCA). A school district's CCA should aim to educate teachers on cultural competence over a six- to seven month period. The CCA obliges teachers to dig deep into this weighty topic at professional development sessions, usually lasting one to three hours, one time a month. The CCA framework is based on the work of art therapist Cheryl Doby-Copeland, who worked with artists going through art therapy school that honed skills in awareness development (learning the racial history of a school district and how that history contributed to the story of the school's community), knowledge development (selected readings and discussion in White privilege, implicit bias, colorism, racial scripts, meritocracy, and implications of an individual's position in relation to race dialogues), and skill development (teachers create culturally responsive teaching methods that value students' languages and cultures). CCA's may have up to seven sessions in a school year. The first three sessions teach participants about the history of their school district. This might include on-sight visits to historical landmarks or guest lectures by local historians. If resources are available, it might necessitate archival research. After establishing trust between the moderator(s) and participants, the third and fourth sessions force participants to take part in discussions centered on implicit bias and an "Identity" activity where they are asked to think about themselves as "Othered" beings. The moderators hang up signs around the room indicating racial, ethnic, gender, religious, and academic degree categories. Participants rotate through the various identity stations. Once at a station, the teachers are asked a series of questions and are forced to talk to one another about their life experiences. This activity certainly makes teachers uncomfortable, as many are told to identify themselves for the first time in their lives. Participants will use the final two professional development sessions to write culturally relevant lesson plans and present those lessons to the group for evaluation.

There are two educators in Oak Ridge, Tennessee, that provide this CCA prototype. Willow Brook Elementary Principal Dr. Sherrie Fairchild-Keyes and Michael Carvella, the Curriculum and Technology Integration Coach for elementary schools in Oak Ridge, launched a Cultural Competency Academy in 2016. Participation in their professional development cohort is not mandated by the Oak Ridge School District; rather faculty members have an array of professional development options from which to choose. Fairchild-Keyes and Carvella meet with cohorts monthly over the duration of a school year. The frequency in professional development opportunities is due to Oak Ridge School District's yearly calendar, which is designed to release students from school early every Wednesday. Fairchild-Keyes' and Carvella's CCA cohorts convene for 90 minutes to two hours during these half days. Similar models can be adapted by school districts across the country.

If creating a Cultural Competency Academy is too much to ask a small number of staff members to manage, there are other proven options. In 1987, Peggy McIntosh, famous for writing "White Privilege: Unpacking the Invisible Knapsack," launched The National Seeking Educational Equity and Diversity (SEED) Project to ensure multiculturalism becomes an integral aspect of curriculum and pedagogy. For over 30 years, McIntosh's SEED project has offered teachers instruction on how to become the leaders of their own multicultural professional development. SEED is both an acronym and a metaphor; it carries a philosophy by which teachers train other teachers about what works in the classroom for Students of Color, students who are disabled, and other non-dominant cultural groups. Thus, teachers effectively become the seed of a district's cultural transformation toward equity and inclusivity. When a district signs on to The National SEED Project, a selected group of faculty members—SEED advises school districts to send eight to 25 participants—undergo an intensive seven-day summer workshop where educators are coached on the skills and provided resources aimed toward making school climate, curricula, and pedagogy more racially and gender cognizant. After the initial SEED training, the local faculty that undergo the weeklong summer workshop then leads monthly, three hour-long professional development sessions with the district's staff during the school year. Through democratized group dialogues at these monthly meetings, educators explore "their own education in relation to race, gender, socioeconomic status, religion, sexual identity, abilities, and age and how these factors currently impact their school [and] classrooms." Since the founding of McIntosh's SEED Project, the organization has trained almost 3,000 K-12 teachers and college professors from 42 states and 15 countries. According to SEED (2020) records, over 30,000 teachers who in turn have impacted the lives of over three million students have experienced in some fashion SEED's cultural competency training. The SEED Program is not free. As of 2020, tuition, materials, meals, lodging, and ongoing assistance from the SEED staff cost $4,600 per participant. SEED makes scholarships available for those who apply.

4) Create an Inter-district Race Project

The high school where I work is part of a school district known to have the best agricultural program in Lancaster County, Pennsylvania. Though the school district is rural, the high school sits on the edge of Lancaster City. In fact, many of Gap's athletic fields are lands purchased from the city. The high school has a diverse student population that rivals most schools in our county. It is a school where owners of John Deere tractors sit shoulder-to-shoulder with Spanish speakers in biology class; it is where Iraqi immigrants do geometry homework with classmates that have never left their small town. About 10 years ago Gap made an effort to get outsiders to see it differently. During the 50th anniversary of the desegregation of Central High School in Little Rock, Arkansas, I invited one of the "Little Rock Nine," Terrence J. Roberts, to speak at an inter-district race symposium. Five area school districts were represented at the event, which included several guest speakers, small group dialogues, and, of course, Roberts's keynote. College students from nearby Franklin and Marshall College volunteered to facilitate the student dialogues. The local Human Rights Commission donated lunches for almost 500 participants.

There is a group in Kansas and Missouri that provides a more enduring example of how to bring students from various school districts together in an initiative that keeps students engaged in conversation about race, ethnicity, and culture during their four years in high school. "The Race Project KC" began when Tanner Colby published *Some of My Best Friends Are Black*. Much of Colby's book addresses the history of residential segregation in Kansas City. The project was born when a group of antiracist public librarians and educators reached out to Colby in 2014. Since then, this organization has offered annual conferences for educators and semiannual symposiums for middle and high school students. The Race Project KC brings students together from schools across Missouri and Kansas, with Kansas City as its focal point, for daylong engagements with Kansas City metro's segregation legacy. After a bus tour with Colby that takes students to key landmarks in the area's civil rights history, students participate in symposiums and engage with guest speakers and small group discussions on how the area's racist past still plagues neighborhoods and schools in Kansas City.

It cannot be taken for granted that arranging an inter-district race project will take a lot of work. Planners must concern themselves with educating students in advance, reserving the venue, raising funds, grant writing, finding guest speakers, ordering an appropriate number of lunches, managing the timing of the various bell and bus schedules for each school, and training any moderators that might facilitate group discussions. Responsibilities, however, can be shared across school districts. To accomplish the goal of training cultural competence among adolescent and teenage students, educators should bring together a broad-based, multifaceted alliance to develop ways of engaging young people in race-based discussions. Participation of antiracist groups, community-focused organizations, faculty at local colleges and universities, curators and directors of local museums, heritage centers and historical landmarks can all become key actors in the learning experience. Of course, the nature and logistics of inter-district race projects will be relative; leaders must decide how often schools will meet as well as select a theme or topic for each meeting. Not only will the experience get easier after each symposium, but also it will always be rewarding. Any time that people of different school cultures and dissimilar backgrounds can come together to share stories will garner more respect and admiration, while ultimately resulting in a healthier community.

5) Write District-wide Equity Standards That (a) Prioritizes Hiring Teachers That Represent Non-dominant Cultural Groups, (b) Creates School Buildings That Are Race Conscious, and (c) Includes a Preemptive and Proactive "Hate Response Team" Ready to Respond to Reported Incidents of Intolerance

The first step in bridging the gap between equal access to a high-quality education and equitable resources that include funding, programs, and supports that target every public school student is the creation of a strong district-wide equity mission statement. If a school district without an administration committed to creating a culturally competent staff, nothing the district tries to do in terms of equity will work. Policies should be guided by a purpose to eliminate race, gender, disability, and family income as predictors of a student's success.

There is a superintendent of a school district in Philadelphia that I will call Spencer that offers a template by which school administrators and board members can write a tailor-made equity policy. The equity doctrine of Spencer School District's superintendent extensively covers everything from hiring for diversity to creating culturally responsive school buildings to forming sustaining partnerships locally, regionally, and nationally. The district has established a system of hiring in which the superintendent is integrally involved. The resume of every applicant sent to Spencer's human resources department is "paper screened" by the superintendent. Spencer also intentionally forms diverse interview committees made up of people who are Black and people who are White, along with a mix of male, female, new, and veteran educators. The committee members are instructed to submit recommendations for interview candidates. During the interview, many of the questions are geared toward receiving culturally responsive answers.

Another achievement in Spencer School District's equity standards has been the acquisition of a vast array of local, regional, and national partnerships. He organizes job fairs to recruit the teachers he wants working in his district. Students of Color in the Spencer School District are given opportunities to explore educational leadership opportunities. The aim has been to create a pipeline of Spencer teachers coming from within its own student body. The program has collaborated with historically Black colleges and universities in the vicinity of Philadelphia. And the district's superintendent has established fellowships with community centers and charitable foundations in the City of Brotherly Love.

Another part of Spencer's equity mission is to mold a culturally profi-cient and responsive workplace at each district building. Principals, teachers, and support staff in every Spencer school must form a "culturally proficiency cadre" responsible for writing a set of equity standards for their respective building. The policy must be drafted as a five-year plan. After each year, however, that five-year plan is reevaluated. Additionally, the staff receives biannual professional development on multiculturalism and must integrate cultural proficiency into pedagogy.

Spencer's equity strategies are inspiring. However, the district's equity mission rests on the shoulders of the superintendent. Albeit, Spencer creates culturally proficiency cadres; yet there is no salaried director or coordinator whose job it is to alleviate pressure that comes with managing the many fac-tors of equity work. One job of an equity coordinator is to manage the district's equity team comprised of all building principals, in addition to several teach-ers, representatives from community-focused organizations, and a few com-munity members that could push the district closer to embracing all cultural and marginalized groups beyond the Black-White binary. In addition to estab-lishing the equity vision, the equity coordinator can see that these teams both implement staff training in each district building and conduct equity audits to measure the quality of interactions between educators and students, especially those historically marginalized students. The equity coordinator should an-swer directly to the superintendent, thus positioning the mission of diversity and inclusion well above the expectations of a middle management position.

The fact that there are predominantly White school districts that sim-ply have zero luck getting educators that represent non-dominant cultural groups to apply for vacant jobs is very real. In this case, school districts should implement a series of standards that establish equitable schools in other ways. First, teachers must make the diversification of the curriculum a priority. Teachers can create syllabi that study experts on critical race and gender topics for virtually any discipline. The scholars include, but are not limited to, Audre Lorde, bell hooks, Derrick Bell, W.E.B. Du Bois, Gary Pel-ler, Richard Delgado, Ian Lopez, Kimberle Crenshaw, Frantz Fanon, Glo-ria Anzaldua, Jack Shaheen, James Baldwin, Michael Eric Dyson, Ta-Nehisi Coates, Tim Wise, Derald Wing Sue, Robin DiAngelo, Joe Feagin, Ibram X. Kendi, Khaled A. Beydoun, Reni Eddo-Lodge, Debby Irving, and Cor-nell West. Earlier in this chapter we explored Diversity Attributes. The im-plementation of Diversity Attributes will ease the curricular transition and help transform the classroom culture into a space of race consciousness. Part of any equity plan should examine what equity work looks like in the classroom. Accordingly, rubrics designed for teacher-evaluation parameters should include a standard that assesses how teachers exhibit culturally re-sponsive classrooms.

Also mentioned in this chapter was the suggestion that White educators should help create spaces where Students of Color, students who are disabled, and LGBTQ+ students can exist away from the day-to-day challenges and stress. School districts that struggle to hire teachers that reflect non-dominant cultural groups (African Americans, transgender, those who are disabled) should mandate its faculty to undergo diversity education. If the expectation for students is to understand the racial and gender inequities of the school and to respect one another for their differences, the same accountability should be placed on the administrative, teaching, and support staffs.

Finally, majority White schools should be ever vigilant and possess the ability to respond swiftly to racist, homophobic, anti–Semitic, and Islamophobic incidents. As discussed in Chapter 3, there is a very real problem of private and structural racism working hand-in-hand wherein White students have a history of mocking their African American, Asian American, Latinx, Jewish, Muslim, and LGBTQ+ counterparts at PWIs. While it might seem that a racist chant by frat brothers at the University of Oklahoma has no correlation to a racist Instagram post from a group of White high school students using the N-word, the historical reconstruction by Lawrence Ross (2015), Khaled A. Beydoun (2018), and other scholars on campus racism indicate otherwise. Additionally, the problem of White blackface costume-party goers is as prevalent today as it was 50 years ago because racist policy and racist culture has a strong grip on educational institutions, which ultimately influence the behavior of students ages 14 to 22. As educators learn about systemic racism, they can begin to take an active role in heading off incidents of racism and bias by creating a school building "Hate Response Team." Colleges and universities have already begun establishing "Campus Climate Response Teams" or "Diversity Response Teams" to provide immediate support for students hurt by biased acts. While there is no silver bullet to eliminate racism, sexism, homophobia, Islamophobia, and anti–Semitism from a school, a Hate Response Team can serve multiple functions to sustain the school as a place of racial tolerance and equity. This team can offer timely responses to incidents of bigotry; a quick and easy procedure (usually digitally) for victims to report an incident; assist victims by providing support or a connection to support services; collect and store data regarding hate crimes that occur to students inside and outside the school, which include racist graffiti, symbols, and parties; facilitate ongoing professional development to staff about hate crimes; and offer best practice recommendations to the administration regarding disciplinary action against an aggressor. The implementation of a Hate Response Team might be easiest as a subcommittee of a Cultural Competency Academy (CCA) discussed earlier this chapter.

6) Get Buy-in from the School Board

The Illinois Association of School Boards (2018) issued in the spring of 2018 "Ten ways school boards can champion racial equity." This online resource is a good start for superintendents and school boards searching for advice on how school board members should support the rollout of equity policies. The Illinois Association of School Boards offer the following suggestions that help districts move toward racial equity:

1. The school board must have a strong commitment to racial equity by embracing the change to a school culture that implements racial equity practices.
2. Adopt an equity statement that serves as a "guidepost" for the district's equity vision.
3. Understand the school district's racial, ethnic, gender, and disability demographics. The board should know the statistics of these identities of residents throughout the district and of the staff and students. The Illinois Association of School Boards says, "It is necessary for the board to have a level of understanding about the intersections of race and education to make decisions about important district-wide equity initiatives."
4. Board members must be willing to engage in their own personal journey to expand their knowledge and understanding of race issues.
5. Be able to create structural changes that support equity for all.
6. While developing goals and policies with a strong equity lens, those policies that support racial, gender, and disability disparities should be dismantled.
7. In accordance to point 6, the school budget should be evaluated to eliminate disparities.
8. Commit to learning the district's data as it pertains to student academic performance, gifted programs, discipline, attendance, dropout and graduation rates, involvement in extracurricular activities, special education classification, and access to student services.
9. Find allies in other school districts and create partnerships with churches and community organizations.
10. Expect opposition and be ready to engage them in "careful and thoughtful responses and strategies."

The bottom line is school boards should receive the same amount of diversity, equity, and inclusion training as the faculty. Boards must provide steadfast support, as the status quo will certainly be challenged, and should assist its central administration come up with readied answers for those occasions when community members question—either in person or in letters to the editor in local newspapers—the direction the district. Enough examples of defiant faculty and resistant community members that challenge the shift toward equity exist at both the micro and macro levels. Expect procedures and trainings to be taken out of context. Anticipate claims of reverse racism. Be ready for people to claim you are telling them to change their beliefs. These criticisms will be both exhausting and infuriating. Therefore, consistency and cohesion between the equity team and school board members will be important. Those who resist the transition are almost exclusively White parents and White faculty members who have never been challenged on issues of race. The job is to not dismiss the concerns of the critics; but rather, have primed and aligned responses. Remember, the job is not to please a few disgruntled individuals; it is about creating the best possible environment that helps all students succeed in school and in life.

Conclusion

An inclusive school culture can change hearts and minds. Be that as it may, the answer to defeating private and institutional racism is not found in the education system alone. No one should be fooled into thinking that a race conscious school system will conquer deep-seated prejudices that are so inextricably ingrained into many aspects of American society; that educating young people the right way is the secret formula that will end stereotyping and biases. Make no mistake, there is no magic wand. Education is critical, but it cannot be the only part of the solution. Consider what President Obama (2016) said at the commencement ceremony at Howard University months before his departure from the Oval Office: "to bring about structural change, lasting change, awareness is not enough. It requires changes in law, changes in custom."

In March 2019, legislation was reintroduced in Congress called the Equality Act to explicitly prohibit discrimination against LGBTQ+ people and racialized individuals. It was first introduced as a comprehensive LGBTQ+ civil rights bill by Senators Jeff Merkley (D-OR) and Tammy Baldwin (D-WI), as well as Representatives John Lewis (D-GA, 5th District) and David Cicilline (D-RI, 1st District) in 2015—shortly after the U.S. Supreme Court's landmark ruling on marriage equality in *Obergefell v. Hodges*. Lawmakers aspire to affix sexual orientation and gender identity to existing civil rights laws, adding sex protection to federal funding so public accommodations could not deny goods and services against a woman because of sex and to remove existing discrimination of women and LGBTQ+ people in employment, housing, public spaces, health care, jury selection, credit, and education. If passed despite the Trump Administration's public condemnation of the bill in May 2019, the Equality Act will modernize the definition of public accommodations to enhance the rights of People of Color, of various religious faiths, and of diverse national origins. A comprehensive piece of legislation like this is critical to build more welcoming schools for People of Color and LGBTQ+ people.

The Equality Act aside, let me be frank: I do not believe there is anything anyone can do to totally eradicate racism, sexism, religious intolerance, and homophobia from the United States, particularly if all that was done depended on curricula and legislation to pull people into the light. I concur with the legal scholar Derrick Bell's ultimate thesis that White supremacy is a permanent fixture in American society. Racism is America's original sin. Accordingly, bigotry is systemic and intergenerational. Bell (1993, 2004) has argued that most White liberals who work for the progress of marginalized communities only do so "when and only so long as policymakers perceive that such advances will further interests that are their primary concern." Bell calls this impulse "interest convergence covenants." Bell's skepticism notwithstanding, the perpetuity of racism hardly means that the work for interracial utopia is futile. Rather, in Bell's words, those "temporary peaks of progress" and "short lived victories"—like Barack Obama's presidential victories—are worth the struggle. This is especially important considering a 2018 survey called "The Holocaust Knowledge and Awareness Study" commissioned by the Conference on Jewish Material Claims Against Germany (CJMCAG) indicated 31 percent of Americans are unaware of how many Jews were killed during the Holocaust. The study, which surveyed 1,350 American adults, also revealed 45 percent of Americans failed to name one of the concentration camps and ghettoes during World War II (Federal Ministry of justice and Consumer Protection). Historian Deborah E. Lipstadt (2012) explains that the CJMCAG's discoveries bring to light a frightening reality: that as the number of Holocaust survivors shrink, there are fewer living voices that can personally challenge deniers who strive to reduce the deaths of six million Jews and another five million enemies of the Nazi state to "contrived … forgeries and falsehoods." If Donald Trump's first term in office is any indication, we have a good picture of how far America will relapse into an apartheid state if social justice warriors in public schools and public offices fall silent.

Therefore, for the welfare of the United States, we not only need Black and non-Black citizens to feel valued in every aspect of society, but LGBTQ+ people, too, must feel safe. That safety needs to be felt across each intersectional community; not just for middle to upper-class college educated and able-bodied dark males, but also for Blacks and Whites of all genders and classes. It must be the same for LGBTQ+ people that are not wealthy, White, college educated and able-bodied males. Since the United States is a racist and sexist society, it is only natural that her citizens since childhood have been exposed to racist and sexist tropes. As a result, there needs to be an intersectional approach to change the cultural consciousness of the American people. This means, in addition to changes that address inequities in the education system and policy, there must be an honest conversation that offers answers to how America's youth sports and popular culture represents stigmatized people.

I was fortunate that my formative years were spent in the capital city of Pennsylvania, where I attended racially and sexually diverse schools. My youth sports coaches were White, Black, young, old, monolingual, bilingual, rich, poor, liberal, conservative, transgender, cisgender, gay, and straight. My experience in Harrisburg was truly a conflation of various cultures. I acknowledge that most White Generation Xers are not as fortunate. If the only interaction that individuals like me had with People of Color was during the crime report on the evening news, or on sitcoms like *The Fresh Prince of Bel Air* and *Martin*, or while *Yo! MTV Raps* offered White folks a glimpse into the Black inner-city experience of New York, Los Angeles, Cleveland, Houston, and Atlanta; it is no wonder that the systemic barriers of racial oppression are as ubiquitous today as they were just after the civil rights movement. Meanwhile, there was just about no representation of LGBTQ+ individuals on television, save *Will & Grace*. A few notable big screen films like *American Beauty* and *Magnolia* in the late 1990s made gay characters an integral part of the plot. Still, much of the 1990s and into the 2000-aughts, romantic comedies made a habit of casting gay men and lesbians in supporting roles to provide the plot some comedic relief, àla *My Best Friend's Wedding*, *Hitch*, and *Easy A*. Though the music industry seemed to offer the public the most LGBTQ+ representation, the profession was already pilloried for sexual innuendo and drug use, while the artists were characterized in fundamental circles as ill repute. The Culture Club's Boy George was the only singer that made adults of the Baby Boom and Silent generations uncomfortable knowing that their Generation X children and grandchildren were observing an individual comfortable in his bisexual and genderqueer appearance. Sure, adults knew Elton John and Freddy Mercury were gay. But to Baby Boomers with children, their reassurances to heteronormativity were reinforced by the fact that no one could tell by looking at them. Then the world bore witness to the 2003 MTV Video Music Awards, which featured a star-laden medley and a beguiling kiss between Madonna and Britney Spears, then Madonna again with Christina Aguilera. The "lesbian kiss," as my then-older colleagues in the teaching profession described it, made Baby Boomers jump out of their socks. However, for me (full disclosure: I am among the youngest of Gen-Xers) the threesome kiss had an educative effect that suggested I not think too deeply about sexuality.

To put this in perspective, a multilateral approach that combines schooling with legislation and the revamping of popular culture would concretely rewrite the curricula of society at large. For decades, educator and author Gloria Ladson-Billings (2003) spoke passionately about "societal curriculum," the form of subconscious learning that occurs when making observations of the surroundings, which has long devalued the contributions and individuality of racialized people (I am including LGBTQ+, the poor, and religious minorities as racialized people). For Ladson-Billings, the answer to resist White supremacy is to make education culturally relevant for Students of Color. She created a paradigm for Black and White educators by paving a path forward to use the school system to advance the cause of cultural competence, shared wealth, and intersectional equity. Her disciples, ranging from Geneva Gay (2000) to Django Paris (2017), and from Gregory Michie (2009) to Christopher Emdin (2017), have advanced the cause of cultural relevance by expanding the field to Latinxs, Asian Americans, Native Americans, women, Islamic Americans, Jews, LGBTQ+ people, and people who are disabled.

This book, however, does not offer strategies for how to get legislation passed. Neither does it expound upon how media and film misrepresents racially minoritized groups like Latinxs and Native Americans, or even Muslims and Jews. Rather, it presents a case for why educators must revise pedagogy and curriculum in a way that is race conscious. About half of these pages focus on why it is important for White students to receive a critical examination of race in America's various institutions. The other half of the book gives teachers strategies for creating a race conscious classroom in addition to offering proactive measures to guard against resentful parents, colleagues, and students. By obliging White students to abandon positions of comfort, power, and privilege; and by making them render themselves open-minded, White children will be better equipped to tackle adult life. Even if the job they eventually obtain lacks Colleagues of Color, they will likely serve Clients of Color. Even if White children grew up in a community without Neighbors of Color, they will possess skills to teach their own children about racial identity development; which will lead to a healthy White identity. As a bonus, White students educated in a race conscious classroom will learn the proper skills for how to think critically, while feeling no pressure to see the world in a particular light. In that sense, White Americans will live happier and more positive lives.

Afterword
by George Yancy

I continue to be profoundly moved and encouraged by Black literary figure and activist James Baldwin whenever I read his indictment of the toxicity, systematicity, and systemic nature of white racism in North America. I am *moved* because Baldwin's chosen discourse speaks courageously to whiteness. It is a discourse that, as Frantz Fanon would say, refuses to be subdued, beautiful, and pure when speaking against the persistence and death-dealing logics of white power and hegemony. I say "death-dealing" as whiteness attempts to preserve itself as "pure" at the expense of Black bodies and non–Black bodies of color that face being constantly pulled into an existential maelstrom of social and physical death by the white state and white proxies of the state. I am *encouraged* because Baldwin exemplifies for us a form of critique of whiteness that is a species of love that has absolutely nothing to do with sentimentality or Hollywood romanticism. In this way, when it comes to critically marking and revealing the entrails, as it were, of whiteness, critique—especially forms of critique formulated based upon anti–Black racism endured by Black bodies—doesn't lose itself in reciprocal hate, but also never loses sight of the necessity for outrage and anger vis-à-vis racial injustice.

Love refuses to leave the world as it is found. Love refuses to placate the insidious ideological, political, social, affective, and phenomenological operations of white racist power. Love refuses to let whiteness off the proverbial hook regarding the latter's self-claimed "innocence." In fact, for Baldwin, the "innocence" of whiteness constitutes the crime. The crime is willful ignorance, the refusal to see whiteness as *the* problem within the context of a thoroughly racialized North American polity, one where, in our current historical moment, whiteness narcissistically grieves, mourns, and laments what is really a reaction to having its mythical status as the "apex" of humanity challenged and repudiated, and its political hegemony and normative monochromatic monopoly called into question.

Whiteness attempts to preserve its "innocence" through the logics of a racialized binary, where whiteness is the transcendental norm. After all, whiteness consumes generative differences and then projects those differences out as "deviant," as "sub-persons," "sub-humans." When white people refuse to see how the logics of whiteness work according to this binary structure, it is to "invite," again, drawing from Baldwin, "their own destruction." He continues, "And anyone who insists on remaining in a state of innocence long after that innocence is dead turns himself [themself] into a monster." In the 21st century, whiteness continues to be a white leviathan of teratological *racist* proportions. Its monstrous reach is sanctioned across a variety of lived social, political, economic, institutional, and geopolitical spaces—on the street, in stores, banks, jobs, and real estate offices, within places of religious worship, within the context of private boardrooms, within tribalistic political parties, within classrooms and on school playgrounds, within pedagogical spaces where canonical and curricular formations take place, within the context of the Global South, within the context of "foreigners" seeking asylum and refugee status, and especially at the "highest" office in the land, the presidency itself.

Yet, isn't this the veil that must be lifted, the reality that must be named and marked, the parrhesia that must be spoken, the de-masking and the painful un-suturing that we must demand of white people?

The book that you hold in your hands, *Race Conscious Pedagogy*, is one within which its author, Todd M. Mealy, responds to the above questions with an affirmative, "YES!" Indeed, the title of the book bespeaks a white temporal rupture and an indictment. Yet, the title also functions as a promise going forward. It implies the author's commitment to, as bell hooks would say, an uncompromisingly audacious process of "talking back" to whiteness. Reading through the book, it is clear that Mealy is aware of how the "we" functions within the title as a specific call to *white people*, especially as Black people and non–Black people of color understand all too well the importance of refusing to be silent.

Mealy's indispensable book is filled with critical sociological exegesis and important sociological empirical data, insightful historical analysis unafraid to show the racist terror of whiteness to itself, keen and unflinching autobiographical excavation, which is necessary for any white person who dares, as Mealy does, to speak truth to white power. While Mealy's book has far reaching implications for whiteness beyond the classroom, his central point of embarkation is a deep and meditative *critical pedagogical* engagement with whiteness. As he makes clear, he does so "by providing readers a close look at the structure, curriculum, and pedagogy" of a critical race studies course that he courageously taught at a predominantly white high school. Having read through the book, Mealy does not falter when it comes to providing such a *close look*.

With clarity, precision, critical self-disclosure, and persuasive argumentation, Mealy demonstrates why public schools ought, which implies the ethical sphere, to make race conscious pedagogy an indispensable part of the school curriculum. He traces the ways in which children, our children, the ones that we love, educationally lose out in terms of not possessing a sharpened critical consciousness when it comes to issues of challenging white racism and how they suffer, or so I would argue, in terms of a diminished ethical vocabulary and critical framework for understanding their own white complicity and the pain this contributes to non-white people because our schools refuse to implement the insights of race conscious pedagogy into the curriculum. Mealy engages the relationship between students of color and what they need in order to ensure their success within often unacknowledged, but problematically white epistemic and pedagogical logics that pervade academic spaces where teachers and staff are predominantly white; and, he addresses the difficult challenges of how white people—who I would argue are both consciously and unconsciously *invested* in the maintenance of whiteness—within North America's pervasively white school systems, which is inclusive of the students themselves, parents, teachers and administrators, can abandon their white power and solace to ensure racially equitable pedagogical spaces.

What makes Mealy's book so rich affectively is his personal communication regarding the existential gravity of the crime of white "innocence." He also conveys, with a sense of urgency, the fact that he cares about his students and understands that, like Baldwin, love requires, within the context of whiteness, historical confrontation, self-confrontation, and the realization that education is a process of "leading out" as the etymology of the word (*educare*) suggests. Being Socratic in spirit and practice, Mealy not only understands how painful educational rebirth can be—the bringing forth of new and radical ideas, the creation of fecund interstitial spaces of profound insight, the transformation of curricular materials and methodologies, and a new and self-critically anti-racist white self on the part of teachers and students—but he also understands what is at stake for him personally in terms of his own compromised sense of safety as he challenges white supremacy.

Regarding the issue of the painful process of leading out, Mealy takes his reader within the classroom itself where students grapple with processes of differential racialization and its psychological, social, economic, and existential impact—indeed, its oppressive and necropolitical blow to the lives of Black and non–Black students of color. Teachers and administrators will be (and certainly should be) empowered by the narratives that Mealy provides of his students as they realize just how white racial logics operate differently for them as opposed to Black and non–Black people of color. Reading through the book, one gets to bear witness to white students as they realize just how whiteness renders their lives safe, predictable, and normative. Such moments are marked with great surprise and by implication, I would argue, the sense of having been misled by white parents and white educators who have failed to educate them about their own whiteness and its toll on non-white people. In short, white ignorance, which *actively* resists knowing otherwise, prevails. While Mealy does not argue this, my sense is that his students have effectively undergone a sense of what I call white double consciousness, where they get to see their own whiteness through the perspectives and critical works of Black people and non–Black people of color. But this is only made possible because of Mealy daring to have his students engage texts (books, films, etc.) by authors that are predominantly not white and who are critical of the structure of whiteness.

Concerning the issue of the threat of white backlash, Mealy frames the discussion through a delineation of my own personal experience of having written a very controversially received article, "Dear White America," for the *New York Times*' philosophy column, "The Stone." That article, published in 2015, received hundreds of horrendously racist responses and involved university police escorts to my classes. Those responses were not only from clearly self-defined white racists, but from white people who would claim, if asked, that they don't have a racist bone in their body. And while Mealy is aware of the differences experienced by me (a Black man) and himself (a white man), and thereby rightly doesn't conflate the experiences, it was crucial that Mealy provided a narrative of some of the white backlash that *he* experienced. The narrative is important for white teachers as they must be made aware of the actual and potential danger they will likely suffer as they dare to mark whiteness within the classroom, the curriculum, the administration, and within themselves. It is the reality of such danger, and such backlash, that unveils, at least in this case, the truth that whiteness is a problem, a problem that white people would rather not confront. From the many who questioned his motives for teaching a critical race studies course at a predominantly white high school, to administrative "surveillance," to very disparaging editorial coverage of his classroom and its assumptions, to distorted memes, and to a defamatory statement posted by a white parent on Facebook that read, "This man has lost his mind," Mealy remained courageous and resolute. Mealy persisted and persists in his pedagogical vision and his understanding of his role as a white teacher who refuses to be silent, and who, in the spirit of the tradition of critical pedagogy, understands critical consciousness and critical discourse as oppositional to hegemonic structures that undermine the importance of a critically engaged demos.

Mealy's indispensable book, *Race Conscious Pedagogy*, is a must read. It is especially important for white teachers, white administrators, white parents, and white legislators, who may not fully understand what is at stake—

urgently so—when they remain silent about the historical and contemporary manifestations of whiteness and how white people, as Baldwin might say, induce their own destruction when they close their eyes to white supremacist reality. Mealy wants all of us, but especially white people who benefit from systems of white power and privilege, to seek to make a difference in the world and to resist all hegemonic structures—from white racism, classism, ableism, heterosexism, cisgenderism, to ethnic exclusions and efforts at and realities of genocide, socioeconomic oppression and pervasive food insecurity, and "anti–Muslim and anti-immigration sentiments in schools." His is a pedagogy designed for those, even if uncertain, who are willing and ready to untie/undo a white Odyssean mindset, where risk is a necessary requirement. Mealy's book is for those white people, and especially for white teachers, who are prepared—unlike Odysseus who tied himself to the mast of a ship—to engage in forms of vulnerability, and educational praxes that are dangerous; and dangerous precisely because they contest the racial/racist status quo. Regardless of the fear and reality of backlash, Mealy wants teachers to risk un-suturing, and to risk the death of white "innocence," white power, and white ethical solipsism. *Race Conscious Pedagogy* is a pedagogical clarion call, an act of Baldwinian love.

George Yancy is a philosopher who works primarily in the areas of critical philosophy of race, critical Whiteness studies, critical phenomenology, and the philosophy of the Black experience. He has authored, edited, or co-edited more than 20 books and over 150 scholarly articles and chapters.

Appendix 1

Response to a Parent, May 2018

Detective,

At 10 o'clock in the evening on May 25, 2018, you, a local police detective, posted a meme on Facebook declaring that I had lost my mind. "This man has no business in the public education system," you wrote. You were apparently reacting to something you saw on a social media parody account. While conceding in the meme that you could not confirm my statement, you then improperly quoted me: "Most Christians are associated with Trump and racism. In fact, Pastors are usually racist."

I was both hurt and frightened the moment I was informed that your meme appeared on Facebook. While given the full support of the [Gap] School District's administrative team, I thought of my wife, who works in the school district, and my two young children. I imagined that if they were a little older, they would have certainly learned of this unfounded assertion from their peers at school and possibly teased about it.

Detective, just like the average citizen has the right to criticize you in your profession, you have the right to criticize me in mine. The public pays both of our salaries. However, neither one of us should make things up when we make those criticisms. You are a detective. I would expect that you invest the same level of inquiry into the comments and credibility of that in which you will ultimately speak publicly on.

Detective, it is not I who has lost his mind. It is you, perhaps because your profession is at the center of national discourse, or possibly for other reasons. Either the pressure of your job or your resistance to a class on race and gender has compelled you to share a slanderous internet meme. Why? You could of chosen to engage with me in a mature and intelligent discussion.

You state, "He brags about how he is untouchable." I'm stunned. Where on earth, Detective, would you think I "brag" about my job security? What is your evidence? You might assume this, as I am involved (rather successfully) in a number of endeavors beyond educating high schoolers. Yet, never have I expressed to anyone that I am "untouchable." In fact, I work very hard at all of my jobs while raising two toddlers with my lovely wife for fear of losing my job and losing the respect of my colleagues.

Detective, you apparently do not know me at all. Would you like me to arrange a meeting with the hundreds of students that have sat in my classes? Or maybe the hundreds colleagues I have worked with at two Lancaster County schools? Perhaps you would like to hear from the countless young men that I have coached at three schools since 1998. Or my peers in graduate school. My family? Would you like to ask any of them if they have heard me say such a thing? You couldn't be more wrong in how you have characterized me.

Detective, you claim that I said to my students, "Most Christians are associated with Trump and racism. In fact, Pastors are usually racist." First, your prose has flaws. "I cant [sic] confirm this statement," you write. Then you placed the following sentence in quotation marks: "Most Christians are associated with Trump and racism. In fact, Pastors are usually racist."

Let us play a game by dissecting this denigration and deviation of the truth.

First, one thing you accused me of saying is: "Most Christians are associated with Trump …" Evangelical ties to Trump have come up in class as a statistic. According to exit polling from the 2016 Presidential Election, 58 percent of Protestants and 52 percent of Catholics voted for Trump. Moreover, 81 percent of White, born-again/evangelical Christians voted for Trump. What, may I ask you, is inaccurate with that comment?

Second, you accuse me of saying, "Most Christians are associated with … racism." You continue the allegation, "In fact, Pastors are usually racist." This might be hard to accept, but most White people are either racists or apathetic toward racism, as I associate racism with the support of policies that wield the power of one group over another, and with privilege. All White people, including pastors, assuming some pastors are White, are either racist or apathetic to racism in that all White people regardless of profession reap hegemonic comfort because of their White skin. When failing to speak out when they should have, or by failing to engage critically in the pain that black people suffer, or fail to challenge poisonous assumptions or jokes that people of color are "inferior" to Whites, or to speak out loudly in the company of Whites who believe that Black identity or White privilege are just terms used in academia, Whites have been complicit with, and have allowed themselves to benefit from, a country that has profited from the labor and culture of Black and Brown people.

But the truth is, I never said pastors are "usually racist." I might say that there have been pastors that participated in the ritual lynching of Black people—in fact I have taught this regularly in my United States history courses. If one is properly educated, this fact should become common knowledge as the primary day of the week when lynchings took place was on Sunday. Yes, church gossip had something to do with that. Sometimes after those lynchings, postcards featuring dismembered and charred Black bodies were manufactured for the public's amusement. Whites, some of them happen to be religious leaders, have been captured in those images. Standing next to those preachers were also teachers, law enforcers, elected officials, and children. And yet independent from ritual lynching, some Christian organizations in American history have certainly strived to improve racial solidarity as there was once a time when racist preachers used Scripture to justify, first, slavery, then, segregation. Two texts I recommend are Sherrilyn Ifill's *On the Courthouse Lawn* (Beacon Press, 2007) and Peter Ehrenhaus and A. Susan Owen's "Race Lynching and Christian Evangelicalism: Performance of Faith" (Taylor & Francis Online, 2007). Detective, you must provide your Facebook followers with context for why topics like that would come up in my class; context that you have not provided in your meme.

Speaking of context, your meme is also missing the fact it was not I who brought up the topic of racism and pastors; rather, it was one of my colleagues who was using my students to practice a lesson on implicit bias for her own class. With me sitting in a student-desk in the back of the room, this teacher used Joel Pares' "Judging America" portrait titled "Full-Time Pastor/Missionary, Jack Johnson" to make the point that there is a generalized stereotype for just about any racial, gender, or occupational intersection existing today. Her approach was powerful. I applaud her and I am sure the lesson with her regular class went well.

The aforementioned hypotheticals notwithstanding, I did *not* say what you claimed I said. I am Catholic. I grew up attending a Catholic church in the City of Harrisburg. I spent much of my adult life as an itinerant worshipper, having visited Lutheran, Pentecostal, Baptist, African Methodist Episcopalian, and nondenominational churches. I spent two years at one of the most conservative churches in Lancaster County, Calvary Church on Landis Valley Road. I made friends at each church and know enough about this world that pastors are not "usually racist."

Harkening back to the Trump and the Evangelical issue, here is a question that I might ask in class: "Is the reason why Evangelicals turned out for Trump in 2016 and continue to support his administration's policies despite the fact that he has lived an immoral life, including his 5 children to 3 wives (not included in the question, though implied, would be the Access Hollywood video, a rumored love-child payoff, his 2000 false and misleading claims over 355 days in office, and his payoffs to an adult movie actor and Playboy model) due to his willingness to wage a culture war on the growing 'brownness' of this country and burgeoning tolerance for LGBTQ issues?" This is a question that addresses the race and gender components of this course. A class discussion would follow my question. Students' answers are opened ended, which means the discussion will go in any direction the students take it. I don't lead student responses in any direction. And I certainly don't "indoctrinate" the minds of my students. I will say more on my method of questioning momentarily.

This brings me to my next point. What is the purpose of Humanities? The Humanities, which includes courses like AP Seminar: Race, Ethnicity, and Gender, teaches students how to problematize issues in the world. Must I remind you, our class motto—voted on by your child and classroom peers—is "Everything is a problem." We put that on our class T-shirt. Humanities students are encouraged to think originally and creatively to develop informed solutions to the world's problems. Without Humanities, academics believe, "democracy could not flourish." Therefore, in AP Seminar: Race, Ethnicity, and Gender, the curriculum is designed to deconstruct American society for the purpose of improving it. For half the school year, my students problematize issues of race and gender in American culture. At the end of each investigation, they offer solutions. That, in essence, is the class your child is enrolled in. It helps students learn that no single version of the "truth" is total and permanent. Fundamentally, my students are taught how to apply new knowledge generated by reading texts written by various race and gender scholars to their analyses of issues, problems, and experiences. It is what separates my course from every other course offered at [Gap] High School.

My job each day is to ask students difficult and thought provoking questions. Not simple questions, but challenging ones that are the types of questions that the students are supposed to ask themselves when they conduct independent research. The procedure goes like such: I ask a question. I listen intently to student responses. I offer commentary once the students have finished responding to my initial question. I then ask a follow up question. That subsequent question might be part of my script or it might have come to mind while listening to the students. I often pose a question that forces the students to think deeper about their peers' comments. Then we have another round of student responses. Class goes on like this for the duration of the lesson. This is supposed to (1) serve as a template of diverse and divergent voices that would later make up their research papers, and (2) offer ideas and skills to help students come up with original research topics. I cannot help it if you do not like the topics we discuss or the responses given by the students (again, in which I summarize in a more articulate way for the benefit of those in the classroom). This class studies race and gender. These are contentious topics. However, just one hour spent in front of the television each evening will show anyone that America has trouble dealing with race and gender. If African Americans are saying there is a problem with how they are policed, that is something this class should discuss. If Islamic Americans say there is a heightened sense of Islamophobia in contemporary society, students in my class should discuss this issue. If women say they are under-represented in leadership positions, that is a topic we should discuss.

I don't have to tell you that the country's demography has changed with the spike in the percentages of minority population in the last two decades. With it has come controversy: upsurges in hate speech, opposition to immigration, some of it taking the form of blogs, talk-radio, and social media trolling. Globalization and outsourcing have removed thousands of jobs, so that the gap in income and family wealth is at one of the highest levels ever. Racial profiling, police profiling, the war on drugs, a swelled prison population, and more problems remain. My class has taken note of all these developments.

Yes, my questions expose certain sensitivities, but isn't that the purpose of a Humanities seminar? Here are a few of the questions I have asked this year: (1) Why is it fair to say that all White people benefit from White supremacy? (2) To what degree is every man in this classroom a sexist? (3) How does every White person in this room harbor racist feelings? Do they benefit from racism? If so, is it because of that comfort that they do nothing to end racism? (4) How is it possible that poor Whites benefit from White privilege? (5) Why is it reasonable that many in the African American community identify with a Black Jesus? (6) How can it be possible that many school shooters have ties to White nationalism? (7) To what extent does the public have a right to criticize law enforcement? With that said, I must state clearly that most of my questions concentrate on the reading of the day. I ask students to identify the author's main argument, supporting claims, credibility of evidence used, values and limitations, and implications. In summary, my class is *not* lecture-based, which would be the appropriate method used to indoctrinate students.

Detective, do you see how these questions might become appropriate research questions for a term paper? According to the Advanced Placement College Board, students' research questions must (1) "require a judgment or evaluation to be made (not just descriptive)," (2) "are researchable," (3) "Involve genuine points of ongoing debate," (4) "Invite engagement with alternative points of view," and (5) "do not contain multiple, nested questions." In summary, developing a good research question must be something "debatable."

Detective, the impression I get is that you would prefer to avoid conversations on these topics. And you apparently don't want your daughter to have these conversations in a classroom. If your reaction is, "I do, but as long as both sides are presented." Well, both sides are always presented. All of my sources are posted on the website I developed for the course. If you don't trust the website, you are welcome to see the handout for the assignments.

It is the difficult conversation about race and racism in America that we must have. And yet, sadly, it is that form of discourse about race that we continue to avoid, that White people especially continue to avoid. My questions in class aim to get students to speak to this. It seems that you don't think it is necessary to have this level of discourse in a classroom setting. Or at least, you don't want your child to engage in the debate. If so, why did your child enrolled in a class about race?

Might I add that this is a social studies credit required by the Commonwealth; my class, however, is an elective. Your child elected to take this course. The Pennsylvania Department of Education requires that every student take one social studies credit per year. [Gap] High School's Social Studies Department offers a multitude of Advance Placement electives. Your child could have chosen any. In a class that has "Race" in its title, did you not expect students to have these conversations? Did you not expect the teacher to bring them up?

In case you've forgotten, Detective, the first, and, well, the only time I heard a concern directly from you was the moment we began discussing Black Lives Matter; which, I assume, you developed an extra sense of indifference about the class because that movement challenges people in your profession to be better. Now, I believe, this has turned into a personal vendetta, not so much against me, but against the existence of a class that spends half the year assessing cultural hegemony. Or maybe you're just upset with a grade your child received on a term paper—a grade, I might add, that was issued because your child did not follow the rubric. Instead of calling into the school to complain, you reposted an internet meme that makes a personal—and false—assault on my character.

Detective, I have taught in public schools for 17 years. Eleven of those have been spent in the [Gap] School District. During my tenure in Millersville, not a single left-leaning official has served on the school board. I live and work in one of the most conservative counties in the Commonwealth. I knew my class would be a lightning rod in the district. I expected complaints. I did not, however, expect to endure slander from a police detective. Slander is demeaning, while gratitude is a powerful gift. I welcome genuine questions or concerns from parents; and, of course, appreciation for the reading, research, writing, and presentation skills that your child learned in my classroom.

Appendix 2
Seminar in Critical Race Studies
Summer Reading Assignment

Todd Mealy, Ph.D.
Social Studies Department
Gap High School

IMPORTANT: Communication between student and teacher is important in this seminar course. Therefore, as per your enrollment in this class, it is expected that you check your email during the summer. Additionally, if for some reason, you withdraw from the class or if you switch sections (move from one block to another), please notify me via email.

Summer Reading Assignment

You are asked to purchase and read one book during the summer. You must prepare an oral presentation that lasts 15 minutes (with an additional 5–10 minutes of discussion). You should outline the book's topic, research question, central argument, supporting claims, important evidence, and comparable sources. No other student will have read the book, so you should be sure to present your summary of the work so that it will be understandable to everyone. You will need to put together a PowerPoint and a handout for your peers in class. Bring the PowerPoint and handout on a USB drive to class on the first day of school.

Notes regarding your handout: (1) place your name and page numbers in the header, (2) proof read and spell check your document before submission on the first day of school.

Below is a suggestion for how to structure the handout (do not include the information in parentheses):

Author's Name and Book Title:

Author's Academic Background:

Author's Publishing Background (List published books and articles):

Source Constellation (What books/articles/documentaries/podcasts are similar to this book? How does this book fit in with other works on the topic?):

Key Terms/Vocab/Names:

Assess the Author's Line of Reasoning:
- Author's central argument (the book's overall thesis) and supporting claims (thesis of each chapter)
- (This is a bulleted list that includes one sentence a piece for the central argument and each claim)
- List the top 3–5 sources used to write the book. (bulleted list)

Summarize the Introduction/Preface (include any important quotes):

Write an essay that responds to the book's argument (either in support or in opposition):
1. Paragraph 1: Have a strong opening sentence/hook. You should include both the title and the name of the author. You might want to include a question that leads you to your thesis. The last sentence of this paragraph should contain a thesis statement.
2. Paragraph 2: You should reflect on one point made in the book. Identify strengths & weaknesses. Be critical or supportive of the author.
3. Paragraph 3: You should reflect on a second point made in the book. Identify strengths & weaknesses. Be critical or supportive of the author.
4. Paragraph 4 (If needed): You should reflect on a third point made in the book. Identify strengths & weaknesses. Be critical or supportive of the author.
5. Paragraph 5: Can you make modern-day connections? How does this contemporary connection strengthen your opinion on the book?

The Reading List (Choose one book)

Foundational Topics
1. Delgado, Richard and Jean Stefancic. 2017. *Critical Race Theory: An Introduction*
2. Diner, Hasia R. 2003. *Hungering for America: Italian, Irish, and Jewish Foodways in the Age of Migration.*
3. Eberhardt, Jennifer. 2019. *Biased: Uncovering the Hidden Prejudice That Shapes What We See, Think, and Do*
4. Kendi, Ibram X. 2019. *How to Be an Antiracist*

Whiteness Studies
5. Diangelo, Robin. 2018. *White Fragility: Why It's So Hard for White People to Talk about Racism*
6. Griffin, John Howard. 1956. *Black Like Me*
7. Harvey, Jennifer. 2018. *Raising White Kids: Bringing Up Children in a Racially Unjust America*
8. Whitman, James. 2018. *Hitler's American Model: The United States and the Making of Nazi Race Law*
9. Wise, Tim. 2011. *White Like Me: Reflections on Race from a Privileged Son*
10. Wray, Matt. 2006. *Not Quite White: White Trash and the Boundaries of Whiteness*

Latinx Studies
11. Molina, Natalia. 2014. *How Race Is Made in America: Immigration, Citizenship, and the Historical Power of Racial Scripts*
12. Paredes, Américo. 1970. *"With His Pistol in His Hand": A Border Ballad and Its Hero*
13. Anzaldua, Gloria. 1999. *Borderlands/La Frontera: The New Mestiza*

African American Studies
14. Alexander, Michelle. 2012. *The New Jim Crow: Mass Incarceration in the Age of Colorblindness*
15. Belcher, Cornell. 2016. *A Black Man in the White House: Barack Obama and the Trigger of America's Racial-Aversion Crisis*
16. Camacho, David E. 1998. *Environmental Injustices, Political Struggles: Race, Class, and the Environment*
17. Dyson, Michael Eric. 2005. *Is Bill Cosby Right? Or Has the Black Middle Class Lost Its Mind?*
18. Fishkin, Shelley Fisher. 1993. *Was Huck Black?: Mark Twain and African American Voices*
19. Hill, Marc Lamont. 2017. *Nobody: Casualties of America's War on the Vulnerable, From Ferguson to Flint*
20. Ifill, Sherrilyn. 2007. *On the Courthouse Lawn: Confronting the Legacy of Lynching in the 21st Century*
21. Turner, Patricia. 1993. *I Heard It Through the Grapevine: Rumor in African-American Culture*

Asian American Studies
22. Nelson, Kim Park. 2016. *Invisible Asians: Korean American Adoptees and Racial Exceptionalism*
23. Yeh, Chiou-Ling. 2008. *Making an American Festival: Chinese New Year in San Francisco's Chinatown*

Jewish American Studies
24. Goldstein, Judith S. 2006. *Inventing Great Neck: Jewish Identity and the American Dream*
25. Heilman, Samuel C. 1995. *Portrait of American Jews: The Last Half of the 20th Century*

Arab American Studies
26. Alsultany, Evelyn. 2012. *Arabs and Muslims in the Media: Race and Representation After 9/11*
27. Bayoumi, Moustafa. 2015. *This Muslim American Life: Dispatches from the War on Terror*
28. Bayoumi, Moustafa. 2009. *How Does It Feel to Be a Problem: Being Young and Arab in America*
29. Beydoun, Khaled A. 2018. *American Islamophobia: Understanding the Roots and Rise of Fear*

Native American Studies
30. Dippie, Brian. 1982. *The Vanishing American*
31. Jenkins, Sally. 2008. *The Real All Americans*
32. Spindel, Carol. 2002. *Dancing at Halftime: Sports and the Controversy Over American Indian Mascots*

Gender Studies

33. Kimport, Katrina. 2013. *Queering Marriage: Challenging Family Formation in the United States*
34. Ware, Susan. 2011. *Game, Set, Match: Billie Jean King and the Revolution in Women's Sports*

Bibliography

Acosta, Curtis, Jose Gonzalez, and Eren McGinnis (2011). *Precious Knowledge*. DVD. Directed by Ari Palos. Tucson, AZ.

Acuña, Rodolfo F. (2017). *Assault on Mexican American Collective Memory, 2010–2015*. Lanham, MD: Rowman & Littlefield.

Adickes, Sandra (2005). *The Legacy of a Freedom School*. Springer, 2005.

American Civil Liberties Union (2018). "Felony Disenfranchisement Laws (Map)." *ACLU*. 2018. https://www.aclu.org/issues/voting-rights/voter-restoration/felony-disenfranchisement-laws-map.

Anderson, Carol (2018). *One Person, No Vote: How Voter Suppression is Destroying Our Democracy*. New York: Bloomsbury Publishing.

Anderson, Monica (2016, July 27). "Blacks with college experience more likely to say they faced discrimination." *Pew Research Center*. Retrieved from https://www.pewresearch.org/fact-tank/2016/07/27/blacks-with-college-experience-more-likely-to-say-they-faced-discrimination/.

Anderson, Monica, and Paul Hilton (2016, August 15). "Social Media Conversation About Race: how social media users see, share, and discuss race the rise of hashtags like #BlackLivesMatter." *Pew Research Center*. http://www.pewinternet.org/2016/08/15/social-media-conversations-about-race/.

Anzaldua, Gloria (1987). *Borderlands/La Frontera: The New Mestiza*. San Francisco: Aunt Lute Books.

Arce, Sean, Dir. Of Mexican Am. Studies Dep't. (2010, Sept. 14). "TUSD Mexican American Studies Department: Presentation to the TUSD Governing Board" (Powerpoint presentation on file with *Arizona Law Review*).

Arenge, Andrew, Stephanie Perry, and Dartunorro Clark (2018). "Poll: 64 percent of Americans say racism remains a major problem." *NBC News*. May 29, 2018. https://www.nbcnews.com/politics/politics-news/poll-64-percent-americans-say-racism-remains-major-problem-n877536.

Arizona State House of Representatives, 49th Legislature, Second Regular Session (2010, May 11) "House Bill 2281, An Act Amending Title 15, Chapter 1, Article 1, Arizona Revised Statutes, By Adding Sections 15–111 and 15–112; Amending Section 15–843, Arizona Revised Statutes; Relating to School Curriculum."

Arizona State Senate Immigration Research Committee (2010, January 15). "Fact sheet for S.B. 1070, immigration; law enforcement; safe neighborhoods." https://www.azleg.gov/legtext/49leg/2r/summary/s.1070pshs.doc.htm.

Asante, Molefi (2003). *Erasing Racism: The Survival of the American Nation*. Amherst, NY: Prometheus Books.

Asim, Jabari (2007). *The N Word: Who Can Say It, Who Shouldn't, and Why*. Boston: Houghton Mifflin.

Badger, Tony (1999, June). "Southerners Who Refused To Sign the Southern Manifesto." *The Historical Journal*, Vol. 42, No. 2.

Baldwin, James (1985) *The Price of the Ticket: Collected Nonfiction, 1948–1985*. New York: St. Martin's Press, 1985.

Bell, Derrick (1980, January). "Brown v. Board of Education and the Interest-Convergence Dilemma." *Harvard Law Review*. Vol. 93, No. 3.

Bell, Derrick (1989). *And We Are Not Saved: The Elusive Quest for Racial Justice*. New York: Basic Books.

Bell, Derrick (1993, 2017). *Faces at the Bottom of the Well: The Permanence of Race*. New York: Basic Books.

Bell, Derrick (2004). *Silent Covenants:* Brown v. Board of Education *and the Unfulfilled Hopes for Racial Reform*. Oxford: Oxford University Press.

Bell, Derrick A., Jr. (1976). "Serving Two Masters: Integration Ideals and Client Interests in School Desegregation Litigation." *Yale Law Journal*. Vol. 85, No. 4.

Beydoun, Khaled A. (2018). *American Islamophobia: Understanding the Roots and Rise of Fear*. Berkeley: University of California Press.

Bieler, Des (2018, September 17). "'Black-ish' actress says 'Thank you' to Colin Kaepernick by wearing Nike to Emmys." *Washington Post*.

Black Panther Party (1971, November 11). "A Talk with the Students of the Huey P. Newton Intercommunal Youth Institute," *Black Panther*.

Black Panther Party (1973, October 27). "Bobby Seal Dedicates New Youth Institute and Son of Man Temple to Community," *Black Panther*.

Bloom, Joshua, and Waldo E. Martin, Jr. (2016). *Black Against Empire: The History and Politics of the Black Panther Party*. Berkeley: University of California Press.

Bolton, Charles C. (2005). *The Hardest Deal of All: The Battle Over School Integration in Mississippi, 1870–1980*. Oxford: University Press of Mississippi.

Bolton, Charles C. (2017). "The Last Stand of Massive Resistance: Mississippi Public School Integration, 1970." *Mississippi History Now*.

Bond, Michaelle (2018, March 18). "Painful saga in Coatesville Area School District ends with ex-Coatesville school chief, figure in racist-text flap, headed to jail." *The Inquirer Philadelphia Daily News*.

Bowie, Harry (1964). "Freedom School Data." *Council of Federated Organizations*. Jackson, MS. Bowie—Freedom Schools, 1964, Jan. 14 - Dec. 2 (Harry J. Bowie papers, 1965–1967; Archives Main Stacks, Mss 31, Box 1, Folder 4).

Brown, David (1954, Oct. 24). "Leader of Citizens Council Drafts Fight on Integration." *Clarion-Ledger* (Jackson, MS). 12.

Brown, Philip, Michael W. Corrigan, Ann Higgins-D'Alessandro (2012). *Handbook of Prosocial Education*. New York: Rowman & Littlefield, 2012.

Brown, Richard W. (1968, April). "Freedom of Choice in the South: A Constitutional Perspective." *Louisiana Law Review*. Vol. 28, No. 3.

"*Brown v. Board of Education of Topeka* (2)" (2018). *The Oyez Project*. Chicago-Kent College of Law at Illinois Institute of Technology. https://www.oyez.org/cases/1940-1955/349us294.

"Byrd Speaks Against Campus Anarchy in Fla." *Charleston Gazette*. May 6, 1969. 6.

Cabrera, Nolan (2014, Sept. 30). "Dr. Nolan L. Cabrera's Letter to the Los Angeles Unified School District, Board of Education."

Cabrera, Nolan, Elisa L. Meza, and Roberto Dr. Cintli Rodriguez (2011, Dec. 8). "The Fight for Mexican American Studies in Tucson." NACLA.

Campbell, Colin (2019). Twitter post. February 6, 2019, 4:44 p.m. https://twitter.com/RaleighReporter/status/1093264208421158912.

Carmichael, Stokely (1971, 2007). *Stokely Speaks: From Black Power to Pan-Africanism*. Chicago: Chicago Review Press.

Caron, Christina (2018). "Officer Who Fired Stun Gun at Unarmed Black Man Will Not Be Suspended." *New York Times*, July 7, 2018. https://www.nytimes.com/2018/07/07/us/lancaster-police-taser-black-man.html.

Carson, Clayborne (Ed.) (1998). *The Autobiography of Martin Luther King, Jr.* New York: Grand Central Publishing.

Census Reporter (2018). "[Gap] School District, ACS 2016." Millersville, PA.

Century Foundation (2016, February 10). "The Benefits of Socioeconomically and Racially

Integrated Schools and Classrooms." Retrieved from https://tcf.org/content/facts/the-benefits-of-socioeconomically-and-racially-integrated-schools-and-classrooms/.

Chang, Alvin (2018, July 31). "White America Is Quietly Self-Segregating." *Vox.* https://www.vox.com/2017/1/18/14296126/white-segregated-suburb-neighborhood-cartoon.

Chen, Grace (2018, September 4). "White Students Are Now the Minority in U.S. Public Schools." *Public School Review.* https://www.publicschoolreview.com/blog/white-students-are-now-the-minority-in-u-s-public-schools.

Cleaver, Eldridge (1970). *Education and Revolution* Washington: Center for Educational Reform.

CNN (2010, May 13). "Ethnic Studies ban racist?" *AndersonCooper360,* YouTube. https://www.youtube.com/watch?v=TgvOdD5bVsg.

Coady, Roxanne (November 29, 2017). "Why Are All the Black Kids Sitting Together in the Cafeteria?" *Just the Right Book Podcast!* Retrieved from http://www.bookpodcast.com/black-kids-sitting-together-beverly-tatum/.

Cobb, Charles E., Jr. (2016). *This Nonviolent Stuff'll Get You Killed: How Guns Made the Civil Rights Movement Possible.* Durham: Duck University Press.

Cobb, Charlie (1982). Prospectus for a Summer Freedom School Program," December 1963, from SNCC, The Student Nonviolent Coordinating Committee Papers, 1959–1972. Sanford, NC: Microfilming Corporation of America.

College Board (2016). "AP Seminar: Part of the AP Capstone Program: Course and Exam Description." New York, NY.

College Board (2018). "AP Seminar Course Overview." The College Board, New York, NY.

College Board AP Central (2018). "AP Capstone Diploma Program." The College Board, New York, NY.

College Reporter (2019, November 10). "Open letter to F&M concerning incidents of racism, need for change in administration, steps that must be taken." Retrieved at https://www.the-college-reporter.com/2019/11/10/open-letter-to-fm-concerning-incidents-of-racism-need-for-change-in-administration-steps-that-can-be-taken/.

Collins, John J. (2007). *The Collins Writing Program Improving Student Performance Through Writing and Thinking Across the Curriculum.* Collins Educational Associates.

Commings, Jeff (2006, May 13). "Silent Protest by Students Greets State Official's Speech." *Arizona Daily Star* (Tucson, AZ). A1 and A5.

Congress of Racial Equality; Mississippi Fourth Congressional District (1964). "Mississippi Freedom Schools." Meridian, McComb, Pike County, Indianola, MS.

Costello, Maureen, Kate Shuster, Hasan Jeffries, and Jeremy Stern (2014). "The State of Civil Rights Education in the United States." *Southern Poverty Law Center.* https://www.tolerance.org/magazine/publications/teaching-the-movement-2014;.

Crenshaw, Kimberle (1989). "Demarginalizing the Intersection of Race and Sex: A Black Feminist Critique of Antidiscrimination Doctrine, Feminist Theory and Antiracist Politics." *University of Chicago Legal Forum.*

Darder, Antonia (2017). *Reinventing Paulo Freire: A Pedagogy of Love.* New York: Routledge.

Davis, Glenn M. Melissa B. Hanzsek-Brill, Mark Carl Petzold, and David H. Robinson (2019). "Students' Sense of Belonging: The Development of a Predictive Retention Model." *Journal of the Scholarship of Teaching and Learning,* Vol. 19, No. 1.

Day, John Kyle (2014). *The Southern Manifesto: Massive Resistance and the Fight to Preserve Segregation.* Oxford: University of Mississippi Press.

Dee, Thomas, and Emily Penner (2017, February 1). "The Causal Effects of Cultural Relevance: Evidence from an Ethnic Studies Curriculum." *American Educational Research Journal.* Vol. 54.

Delgado, Richard, and Jean Stefancic (2000). *Critical Race Theory: The Cutting Edge.* Philadelphia: Temple University Press.

Delgado, Richard, and Jean Stefancic (2017). *Critical Race Theory: An Introduction.* New York: New York University Press.

Department of Education Office for Civil Rights (2014). "Civil Rights Data Collection: Data Snapshot: School Discipline." Issue Brief No. 1. https://www2.ed.gov/about/offices/list/ocr/docs/crdc-discipline-snapshot.pdf.

Dependbrock, Julie (2017, August 13). "Ethnic Studies: A Movement Born of a Ban." *NPR.*

https://www.npr.org/sections/ed/2017/08/13/541814668/ethnic-studies-a-movement-born-of-a-ban.

Desilber, Drew, and Kristen Bialik (2017, January 10). "Blacks and Hispanics Face Extra Challenges in Getting Home Loans." *Pew Research Center.* http://www.pewresearch.org/fact-tank/2017/01/10/blacks-and-hispanics-face-extra-challenges-in-getting-home-loans/.

Dewey, John (1915). *The School and Society.* Chicago: University of Chicago Press.

DiAngelo, Robin (2018). *White Fragility: Why It Is So Hard for White People to Talk About Race.* Boston: Beacon Press.

Dickinson College (2018). "Diversity and Inclusion: Dickinson's Strategic Framework." https://www.dickinson.edu/download/downloads/id/9684/strategic_framework.pdf.

Diehl, Digby (1972, October 4). "Revolt of Huey Newton: Panther leader tells it as he sees it." *Arizona Republic* (Phoenix, AZ). D-9.

Dimock, Michael (2017, January 10). "How American Changed During Barack Obama's Presidency." *Pew Research Center.* http://www.pewresearch.org/2017/01/10/how-america-changed-during-barack-obamas-presidency/.

Dittmer, John (1994). *Local People: The Struggle for Civil Rights in Mississippi.* Urbana: University of Illinois Press.

Douglas, Davison M. (2012). *Reading, Writing and Race: The Desegregation of the Charlotte School.* Chapel Hill: University of North Carolina Press.

@DrDavidDuke (2017, August 15). "Thank you President Trump for Your Honest & Courage to Tell the Truth About #Charlottesville & Condemn the Leftist Terrorist in BLM/Antifa." [Twitter] Retrieved from https://twitter.com/DrDavidDuke/status/897559892164304896?ref_src=twsrc%5Etfw%7Ctwcamp%5Etweetembed%7Ctwterm%5E897559892164304896&ref_url=https%3A%2F%2Fwww.vox.com%2Fidentities%2F2017%2F8%2F15%2F16153736%2-2Fwhite-supremacists-neo-nazis-trump-honest-charlottesville-tweets.

Du Bois, W.E.B. (1935). "Does the Negro Need Separate Schools?" *The Journal of Negro Education* Vol. 4, No. 3

Du Bois, W.E.B. (1950). "The World of William Howard Day." Harrisburg, PA: The Historical Society of Dauphin County, William Howard Day File.

Du Bois, W.E.B. (1968). *The Souls of Black Folk; Essays and Sketches.* Chicago, A.G. McClurg, 1903. New York: Johnson Reprint Corp.

Du Bois, W.E.B. (1980). *Prayers for Dark People:* Boston: University of Massachusetts Press.

Dugan, Margaret Garcia (2006, May 12). "Full Text of Dugan's speech." *Tucscon.com.*

Duggan, Paul (2018, October 2). "Four Alleged Members of Hate Group Charged in 2017 'United the Right' Rally in Charlottesville." *Washington Post.* https://www.washingtonpost.com/local/public-safety/federal-officials-to-announce-additional-charges-in-2017-unite-the-right-rally-in-charlottesville/2018/10/02/60881262-c651-11e8-9b1c-a90f1daae309_story.html?utm_term=.bdea9bad3b35.

Dum, Larry (1969, November 24). "Man Who Isn't There Haunts Hayakawa." *San Francisco Examiner.*

Duncan, Jericka, Christopher Zawistowski, and Shannon Luibrand. February 19, 2020. "50 States, 50 Different Ways of Teaching America's Past." *CBS News.* Retrieved at https://www.cbsnews.com/news/us-history-how-teaching-americas-past-varies-across-the-country/.

Dyson, Michael Eric (2018). *What Truth Sounds Like: Robert F. Kennedy, James Baldwin, and Our Unfinished Conversation About Race in America.* New York: St. Martin's Press.

Dyson, Omari L. (2014). *The Black Panther Party and Transformative Pedagogy: Placed-Based Education in Philadelphia.* New York: Lexington Books.

Eberhardt, Jennifer L. (2019). *Biased: Uncovering the Hidden Prejudice That Shapes What We See, Think, and Do.* New York: Viking Press.

Eddo-Lodge, Reni (2017). *Why I'm No Longer Talking to White People About Race.* New York: Bloomsbury Publishing.

Emdin, Christopher (2016). *For White Folks Who Teach in the Hood ... and the Rest of Y'all Too: Reality Pedagogy and Urban Education.* Boston: Beacon Press.

"Ethnic Studies Law" (2010, May 13). *Arizona State University, PBS.*

Fattal, Isabel (2018, October 28). "A Brief History of Anti-Semitism Violence in America." *The Atlantic.* https://www.theatlantic.com/politics/archive/2018/10/brief-history-anti-semitic-violence-america/574228/.

Federal Bureau of Investigation (2017, January). "About Hate Crimes Statistics, 2016 and Recent Developments." *Criminal Justice Information Services Division.* https://ucr.fbi.gov/hate-crime/2016.

Federal Bureau of Investigation (2017). "U.S. Dept. of Justice, Federal Bureau of Investigation, Nov. 23, 2018. Federal Crime Data, 2017." https://ucr.fbi.gov/crime-in-the-u.s/2017/crime-in-the-u.s.-2017/additional-data-collections/federal-crime-data/federal-crime-data.pdf.

Federal Ministry of Justice and Consumer Protection (1967). "List of Concentration Camps and Their Outposts." Retrieved at http://www.gesetze-im-internet.de/begdv_6/anlage.html.

Fields, Barbara J. (1982). "Ideology and Race in American History" from *Region, Race, and Reconstruction: Essays in Honor of C. Vann Woodward.* Ed. J. Morgan Kousser and James M. McPherson. New York: Oxford University Press.

Fischer, Howard (2006, May 20). "Legislator Asks Official Ruling on Huerta Talk." *Arizona Daily Star* (Tucson, AZ). B1-B2.

Fischer, Howard (2017, Dec. 20). "Douglas Decries Ethnic Studies Ban Ruling." *Arizona Daily Sun* (Flagstaff, AZ). A3.

Freire, Paulo (1970, 2018). *Pedagogy of the Oppressed: 50th Anniversary Edition.* London: Bloomsbury Publishing.

Freire, Paulo (1985, January). "Reading the World and Reading the Word: An Interview with Paulo Freire." *Language Arts,* Vol. 62, No. 1 Making Meaning, Learning Language (National Council of Teachers of English).

French, Bonnie E. (2017). *Race at Predominantly White Independent Schools: The Space Between Diversity and Equity.* Lanham, MD: Lexington Books.

Frey, William H. (2016) "White Neighborhoods Get Modestly More Diverse, New Census Data Show." *Brookings Institute.* Retrieved at https://www.brookings.edu/blog/the-avenue/2016/12/13/white-neighborhoods-get-modestly-more-diverse-new-census-data-show/.

Frey, William H. (2018). "Black-White Segregation Edges Downward Since 2000, Census Shows." *Brookings Institute.* Retrieved at https://www.brookings.edu/blog/the-avenue/2018/12/17/black-white-segregation-edges-downward-since-2000-census-shows/.

Funk, Cary, Meg Hefferon, Brian Kennedy, and Courtney Johnson (2019, August 2). "Trust and Mistrust in Americans' View of Scientific Experts." *Pew Research Center.* Retrieved at https://www.pewresearch.org/science/2019/08/02/trust-and-mistrust-in-americans-views-of-scientific-experts/.

Fuso, Liz (1964, November). "Deeper Than Politics." *The Mississippi Freedom Schools.*

Gadotti, Moacir (1994). *Reading Paulo Freire: His Life and Work.* New York: SUNY Press.

Gap School District (2017, April 25). "[Gap] HS Earns Third Straight Silver Award from U.S. News." Millersville, PA.

Gap School District (2019). "2018/2019 Equity Audit." [Gap] School District, Millersville, PA.

Gap School District, Guidance Department (2009, October 26). "Dual Enrollment Info." Millersville, PA.

Gap School District, Guidance Department (2018-2019). "Graduation Requirements and Course Selection Procedures." Millersville, PA.

Gay, Geneva (2000). *Culturally Responsive Teaching: Theory, Research, and Practice.* New York: Teachers College Press.

Geiger, Abigail (2018, August 27). "America's Public Schools Teachers Are Far Less Racially and Ethnically Diverse Than Their Students." *Pew Research Center.*

Gewertz, Catherine (2019, August 27). "California's Proposal to Get an Overhaul." *Education Week.* Retrieved at https://www.edweek.org/ew/articles/2019/08/28/ethnic-studies-curriculum-deemed-anti-jewish.html.

Ginzberg, Abby, and Frank Dawson (2016, February 11). "Agents of Change." Documentary. Kanopy.

Giroux, Henry A. (2011). *On Critical Pedagogy.* New York: A&C Black, The Continuum International Publishing Group.

Giroux, Henry A. (2018). *American Nightmare: Facing the Challenges of Fascism.* San Francisco, CA: City Light Books, Open Media Series.

Glaude, Jr., Eddie S. (2016). *Democracy in Black: How Race Still Enslaves The American Soul.* New York: The Crown Publishing Group.

Goodman, Walter (198,4 May 17). "*Brown v. Board of Education*: Uneven Results 30 Years Later." *New York Times.*

Gottesman, Issac (2016). *The Critical Turn In Education: From Marxist Critique to Poststructuralist Feminism to Critical Theories of Race.* New York: Routledge.

Grand Jury, Chester County 18th Investigating Grand Jury's Report RE: Coatesville Area School District (pp. 1–118, Rep. No. No. 874 Misc 2013) (December 3, 2014). Coatesville, PA.

Griffith, Janelle (2019, May 29). "Black Students Were Cast as Slaves in New York Teacher's Mock 'Auctions,' State Finds." *NBCNews.* Retrieved at https://www.nbcnews.com/news/nbcblk/black-students-were-cast-slaves-new-york-teacher-s-mock-n1011361?cid=sm_npd_nn_tw_ma.

Grussendorf, Jeannie (2012). "Teaching Peace When Students Don't Know (About) War." *APSA 2012 Teaching and Learning Conference Paper*

Hale, Jon N. (2016). *The Freedom Schools: Student Activists in the Mississippi Civil Rights Movement.* New York: Columbia University Press.

Halley, Jean, Amy Eshleman, and Ramya Mahadevan Vijaya (2001). *Seeing White: An Introduction to White Privilege and Race.* Lanham, MD: Rowman & Littlefield Publishing Group.

Hannah-Jones, Nikole (2015, July 31). "The Problem We All Life With—Part One." *This American Life* Podcast. Retrieved at https://www.thisamericanlife.org/562/the-problem-we-all-live-with-part-one.

Hannah-Jones, Nikole (2018). "School Segregation in 2018 with Nikole Hannah-Jones." *Why Is This Happening? With Chris Hayes* Podcast.

Harwood, S.A., Choi, S., Orozco, M., Browne Huntt, M., & Mendenhall, R. (2015). "Racial Microaggressions at the University of Illinois at Urbana-Champaign: Voices of Students of Color in the Classroom." *University of Illinois at Urbana-Champaign.*

Hawkes, Jeff (2017, September 10). "In the Era of Charlottesville and Kaepernick, Some Lancaster County Educators Look to Address Race in the Classroom." *Lancaster Newspaper.*

Heitzeg, Nancy A. (2016). *The School-to-Prison Pipeline: Education, Discipline, and Racialized Double Standards.* Santa Barbara, CA: ABC-CLIO.

Hengler, Greg (2010, May 14). "Black Professor: Ethnic Studies 'Never' Teaches Ethnic Solidarity." MSNBC, YouTube. https://www.youtube.com/watch?v=-GO45D8wUfQ.

Hilliard, David (2001). *This Side of Glory: The Autobiography of David Hilliard and the Story of the Black Panther Party.* Lawrence Hill Books.

Hills, Charles M. (1955, October 23). "Citizens Councils Being Organized in Many Sections of State by Golding." *Clarion-Ledger* (Jackson, MS). 15.

Himle, J.A., Baser, R.E., Taylor, R.J., Campbell, R.D., & Jackson, J.S. (2009). "Anxiety Disorders Among African Americans, Blacks of Caribbean Descent, and Non-Hispanic Whites in the United States." *Journal of Anxiety Disorder.*

Hobbs, Lisa (1968, Dec. 25). "State's Hare: Cotton Picking Kid Toughened by His Time." *San Francisco Examiner.*

hooks, bell (1994). *Teaching to Transgress: Education as the Practice of Freedom.* New York: Routledge.

Horne, Gerald (1995). *Fire This Time: The Watts Uprising and the 1960s.* Charlottesville: University Press of Virginia.

Horne, Tom (2007, February 3). "Racist Views Are Poor Use of School Funding." *Arizona Republic* (Phoenix, AZ). B7.

Horne, Tom (2007, December 5). Opinion, "Horne Takes to Task Raza Studies Teachers," *Arizona Daily Star.*

Horne, Tom (2008, August 10). "Ethnic Studies Must Be Put on New Track." *Arizona Republic* (Phoenix, AZ). V1 and V3.

Horne. Tom (2012, June 11). "Race-Based Studies Can't Be Justified." *Arizona Republic* (Phoenix, AZ). B7.

Horowitz, Juliana Menasce, Anna Brown, and Kiana Cox (2019, April 9). "Race in America 2019." *Pew Research Center.* Retrieved from https://www.pewsocialtrends.org/2019/04/09/race-in-america-2019/.

Howard, Tyrone C. (2010). *Why Race and Culture Matter in Schools: Closing the Achievement Gap in America's Classrooms.* New York: Teacher's College Press.

@HuffPost (2018, March 5). "HuffPost Discovered That Florida Teacher Dayanna Volitich Was Promoting White Nationalist Views Online Under the Pseudonym 'Tiana Dalichov.' Now She's Been Removed from the Classroom." [Twitter post] Retrieved from https://twitter.com/HuffPost/status/971124510555488256.

Huppenthal, John (2017, Aug. 27). "Judge's Finding of Racism at Variance with the Facts." *Arizona Daily Star* (Tucson, AZ). A7.

Illinois General Assembly (2018). Bill Status of HB4346, 100th General Assembly. http://www.ilga.gov/legislation/billstatus.asp?DocNum=4346&GAID=14&GA=100&DocTypeID=HB&LegID=109012&SessionID=91&SpecSess=.

Ingersoll, Richard, and Henry May (September 2011). "Recruitment, Retention and the Minority Teacher Shortage." *The Consortium for Policy Research in Education, University of Pennsylvania and the Center for Educational Research in the Interest of Underserved Students, University of California, Santa Cruz.*

Ingram, Bob (1954, Dec. 5). "White Citizen Units Are Growing Swiftly." *Montgomery Advertiser* (Montgomery, AL). 11.

Irvine, Jacqueline Jordan (2003). *Educating Teachers for Diversity: Seeing With a Cultural Eye.* New York: Teachers College Press.

Irving, Debby (2014). *Waking Up White: And Finding Myself in the Story of Race.* Elephant Room Press.

Israel, Elfie (2002). "Examining Multiple Perspectives in Literature." *Inquiry and the Literary Text: Constructing Discussions in the English Classroom.* James Holden and John S. Schmit, eds. Urbana, IL: NCTE.

Jennings, Regina (1993). "Why I Joined the Party: An Africana Womanist Reflection," in Charles E. Jones, *Black Panther Party Reconsidered.* Boston: Little, Brown.

Jensen, Robert (2005). *The Heart of Whiteness: Confronting Race, Racism, and Whiteness.* City Lights Publishers.

Johnson, Rucker (2019). *Children of the Dream: Why School Integration Works.* New York: Basic Books.

Johnson, Rucker. *Race in America* (2019, April 16). "The Success of Integrating Schools with Rucker Johnson." Podcast.

Jordan, Reed (2014, October 29). "Millions of Black Students Attend Public Schools That Are Highly Segregated by Race and by Income." *Urban Wire: Education and Training.* Retrieved at https://www.urban.org/urban-wire/millions-black-students-attend-public-schools-are-highly-segregated-race-and-income.

Joseph, Peniel E. (2006). *The Black Power Movement: Rethinking the Civil Rights-Black Power Era.* New York: Routledge.

Julian, Liam (2008, July 2). "'Raza Studies' Defy American Values." CBS News.

Kanter, Jonathan W., Monnica T. Williams, Adam M. Kuczynski, Tatherine E. Manbeck, Marlena Debreaux, and Daniel C. Rosen (2017, August 30). "A Preliminary Report on the Relationship Between Microaggressions Against Black People and Racism Among White College Students." *Race and Social Problems*, Vol. 9, Issue 4. Retrieved at https://link.springer.com/article/10.1007/s12552-017-9214-0.

Kay, Matthew R. *Not Light, but Fire: How to Lead Meaningful Race Conversations in the Classroom.* Portsmouth, NH: Stenhouse Publishers, 2018.

Kendi, Ibram X. (2016). *Stamped from the Beginning: The Definitive History of Racist Ideas in America.* New York: Hachette Brook Group, Nation Books.

Kendi, Ibram X. (2019). *How to Be an Antiracist.* New York: One World, Random House Publishing Group.

Kennedy, Randall L. (1999–2000). "Who Can Say "Nigger"? and Other Considerations." *The Journal of Blacks in Higher Education,* The JBHE Foundation, Inc.

Kennedy, Randall L. (2002, 2003). *Nigger: The Strange Case of a Troublesome Word.* New York: Vintage Books.

Khan-Cullors, Patrisse, and asha bandele (2018). *When They Call You a Terrorist: A Black Lives Matter Memoir.* New York: St. Martin's Press.

Kincheloe, Joe L., Shirley R. Steinberg, et al. (1998). *White Reign: Deploying Whiteness in America.* Basingstoke, United Kingdom: Palgrave Macmillan.

King, Bernice A. @BerniceKing (2018, December 21). "Andrew Johnson's teammates and coaches protesting on his behalf would have been a true reflection of 'team' and dignity, @ MikeFrankelSNJ. Please discontinue framing this as a 'good' story. It's actually a reflection of bias and acquiescence to bias." [Twitter] Retrieved from https://twitter.com/BerniceKing/status/1076162511655878656;.

King, Martin Luther, Jr. (1967, April 4). "Beyond Vietnam: A Time to Break Silence" delivered at Riverside Church, New York City, April 4, 1967. This version was published in *"A Single Garment of Destiny": A Global Vision of Justice*. Boston: Beacon Press, 2012.

Kishi, Katayoun (2017, November 15). "Assaults Against Muslims in U.S. Surpass 2001 Level." *Pew Research Center*. http://www.pewresearch.org/fact-tank/2017/11/15/assaults-against-muslims-in-u-s-surpass-2001-level/.

Kotler, Jennifer, Tanya Haider, and Michael H. Levine (2019). "Identity Matters: Parents' and Educators' Perceptions of Children's Social Identity Development." *Sesame Workshop and NORC at the University of Chicago*.

Krogstad, Jens Manuel, and Richard Fry (2014, August 18). "Dept. of Ed. Projects Public Schools Will Be 'Majority-Minority' This Fall." *Pew Research Center*.

Ladson-Billings, Gloria (1999). "Preparing Teachers for Diverse Student Populations: A Critical Race Theory Perspective. *Review of Research in Education*.

Ladson-Billings, Gloria (2003). *Critical Race Theory Perspectives on Social Studies: The Profession, Policies, and Curriculum*. Greenwich, CT.

Lancaster Newspapers Editorial Board (2017, September 17). "There Is Room in School to Talk About Race." *Lancaster Sunday News*.

Lassiter, Michael D., Matthew D. Lassiter, and Andrew B. Lewis (1998). *The Moderates' Dilemma: Massive Resistance to School Desegregation in Virginia*. Charlottesville: University of Virginia Press.

Lee, Spike (2016). "Two Fists Up." *ESPN Presents A Spike Lee Joint*, April 21, 2016.

Lehew, Dudley (1964, July 10). "'Freedom Schools' Springing Up Throughout Mississippi." *Hattiesburg American* (Hattiesburg, MS). 6.

Lichter, Daniel, et al. (2015). "Toward a New Macro-Segregation? Decomposing Segregation Within and Between Metropolitan Cities and Suburbs," *American Sociological Review* Vol. 80(4).

Lilienfeld, Scott O. (2017). "Microaggressions: Strong Claims, Inadequate Evidence." *Association for Psychological Science*. Vol. 12(1).

Lipstadt, Deborah E. (2012). *Denying the Holocaust: The Growing Assault on Truth and Memory*. New York: Simon & Schuster.

Lott, Juanita Tamoayo (2018). *Golden Children: Legacy of Ethnic Studies, SF State, A Memoir*. Berkeley, CA: Eastwind Books of Berkeley.

Love, Bettina (2019). *We Want to Do More Than Survive: Abolitionist Teaching and the Pursuit of Educational Freedom*. New York: Beacon Press.

Lowery, Wesley (2016). *They Can't Kill Us All: The Story of the Struggle for Black Lives*. New York: Little, Brown, 2016.

"Lowndes Co. Forms Citizens Council" (1954, October 28). Greenwood Commonwealth (Greenwood, MS). 1.

Lynd, Staughton, and Harold Baranelli, Congress of Racial Equality, Mississippi Fourth Congressional District (1964). "CORE—Freedom Schools (COFO) - Memoranda (Congress of Racial Equality, Mississippi 4th Congressional District records, 1961–1966.

Lynn, Marvin (1999). "Toward a Critical Race Pedagogy: A Research Note." *Urban Education*, vol. 33.

MacPherson Institute (2015, Oct. 22). "Henry Giroux: Where Is the Outrage? Critical Pedagogy in Dark Times." Retrieved from https://www.youtube.com/watch?v=CAxj87RRtsc

Malik, Rasheed (2017, November 6). "New Data Reveal 250 Preschoolers Are Suspended or Expelled Every Day." *Center for American Progress*.

Mays, David J. (2008). *Race, Reason, and Massive Resistance*. Athens: University of Georgia Press.

Mazzacco, Philip J. (2017). *The Psychology of Racial Colorblindness: A Critical Review*. Basingstoke, UK: Palgrave Macmillan.

McCrone, Brian X., Vince Lattanzio, and David Chang (2016). "Racist Texts Sent to Black U. Penn. Students; 3 Arrested." *NCB San Diego, US & World*. November 14, 2016. https://

www.nbcsandiego.com/news/national-international/University-of-Pennsylvania-Students-Received-Racist-Texts-From-Unknown-Source-400872511.html.

McLaren, Peter, and Joe L. Kincheloe (2007). *Critical Pedagogy: Where Are We Now?* New York: Peter Lang.

McLaughlin, Eliott C., and Tina Burnside (2017, May 17). "Bananas, Nooses at American University Spark Protests, Demands." CNN. Retrieved at https://www.cnn.com/2017/05/17/us/american-university-bananas-nooses-hate-crime-protests/index.html.

Mealy, Todd (2010). *Aliened American: A Biography of William Howard Day, 1825–1900, Volume II.* Frederick, MD: PublishAmerica.

Mealy, Todd (2017). *This Is the Rat Speaking: Black Power and the Promise of Racial Consciousness at Franklin and Marshall College in the Age of the Takeover.* Bloomington, IN: iUniverse.

Michie, Gregory. 2009. *Holler If You Hear Me: The Education of a Teacher and His Students.* New York: Teachers College Press.

@MikeFrankelJSZ (2018, December 20). "Epitome of a Team Player." [Twitter] Retrieved from https://twitter.com/MikeFrankelSNJ/status/1075811774954463235.

Mississippi Summer Project Staff to Mississippi Freedom School Teachers (1964, May 5). "Overview of the Freedom Schools." Jackson, MS.

Mitchell, John N. (2011, October 27). "Report: Schools Fall Short on Civil Rights History." *The Philadelphia Tribune.*

Mondale, Sarah, and Sarah B. Patton (2001). *School: The Story of American Public Education.* Boston: Beacon Press.

Monteiro, Kenneth (2018). "Ethnic Studies Contributes to College Students' Success." *Cesar Chavez Institute, College of Ethnic Studies, San Francisco State University* cited by Ashley A. Smith (2018, July 9). "The Benefits of Ethnic Studies Courses." *Inside Higher Education.* Retrieved at https://www.insidehighered.com/news/2018/07/09/san-francisco-state-finds-evidence-ethnic-studies-students-do-better.

Moses, Michele S. (2002). *Embracing Race: Why We Need Race-Conscious Education Policy.* New York: Teachers College Press.

Mthethwa-Sommers, Shirley (2014). *Narratives of Social Justice Educators.* New York: Springer Cham Heidelberg.

Mullane, JD (2017, September 19). "The Unbearable Whiteness of Detectors of Disrespect." *Bucks County Courier Times.*

Murch, Donna Jean (2010). *Living for the City: Migration, Education, and the Rise of the Black Panther Party in Oakland, California.* Chapel Hill: University of North Carolina Press.

Nagai, Althea (2017, March 29). "The Pseudo-Science of Microaggressions." *National Association of Scholars.*

National Center of Education Statistics (NCES) (2018, May). "Public High School Graduation Rates." Retrieved from https://nces.ed.gov/programs/coe/indicator_coi.asp.

National Public Radio (2014, March 21). "Black Preschoolers Far More Likely to Be Suspended." https://www.npr.org/sections/codeswitch/2014/03/21/292456211/black-preschoolers-far-more-likely-to-be-suspended.

National SEED Project (2019). "History." Seeking Educational Equity and Diversity. Accessed on January 1, 2019. https://nationalseedproject.org/about-us/history.

Newport, Frank, David W. Moore, and Lydia Saad (1999, Dec. 6). "The Most Important Events of the Century from the Viewpoint of the People." *Gallup News Service.*

Newton, Casey (2010, Feb. 10). "Horne Set to Run for Attorney General." *Arizona Republic* (Phoenix, AZ). 3.

Newton, Huey P., and Bobby Seal (1967, May 15). "Ten Point Program." *The Black Panther.*

Obama, Barack (2016, May 6). "Howard University Commencement Address" quoted in *Politico* (2016, May 7). "Obama's Full Remarks at Howard University Commencement Ceremony." Retrieved from https://www.politico.com/story/2016/05/obamas-howard-commencement-transcript-222931.

Ogletree, Charles (2004). *All Deliberate Speed: Reflections on the First Half-Century of Brown v. Board of Education.* New York: W.W. Norton and Company.

Oluo, Ijeoma (2018). *So You Want to Talk About Race.* Berkeley, CA: Seal Press.

Orfield, Gary, Erica Frankenberg, Jongyeon Ee, and John Kuscera (2014, May 15). "Brown at 60: Great Progress, a Long Retreat and an Uncertain Future." The Civil Rights Project.

Retrieved at https://www.civilrightsproject.ucla.edu/research/k-12-education/integration-and-diversity/brown-at-60-great-progress-a-long-retreat-and-an-uncertain-future/.

Palko, Chris (2010, March 15). "America's 100 Most Conservative-Friendly Counties." *Daily Caller.* https://dailycaller.com/2010/03/15/americas-100-most-conservative-friendly-counties-numbers-81-100/.

Paris, Django (2016). "On Educating Culturally Sustaining Teachers." *TeachingWorks Working Papers, University of Michigan.*

Paris, Django (2017). *Culturally Sustaining Pedagogies: Teaching and Learning for Justice in a Changing World.* New York: Teachers College Press.

Paris, Django, and H. Samy Alim (2014, March 31). "Pedagogy Beyond the White Gaze." *Harvard Education Publishing Group.*

Parker, Nate, and James Lopez (2014). *AmeriCAN.* Drama/Short.

Patterson, John, quoted in Teda Skocpol and Vanessa Williamson (2016). *The Tea Party and the Remaking of Republican Conservatism.* Oxford: Oxford University Press.

PBS News Hour (2010, December 30). "Whose Version of History is Taught? Arizona Law Bans Ethnic Studies Classes." YouTube. https://www.youtube.com/watch?v=4QVM4UpxXfM.

Pearl, Mike (2016, November 22). "How to Tell If Your Alt-Right Relative Is Trying to Redpill You at Thanksgiving." *Vice.* https://www.vice.com/en_us/article/nnk3bm/how-to-tell-if-your-alt-right-relative-is-trying-to-redpill-you-at-thanksgiving.

Peller, Gary (1990). "Race Consciousness." *Duke Law Journal.*

Pennsylvania Department of Education (2002). "Academic Standards for History." 22 Pa. Code, Chapter 4, Appendix C (#005–275).

Perlstein, Daniel (2002). "Minds Stayed on Freedom: Politics and Pedagogy in the African American Freedom Struggle." *American Educational Research Journal,* Vol. 39, No. 2, Education and Democracy.

Petersen, William (1966, January 9). "Success Story, Japanese-American Style." *New York Times.*

Picower, Bree, and Rita Kohli (2017). *Confronting Racism in Teacher Education: Counternarratives of Critical Practice.* New York: Routledge.

Pilgrim, David (2015). *Understanding Jim Crow: Using Racist Memorabilia to Teach Tolerance and Promote Social Justice.* Ferris State University and PM Press.

Pollock, Mica, Sherry Deckman, Meredith Mira, and Carla Shalaby (2010). "'But What Can I Do?': Three Necessary Tensions in Teaching Teachers About Race." *Journal of Teacher Education,* American Association of Colleges of Teacher Education.

Potok, Mark (2017, February 15). "The Trump Effect." *Southern Poverty Law Center.* https://www.splcenter.org/fighting-hate/intelligence-report/2017/trump-effect.

Price, Bem (1954, Nov. 21). "AP Surveys South's New Type of Anti-Negro Vigilante." *Clarion-Ledger* (Jackson, MS). 8.

Prose, J.D. (2014, March 31). "Pa. Earns "D" in Civil Rights Teaching, Study Says." *Beaver County Times.*

Quillian, Lincoln, and Devah Pager (2001). "Black Neighbors, Higher Crime? The Role of Racial Stereotypes in Evaluations of Neighborhood Crime." *American Journal of Sociology* 107, no. 3.

Reilly, Katie (2016, November 12). "University of Pennsylvania Black Students Targeted in Racist Group Message." *Time.*

Resnick, Gideon (2017, August 17). "The Remarkable Self Harm of the White Supremacists Who Gathered in Charlottesville." *The Daily Beast.*

@RichardBSpencer (2017, August 15). "Trump's statement was fair and down to earth. #Charlottesville could have been peaceful, if police did its job." [Twitter] Retrieved from https://twitter.com/RichardBSpencer/status/897572085052190723?ref_src=twsrc%5Etfw%7Ctwca mp%5Etweetembed%7Ctwterm%5E897572085052190723&ref_url=https%3A%2F%2Fwww. usatoday.com%2Fstory%2Fnews%2Fpolitics%2Fonpolitics%2F2017%2F08%2F15%2Fdavid-duke-reaction-trump-news-conference%2F570517001%2F.

Richardson, Judy (1964, September 6). "Memo to SNCC Executive Committee RE: Residential Freedom School.," 1964, SNCC Papers, A=II=4, 0367.

Richardson, Judy (1965). "Residential Freedom School Report," August 1965, 3, 6, 12, 13, ANCC Papers, reel 20, 0101.

Rock, Amy (2017, December 4). "Black Preschoolers 3.6 Times More Likely to Be Suspended than White Students." *Campus Safety*. Retrieved from https://www.campussafetymagazine.com/safety/black-preschoolers-suspension/.

Rogers (Kendi), Ibram (2012). *The Black Campus Movement: Black Students and the Racial Reconstitution of Higher Education, 1965–1972*. New York: Palgrave, MacMillan.

Rollin, Francis (1883). *The Life and Public Services of Martin R. Delany*. Boston: Lee and Shepard.

Romero, Augustine F. (2008, Aug. 10). "Defense of Tucson's Raza Studies." *Arizona Republic* (Phoenix, AZ). V1 and V3.

Ross, Lawrence (2015). *Blackballed: The Black and White Politics of Race on America's Campuses*. New York: St. Martin's Press.

Rothman, Lily (2015, April 28). "What Martin Luther King Really Thought About Riots." *Time*. http://time.com/3838515/baltimore-riots-language-unheard-quote/?scrlybrkr=35905b1e.

Savage-Williams, Pat (2018, March/April). "Ten Ways School Boards Can Champion Racial Equity." *Illinois Association of School Boards*. https://www.iasb.com/journal/j030418_03.cfm.

Scapinato, Daniel (2006 April 26). "Tucson High Will Get GOP Speaker." *Arizona Daily Star* (Tucson, AZ), B1-B3.

Scarpinato, Daniel (2006, April 14). "Labor Activist's Speech Gets Attention of O'Reilly Factor." *Arizona Daily Star* (Tucson, AZ). 1–3.

Schugurensky, Daniel (2014). *Paulo Freire*. London: Bloomsbury Publishing.

Schultz, Katherine (2019). *Distrust and Educational Change: Overcoming Barriers to Just and Lasting Reform*. Cambridge, MA: Harvard Education Press.

Schwartz, Lara, and Daniel Ritter (Winter 2019). "Civil Discourse in the Classroom." *American University of University Professors*. Retrieved at https://www.aaup.org/article/civil-discourse-classroom#.XbpFz-hKhPY.

Sealey-Ruiz, Yolanda. Future for Learning (2018, December). *Yolanda Sealey-Ruiz: The Archaeology of the Self*. [Video file]. Retrieved from https://vimeo.com/299137829.

Seymour, Sean, and Julie Ray (2015). "Grads of Historically Black Colleges Have Well-Being Edge." *Gallup*. Retrieved from https://news.gallup.com/poll/186362/grads-historically-black-colleges-edge.aspx?g_source=CATEGORY_WELLBEING&g_medium=topic&g_campaign=tiles.

Shaw, Terri (1964, July 7). "COFO Worker Explains Summer Project Aims." *Hattiesburg American* (Hattiesburg, MS). 5.

Shreveport Times (Shreveport, Louisiana). "A Wise Ruling by Judge Ellis." May 26, 1962, 6.

Simpson, Douglas, and Sally McMillan (2008). "Is It Time to Shelve Paulo Freire?" *Journal of Thought*. Spring/Summer 2008, Vol. 43, Issues 1 and 2.

Small, Deborah (2001). "The War on Drugs Is a War on Racial Justice." *Social Research,* Vol. 6, No. 3, Altered States of Consciousness.

Solomon, Akiba, and Kenrya Rankin (2019). *How We Fight White Supremacy: A Field Guide to Black Resistance*. New York: Bold Type Books.

Sommers, Samuel R., Evan P. Apfelbaum, Kristin N. Dukes, Negin Toosi, and Elsie J. Wang (2006). "Race and Media Coverage of Hurricane Katrina: Analysis, Implications, and Future Research Questions. *Analyses of Social Issues and Public Policy*. Vol. 6. No. 1.

Southern Poverty Law Center (2016, April 13). "The Trump Effect: The Impact of the Presidential Campaign on Our Nation's Schools." https://www.splcenter.org/20160413/trump-effect-impact-presidential-campaign-our-nations-schools.

Sparks, Colleen (2002, November 25). "Students Say Ethnic Classes Give School More Meaning." *Arizona Daily Star*.

"Spokesmen for Citizens Councils Deny Accusations of Left Wingers" (1955, June 10). *Greenwood Commonwealth* (Greenwood, MS). 1.

Stancil, Will (2018, March 14). "School Segregation Is Not a Myth." *The Atlantic*. Retrieved from https://www.theatlantic.com/education/archive/2018/03/school-segregation-is-not-a-myth/555614/.

Steinbuch, Yaron (2018, December 10). "White Columbia University Student Goes on Racist Tirade." *New York Post*.

Stern, Alexandra Minna (2019). *Proud Boys and the White Ethnostate: How the Alt-Right Is Warping the American Imagination*. Boston: Beacon Press.

Stevens, Matt (2018, March 7). "Florida Teacher Says Her Racist Podcast Was 'Satire.'" *New York Times.*

Stevens Point Area Public School District (2013). "Graduation Requirements Task Force Final Report, 2012–2013."

Stuyk, Ryan (2017, August 15). "By the Numbers: 7 Charts That Explain Hate Groups in the United States." *CNN Politics.* https://www.cnn.com/2017/08/14/politics/charts-explain-us-hate-groups/index.html.

Sue, Derald Wing (2003). *Overcoming Our Racism: The Journey to Liberation.* San Francisco, CA: John Wiley & Sons, Inc.

Sue, Derald Wing (2010). *Microaggressions and Marginality: Manifestation, Dynamics, and Impact.* Hoboken, NJ: John Wiley & Sons.

Sue, Derald Wing (2010). *Microaggressions in Everyday Life: Race, Gender, and Sexual Orientation.* Hoboken, NJ: John Wiley & Sons.

Sue, Derald Wing (2015). *Race Talk and the Conspiracy of Silence: Understanding and Facilitating Difficult Dialogues on Race.* Hoboken, NJ: John Wiley & Sons, Inc.

Tatum, Beverly Daniel (1997). *Why Are All the Black Kids Sitting Together in the Cafeteria?: And Other Conversations About Race.* New York: Basic Books.

Tatum, Beverly Daniel (2007). *Can We Talk About Race? And Other Conversations in an Era of School Resegregation.* Boston: Beacon Press.

Tatum, Beverly Daniel (December 13, 2017). "The Backstory: The Cost of Silence." *Wesleyan University Magazine.* Retrieved at http://magazine.blogs.wesleyan.edu/2017/12/13/the-backstory-the-cost-of-silence-by-beverly-daniel-tatum-75/.

Tefft, Pearce (2017, August 14). "Letter: Family Denounces Tefft's Racist Rhetoric and Actions." *In Forum.* https://www.inforum.com/opinion/letters/4311880-letter-family-denounces-teffts-racist-rhetoric-and-actions.

Thurmond, Strom, and Richard Russell (1956, March 11). "Declaration of Constitutional Principles." *Southern School News.* April 1956; 102 Cong. Red. 4459–61 (1956) (statement of Sen. Walter George).

Tiede, Tom (1969, June 4). "Shock Waves of Cornell Takeover Still Being Felt." *Daily Tribune* (Wisconsin Rapids, WI).

Tochluk, Shelly (2010). *Witnessing Whiteness: The Need to Talk About Race and How to Do It.* New York, Toronto, Plymouth, UK: Rowman and Littlefield Education.

Toppo, Greg (April 28, 2004). "Thousands of Black Teachers Lost Jobs." *USA Today.* Retrieved at http://usatoday30.usatoday.com/news/nation/2004-04-28-brown-side2_x.htm.

Troy, Tevi (2009, December 13). "Cornell's Straight Flush." *City-Journal.org.*

Uggen, Christopher, Ryan Larson, and Sarah Shannon (2016, October 6). "6 Million Lost Voters: State-Level Estimates of Felony Disenfranchisement." *The Sentencing Project.* https://www.sentencingproject.org/publications/6-million-lost-voters-state-level-estimates-felony-disenfranchisement-2016/.

United Press International (1969, April 21). "Peace Prevails at Cornell. Amnesty for Demonstrators." *Kingston Daily Freeman* (Kingston, NY).

United States Census Bureau (2010). "American Fact Finder." https://factfinder.census.gov/faces/tableservices/jsf/pages/productview.xhtml?pid=ACS_10_3YR_C04006&prodType=table.

Walker, Vanessa Siddle (2000). *Their Highest Potential: An African American School Community in the Segregated South.* Chapel Hill, NC: The University of North Carolina Press.

Walker, Vanessa Siddle (2018). *The Lost Education of Horace Tate: Uncovering the Hidden Heroes Who Fought for Justice in Schools.* New York: The New Press.

Wallis, Jim (2016). *America's Original Sin: Racism, White Privilege, and the Bridge to a New America.* Grand Rapids, MI: Brazos Press.

Washington, Jesse (2019, September 18). "The Untold Story of Wrestler Andrew Johnson's Dreadlocks." *The Undefeated.* Retrieved at https://theundefeated.com/features/the-untold-story-of-wrestler-andrew-johnsons-dreadlocks/.

Watkins, William Henry (2005). *Black Protest Thought and Education.* Peter Land.

Watson, Bruce (2010). *Freedom Summer: The Savage Season That Made Mississippi Burn and Made American a Democracy.* New York: Penguin Group.

Waxman, Laura (2017, Aug. 22). "Social Justice at the Fore for SFUSD." *San Francisco Examiner* (San Francisco, CA). A4.

Weissert, Will (2018, April 12). "Texas Oks Mexican-American Studies Curriculum, but Under 'Ethnics Studies." *Monitor* (McAllen, TX). A5.

White, William S. (1956, March 13). "Manifesto Splits Democrats Again," *New York Times*.

"White Citizens Councils Unfold Their Strategy" (1956, July 13). *Alabama Tribune* (Montgomery, AL) 1.

Williams, M.T., Malcoun, E., Sawyer, B., Davis, D.M., Bahojb-Nouri, L.V., & Leavell Bruce, S. (2014). "Cultural Adaptations of Prolonged Exposure Therapy for Treatment and Prevention of Posttraumatic Stress Disorder in African Americans." *Behavioral Sciences,* 4(2).

Williamson, Joy Ann (2000, April). "Educate to Liberate! SNCC, Panthers, and Emancipator Education." Paper presented at the annual meeting of the American Educational Research Association.

Yancy, George (2018). *Backlash: What Happens When We Talk Honestly About Racism in America*. New York: Rowman and Littlefield.

Young, Iris. "Five Faces of Oppression." Published by Lisa Heldke and Peg O'Connor. *Oppression, Privilege, and Resistance*. Boston: McGraw-Hill, 2004.

Zoya Zeman Freedom Summer College (1964, June 21–25). "Philadelphia Mississippi Case: Chronology of Contact with Agents of the Federal Government."

Zubrzycki, Jackie (2017, July 10). "Did Arizona Ethnic-Studies Law Come with Discriminatory Intent?" *Edweek*. https://blogs.edweek.org/edweek/curriculum/2017/07/Mexican_Studies_Law_Court_Tucson.html.

Index